# 123 scrapbooks

QUARRY

First published in the United States of America by:
Quarry Books, a member of
Quayside Publishing Group
33 Commercial Street
Gloucester, Massachusetts 01930-5089
Telephone: (978) 282-9590
Fax: (978) 283-2742
www.rockpub.com

**Library of Congress Cataloging-in-Publication Data available**

ISBN 1-59253-143-1

10 9 8 7 6 5 4 3 2 1

Production: Joan Lockhart
Cover Design: laura mcfadden design, inc.

Printed in China

GLOUCESTER MASSACHUSETTS

# 123 scrapbooks

## EVERYTHING YOU NEED TO KNOW TO MAKE AMAZING PAGES

### TRICE BOERENS AND SANDI GENOVESE

QUARRY BOOKS

# Contents

6    **Introduction**

8    **Project Recipes**

8     Folded Borders

11    Paper Clay

14    Fusible Fabric

17    Appliqué

20    Shaped Wire

23    Quilling

26    Pencil Shadowing

29    Eyelets

32    Sequins

35    Lace-ups

38    Weaving

41    Ribbon Embroidery

44    Shrink Plastic

47    Yarn Painting

50    Cross-Stitch

53    Quilting

56    Machine Stitching

59    Found-Object Collage

62    Paper-Piecing

65    Stenciling

68    Wrapped Thread

71    Gold Leafing

74    Sand Painting

77    Micro Beads

80    Dip-Dyeing

83    Aged Paper

86    Stamping

89    Decoupage

92    Marbling

95    Mosaics

98    Layered Borders

101   Tassels

104 **Borders, Corners, and Frames**

184 **Dimensional Pages**

184    Basics

186    Paper

204    Fabric

224    Metal

246    Keepsakes

258    Beads and Baubles

274    Exotic Elements

284 **Templates**

298 **Resources**

302 **Contributors**

304 **About the Authors**

# Introduction

The recent surge in the popularity of scrapbooking has turned placing photographs and captions into blank books into an art form. Now, complete montages of photographs, ephemera, and embellishments accompany journaled text, poetry, and quotations. Though traditional scrapbooks have remained popular, many hobbyists are choosing those that use several layers of design detail. Even traditionalists are learning that the addition of just one color or texture to a page enhances the overall scrapbook page's design. What may seem like the simplest touch may hold the key to creating your most original scrapbook page yet.

*1-2-3 Scrapbooks* covers all aspects of scrapbooking, from basic tools needed to techniques for the most intricate details. With Quarry Books' guide to creating wonderfully innovative pages at your side, you can tailor your pages by incorporating borders, frames, and corners. Glass, metals, fabrics, ribbons, die-cuts, and beads, as well as natural embellishments, such as seashells, flowers, and leaves, can also be added to your pages for extra dimension. You will learn quilling, wire shaping, and gold leafing, among other techniques, for adding hand-crafted effects. A gallery of artists' projects are featured, accompanied by detailed visuals that are sure to spark your own creative ideas.

Your photographs can now be displayed in innumerable styles and setups—all of which will enhance your chosen message. From the simplest add-ons to the most ornate embellishment, the tips, techniques, and projects in *1-2-3 Scrapbooks* will complement your scrapbook pages for years to come.

**recipe #**

# 1

# Folded Borders

Paper is everywhere in our lives and has become so commonplace that its beauty and versatility are sometimes unappreciated. Scrapbook enthusiasts, however, regard paper as a treasure and delight in transforming it into art. Use folding to make paper borders that virtually jump off the page. These folded-paper flowers add dimension without adding bulk. A few well-placed folds and a little sleight of hand can turn a paper square into a beautiful blossom. In fact, two of these flower variations begins with a simple square.

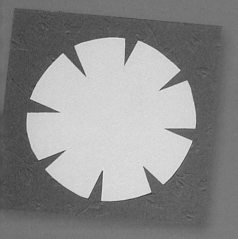

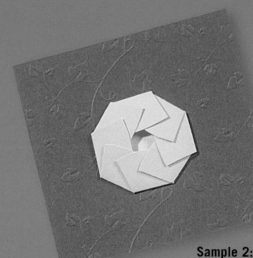

**Sample 1:** To make a folded flower, cut out the center flower shape.

**Sample 2:** Overlapping the petals, fold them to the center of the flower.

**Sample 3:** Layer the flat and folded shapes, then attach them to the page.

# Sorority Sisters

Throw open the windows and let the outside in with this happy border of morning glories.

**Materials**

- photos
- one 12" x 12" (30.5 cm x 30.5 cm) sheet purple paper
- one 12" x 12" (30.5 cm x 30.5 cm) sheet cream paper
- one 8 1/2" x 11" (21.5 cm x 28 cm) sheet blue patterned paper with white reverse side
- one 8 1/2" x 11" (21.5 cm x 28 cm) sheet green patterned paper
- one 8 1/2" x 11" (21.5 cm x 28 cm) sheet yellow paper
- white quilling paper
- turquoise micro beads
- archival-quality adhesive spray
- double-sided adhesive sheet, such as Peel-N-Stick

**Tools**

- metal-edged ruler
- craft knife
- scissors
- pencil
- tracing paper
- kneaded rubber eraser
- black fine-tip marker

## Instructions

1. With the ruler and knife, trim the cream paper to 9 1/2" x 12" (24 cm x 30.5 cm). Tear the right edge of the rectangle. Place the cream paper 2 3/8" (6 cm) from the left edge of the purple paper. Using a pencil, lightly mark the purple paper at the left edge of the cream paper for placement. Following the manufacturer's directions for the adhesive spray, coat the back of the cream paper. Press in place.

2. Using the scissors, trim the photos to the following sizes, clockwise from left: 2 1/2" x 4 1/4" (6.5 cm x 11 cm), 5 1/8" x 2 3/4" (13 cm x 7 cm), and 4" x 6" (10 cm x 15 cm). Place the small photo 2" (5 cm) from the left edge and 3 1/2" (9 cm) from the bottom edge of the purple paper. Place the top photo 2 3/4" (7 cm) from the right edge of the purple paper and 5/8" (1.5 cm) from the top edge of the cream paper. Place the bottom photo 3" (7.5 cm) from the right edge of the purple paper and 3/4" (2 cm) from the bottom edge of the cream paper. Mark the cream paper at the corners of the photos for placement. Coat the backs of the photos with adhesive spray. Press in place.

3. From the yellow paper, cut one 1/4" x 11" (0.6 cm x 28 cm) strip. Loosely wrap one or two lengths of quilling paper around the yellow strip. Press the quilling paper flat. From the double-sided adhesive sheet, cut one 1/8" x 9" (0.3 cm x 23 cm) strip. Peel off the protective paper, and attach the adhesive sheet to the back of the yellow strip. Mark a vertical line on the cream paper 1 1/8" (3 cm) from the right edge of the purple paper. From the quilling paper, cut six 2" (5 cm) lengths. Place them at various angles on the marked line. Remove the remaining protective paper from the adhesive sheet, and press the wrapped strip in place on the marked line.

4. Using the tracing paper, make the template for the leaf shape. From the green patterned paper, cut five leaf shapes. From the double-sided adhesive sheet, cut five 1/2" (1 cm) squares. Peel off the protective paper, and attach the squares to the backs of the leaf shapes. Remove the remaining protective paper. Referring to the photo for placement, press the leaf shapes in place. From the blue-and-white patterned paper, cut one 1 3/4" (4.5 cm) square. Referring to Diagram A, fold the corners of the square into the center. Trim the center corners to

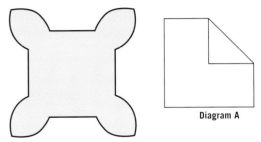

**Leaf Template (Photocopy at 100%)**

**Diagram A**

make a small window. Trim the folded corners. Cut a small rectangle from the double-sided adhesive sheet. Peel off the protective paper, and attach the adhesive sheet to the center of the flower. Remove the remaining protective paper from the adhesive sheet. Sprinkle the exposed adhesive sheet with the micro beads, removing any excess beads. Repeat to make four more flowers. From the double-sided adhesive sheet, cut five 1/2" (1 cm) squares. Peel off the protective paper, and attach the adhesive sheet to the backs of the flowers. Remove the remaining protective paper. Referring to the photo for placement, press the flowers on the leaf shapes. Trim the ends of the quilling paper, if necessary.

5. Using the marker, write the title. Using the kneaded rubber eraser, remove all pencil marks.

# Paris in Springtime

The climbing paper vines lead the eye up, as does the spire in the photo.

## Materials

- photo
- one 12" x 12" (30.5 cm x 30.5 cm) sheet blue paper
- one 8 1/2" x 11" (21.5 cm x 28 cm) sheet green paper with white reverse side
- one 8 1/2" x 11" (21.5 cm x 28 cm) sheet pink paper
- one 8 1/2" x 11" (21.5 cm x 28 cm) white paper
- one 8 1/2" x 11" (21.5 cm x 28 cm) sheet yellow patterned paper
- white quilling paper
- archival-quality adhesive spray
- double-sided adhesive sheet, such as Peel-N-Stick
- red pencil
- pink pencil

## Tools

- metal-edged ruler
- craft knife
- scissors
- pencil
- tracing paper
- kneaded rubber eraser
- black fine-tip marker (optional)

## Instructions

**1.** Using the ruler and knife, trim the photo to 7 3/8" x 9 1/4" (18.5 cm x 23.5 cm). Place the photo 1 1/4" (3 cm) from the left edge and 5/8" (1.5 cm) from the top edge of the blue paper. With the pencil, lightly mark the blue paper at the corners of the photo for placement. Following the manufacturer's directions, coat the back of the photo with adhesive spray. Press in place.

**2.** From the yellow patterned paper, cut one 1/4" x 11" (0.6 cm x 28 cm) strip. Loosely wrap one or two lengths of quilling paper around the yellow strip. Press the quilling paper flat. From the double-sided adhesive sheet, cut one 1/8" x 9" (0.3 cm x 23 cm) strip. Peel off the protective paper, and attach the adhesive sheet to the back of the yellow strip. Mark a vertical line 1 1/4" (3 cm) from the right edge of the blue paper. Remove the remaining protective paper from the adhesive sheet, and press the wrapped strip in place on the marked line.

**3.** From the pink paper, cut one 1 3/4" (4.5 cm) square. Draw a diagonal line on the square from the bottom-left corner to the top-right corner. Referring to Diagram A, fold the bottom right corner of the square into the center to meet the marked line. Fold the top left corner of the square into the center at the marked line. Referring to Diagram B, fold the top-right corner in 1/4" (0.6 cm). Use the kneaded rubber eraser to erase the line. Use the scissors to trim the bottom-left corner. Using the red pencil, draw one or two small circles beneath the folded corner. Repeat to make two more pink flowers. From the green-and-white paper, cut one 3/8" x 3 1/2" (1 cm x 9 cm) strip. With the white side facing up, wrap the strip around the bottom of one flower, and angle the ends up behind the flower. Trim the ends of the strip, if necessary. Repeat with the remaining two flowers. From the double-sided adhesive sheet, cut three 1/2" (1 cm) squares. Peel off the protective paper, and attach the squares to the backs of the flowers and the leaves. Remove the remaining protective paper. Referring to the photo for placement, press the flowers in place.

**4.** From the white paper, cut one 1 1/2" (4 cm) square. Fold the corners of the square into the center. Trim the center corners to make a small window. Unfold the white square. From the green-and-white paper, cut one 1/2" (1 cm) square. From the double-sided adhesive sheet, cut one

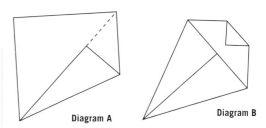

**Diagram A**     **Diagram B**

1/4" (0.6 cm) square. Peel off the protective paper, and attach the square to the back of the green square. Remove the remaining protective paper from the adhesive sheet, and press the square in place in the center of the white square. Refold the paper, and fold the corners in 1/4" (0.6 cm). Repeat to make three more white flowers. From the double-sided adhesive sheet, cut four 1/2" (1 cm) squares. Peel off the protective paper, and attach the squares to the backs of the white flowers. Remove the remaining protective paper. Referring to the photo for placement, press the flowers in place.

**5.** On the white paper, print the title using the black marker (or do this on a computer). Trim the title box to 7" x 3/4" (18 cm x 2 cm). Coat the back of the title box with adhesive spray. Referring to the photo for placement, press the title box in place.

**6.** Use the kneaded rubber eraser to remove all pencil marks.

# Paper Clay

Lightweight, air-hardening modeling clays are widely available and are perfect for enhancing scrapbooks with simple sculptural shapes. The material can be molded and shaped while it's still moist, and it air-dries naturally without needing to be baked or fired in a kiln. Once the clay is dry, it can be painted with tempera, watercolor, or acrylic paint. These nontoxic clays contain all-natural ingredients and can be used by people of any skill level. They are available in a wide range of blendable colors, from natural stone and marble tints to brights, pearlescents, and metallics. The samples here show some of the many techniques that can be applied to air-hardening clay.

**Sample 1:** Trace and cut out a simple leaf shape from rolled-out clay. Embed a piece of plastic-coated wire as the stem, and let dry.

**Sample 2:** Use pinking shears or other decorative scissors to cut a simple square from rolled-out clay. Embed coins or other found objects, and let dry.

**Sample 3:** Use decorative scissors to cut a border from rolled-out clay. Press in buttons. Use a pencil tip to imprint the background with dots. Let dry.

# Little Cowboys

In this page design, the acorn clay tiles illustrate the quote, adding a horizontal design element that nicely balances the vertical silhouette of the tree.

## Materials

- photo
- one 12" x 12" (30.5 cm x 30.5 cm) sheet mustard paper
- one 12" x 12" (30.5 cm x 30.5 cm) sheet cream paper
- one 9" x 12" (23 cm x 30.5 cm) sheet black textured paper
- one die-cut tree shape or one 12" x 12" (30.5 cm x 30.5 cm) sheet light brown paper
- air-hardening modeling clay, such as PaperClay
- acorn rubber stamp with 1³/₈" x 1³/₈" (3.5 cm x 3.5 cm) image size
- tan acrylic craft paint
- double-sided adhesive sheet, such as Peel-N-Stick
- four self-adhesive foam spacers
- brown chisel-point marker
- archival-quality adhesive spray

## Tools

- waxed paper
- rolling pin
- craft knife
- metal-edged ruler
- pencil
- kneaded rubber eraser
- fine-grain sandpaper
- tan acrylic craft paint
- white craft glue
- paintbrush
- paper towel
- tracing paper (optional)

## Instructions

1. Using the rolling pin, roll the clay on the waxed paper to approximately ¹/₈" (0.3 cm) thick. (Trimmed clay tiles are 1⁷/₈" (5 cm) square, so create enough surface area for three tiles.) Press the stamp in the clay three times, allowing ¹/₂" (1 cm) around each image. Let dry.

2. Center the images, and using the ruler and knife, cut out three 1⁷/₈" (5 cm) square tiles. Dried clay is dense and requires several passes with the knife. Use the sandpaper to slightly sand the edges.

3. Dilute the acrylic craft paint to approximately three parts water to one part paint. Paint the tiles. Blot the tiles with the paper towel, if necessary. Let dry. Apply one light coat of craft glue to the backs of the tiles to seal. Let dry.

4. Place the die-cut tree shape on the center-left of the mustard paper. Or, using the tracing paper, make the template for the tree shape. (See Tree template on page 284.) From the light brown paper, cut one tree shape. Use the pencil to mark lightly the mustard paper at chosen reference points on the tree for placement. Following the manufacturer's directions, coat the back of the tree with adhesive spray. Press in place.

5. Using the ruler and knife, cut one 12" x 1³/₄" (30.5 cm x 4.5 cm) strip from the cream paper. Place the strip 1¹/₄" (3.5 cm) from the bottom edge of the mustard paper. Mark the mustard paper at the top edge of the strip for placement. Coat the back of the strip with adhesive spray. Press in place.

6. From the double-sided adhesive sheet, cut three 1¹/₂" (4 cm) squares. Peel off the protective paper, and attach the squares to the backs of the clay tiles. Remove the remaining protective paper from the adhesive sheet. Center one tile on the cream strip, and press in place. Attach the remaining tiles, allowing 1³/₄" (4.5 cm) between each.

7. Using the ruler and knife, trim the photo to 3¹/₂" x 5⁵/₈" (9 cm x 14 cm). Coat the back of the photo with the adhesive spray. Place the photo on the black paper, and press to adhere. Centering the photo, trim the black paper to 4" x 6¹/₈" (10 cm x 15.5 cm). Place the mounted photo 2¹/₄" (6 cm) from the left edge and 2¹/₂" (6.5 cm) from the top edge of the mustard paper. Use the pencil to mark the mustard paper at the corners of the mounted photo for placement. Attach the foam spacers to the back of the black paper at the corners. Peel the protective paper from the foam spacers, and press the photo in place.

8. Use the marker to write the quote, names, and date.

9. Use the kneaded rubber eraser to remove all pencil marks.

# Western Vistas

The organic swirl shapes in the clay border echo the natural curves of the clouds and mountaintops in the photos. The white clay highlights the white, handwritten captions.

**Materials**

- photos
- one 12" x 12" (30.5 cm x 30.5 cm) sheet dark brown paper
- air-hardening modeling clay, such as PaperClay
- swirl stamp with 1 ½" x 1 ½" (4 cm x 4 cm) image size
- white pencil
- double-sided adhesive sheet, such as Peel-N-Stick
- archival-quality adhesive spray

**Tools**

- waxed paper
- rolling pin
- craft knife
- metal-edged ruler
- pencil
- kneaded rubber eraser
- white craft glue
- fine-grain sandpaper

**Instructions**

1. Using the rolling pin, roll the clay on the waxed paper to approximately ⅛" (0.3 cm) thick. Press the stamp in the clay in a random pattern within a 2" x 12" (5 cm x 30.5 cm) surface area. Let dry.

2. Using the ruler and knife, trim one side of the clay to create a straight border. Dried clay is dense and requires several passes with the knife. Use the knife to trim carefully around the swirls on the opposite side of the border. Use the sandpaper to sand the edges of the trimmed border lightly. Apply one light coat of craft glue to the back of the clay border to seal. Let dry.

3. Using the ruler and knife, trim the photos to 7" x 3 ⅜" (18 cm x 8.5 cm). Place the top photo 2 ⅛" (5.5 cm) from the right edge, and ⅝" (1.5 cm) from the top edge of the brown paper. Center the remaining photos under the top photo, allowing ⅜" (1 cm) between each. Use the pencil to lightly mark the brown paper at the corners of the photos for placement. Following the manufacturer's directions, coat the backs of the photos with adhesive spray. Press in place.

4. Using the white pencil, write the captions.

5. From the double-sided adhesive sheet, cut one shape that matches the clay border. Peel off the protective paper, and attach the adhesive shape to the back of the clay border. Remove the remaining protective paper, and attach the clay border to the right edge of the brown paper.

6. Use the kneaded rubber eraser to remove all pencil marks.

# recipe # 3

# Fusible Fabric Appliqué

For centuries, appliqué has been the favorite pastime of quilters. Combine the variety of available fabrics with the versatility of the technique, and the design possibilities are endless. However the traditional needle-turn method is time-consuming and requires many tiny hand stitches. With the introduction of fusible web, fast and easy iron-on appliqué is now possible. Fusible web is paper-backed adhesive that is activated by the heat from an iron. It is sold by the yard in craft and fabric stores. Patterns can be drawn on the smooth, paper side of the web. The rough side is coated with adhesive crystals that melt when heated by a hot iron. Fusible web enables scrapbook enthusiasts to make fabric appliqués by fusing fabric to paper and then attaching the paper-backed appliqués to the page. Designs can be ironed directly onto the page, but, unfortunately, the heat from the iron can warp the paper. Experiment with mixing patterns and textures of interesting fabrics to enhance your pages.

**Sample 1.** Use cheery pink fabric to line this puffy paper envelope.

**Sample 2.** Snip many tiny squares from fabric that has first been fused to paper. Then construct this patchwork quilt to enhance a photo of your favorite baby.

**Sample 3.** Make a statement. Cut letters or numbers from fused fabric and string them together for titles or captions.

# Art Deco Flowers

Fabric absorbs more light and has a softer-appearing surface than paper. To stabilize the fabric and achieve a clean-cut edge, fused the paper to the wrong side of the fabric. After fusing, cut the fabric into curvy silhouette shapes, such as these Art Deco flowers.

**Materials**

- photo
- one 12" x 12" (30.5 cm x 30.5 cm) sheet wine paper
- one 8 1/2" x 11" (21.5 cm x 28 cm) sheet burgundy paper
- one 8 1/2" x 11" (21.5 cm x 28 cm) sheet gray vellum
- two sheets typing paper
- scrap burgundy print fabric
- scrap green print fabric
- 4 1/2" (11.5 cm) fusible web
- archival-quality adhesive spray
- double-sided adhesive sheet, such as Peel-N-Stick

**Tools**

- craft knife
- metal-edged ruler
- pencil
- iron
- scissors
- kneaded rubber eraser

## Instructions

**1.** From the fusible web, cut one 4 1/2" x 7" (11.5 cm x 18 cm) rectangle. From the green fabric, cut one 5" x 7 1/2" (12.5 cm x 19 cm) rectangle. Following the manufacturer's directions, center and fuse the web to the wrong side of the green fabric. Let cool. On the typing paper, trace three stems 1/4" (0.6 cm) apart. (See Flower template on page 284.) Because the typing paper is on the back of the fabric appliqués, all templates are reversed. Peel the protective paper from the web. Place the fabric, adhesive side up, on the ironing surface. Center the stems on the fabric, and use an iron to fuse the typing paper to the fabric. Let cool. Cut out the stems.

**2.** From the fusible web, cut one 1 1/2" x 4" (4 cm x 25.5 cm) rectangle. From the burgundy fabric, cut one 2" x 4 1/2" (5 cm x 11.5 cm) rectangle. Center and fuse the web to the wrong side of the burgundy fabric. Let cool. Trace three flowers 1/4" (0.6 cm) apart on the typing paper. Peel

the protective paper from the web. Place the fabric, adhesive side up, on the ironing surface. Center the flowers and fuse the typing paper to the fabric. Let cool. Cut out the flower sections.

**3.** Place one stem 1 5/8" (4 cm) from the left edge and 3/4" (2 cm) from the bottom edge of the wine paper. Align them horizontally, and place the remaining two stems on the wine paper, allowing 1" (2.5 cm) between each stem. Use the pencil to mark lightly the wine paper at the top and the bottom of each stem for placement. Following the manufacturer's directions, coat the backs of the stems with the adhesive spray. Press in place. Coat the backs of the flower sections with the adhesive spray. Press in place.

**4.** Using the ruler and the knife, trim the photo to 4 1/2" x 6 3/4" (11.5 cm x 17 cm). Coat the back of the photo with the adhesive spray. Place the photo on the burgundy paper, and press. Centering the photo, trim the burgundy paper to 4 3/4" x

7" (12 cm x 18 cm). Place the mounted photo 1 1/4" (3 cm) from the right edge and 1 1/2" (4 cm) from the top edge of the wine paper. Use the pencil to mark the wine paper at the corners of the mounted photo for placement. Coat the back of the burgundy paper with the adhesive spray. Press in place.

**5.** Use the pencil to print a message on the gray vellum. Trim the gray vellum to 3 1/4" x 2" (8.5 cm x 5 cm). From the double-sided adhesive sheet, cut four small triangles. Peel off the protective paper, and attach the adhesive sheet to the corners of the message box. Remove the remaining protective paper from the adhesive sheet. Align the message box with the right side of the mounted photo, and press it in place below the photo.

**6.** Use the kneaded rubber eraser to remove all pencil marks.

# Fused Frame

This combination of vintage fabrics creates a tactile, textured frame that enhances the antique quality of this family photo. The buttons echo the paper pattern and add a three-dimensional appeal to the presentation.

## Materials

- photo
- one 12" x 12" (30.5 cm x 30.5 cm) sheet blue patterned paper
- one 8 1/2" x 11" (21.5 cm x 28 cm) sheet oatmeal paper
- one sheet typing paper
- 1/4 yard (23 cm) blue print fabric
- 1/4 yard (23 cm) blue velveteen fabric
- 1/4 yard (23 cm) fusible web
- double-sided adhesive sheet, such as Peel-N-Stick
- archival-quality tape
- three assorted buttons
- blue thread
- white milky pen

## Tools

- craft knife
- metal-edged ruler
- pencil
- iron
- scissors
- needle
- kneaded rubber eraser

## Instructions

1. From the fusible web, cut one 8" x 10" (20.5 cm x 25.5 cm) rectangle. From the blue print fabric, cut one 8 1/2" x 10 1/2" (21.5 cm x 26.5 cm) rectangle. Center the web, and, following the manufacturer's instructions, use the iron to fuse the web to the wrong side of the blue print fabric. Let cool. Referring to Diagram A, draw a frame on the typing paper. Peel the protective paper from the web. Place the fabric, adhesive side up, on the ironing surface. Center the frame on the fabric, and use the iron to fuse the typing paper to the fabric. Let cool. Cut out the frame.

2. Draw the scalloped border for the frame on the paper side of the fusible web. (See Scalloped Frame Border template on page 285.) Use the scissors to cut around the border, allowing 1/2" (1 cm) around the marked lines. Use the iron to fuse the border piece to the wrong side of the velveteen fabric. Let cool. Using the scissors, cut the scalloped border along the marked lines. Peel the protective paper from the

fusible web. Place the blue print frame, right side up, on the ironing surface. Place the border, right side up, on the frame. Align the inside of the border with the inside of the frame, and use the iron to fuse the border to the frame. Let cool.

3. Place the fabric frame 1 1/2" (4 cm) from the right edge and 1" (2.5 cm) from the top edge of the blue paper. Use the pencil to mark lightly the blue paper at the corners of the frame for placement. Following the manufacturer's directions, coat the back of the frame with the adhesive spray. Press in place.

4. Using the ruler and the knife, trim the photo to 6 5/8" x 4 3/4" (17 cm x 12 cm). Coat the back of the photo with the adhesive spray. Center the photo in the frame, and press to adhere.

5. Using the needle and the thread, stitch one button to the top-left corner of the frame. From the oatmeal paper, cut two circles that are slightly larger in diameter

than the remaining buttons. Referring to the photo for placement, stitch circles and buttons to the frame and the blue paper. With the tape, square the ends of thread to the back of the paper.

6. Use the pen to write the caption.

7. Use the kneaded rubber eraser to remove all pencil marks.

### Diagram A

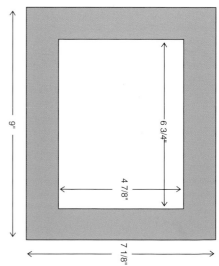

# Silk Flower Appliqué

The ubiquitous silk flower can easily dress up any page. Take the flower apart, and attach the petals and leaves to the paper using fusible web or double-sided adhesive. Or stitch the flower parts to a scrap of fabric, and attach the fabric to the paper. Silk petals and leaves are more durable than paper, are articulated with fine detail, and are colored with lovely variegated shading.

**Sample 1.** Layer petals and leaves randomly on gauzy ribbon. Machine-stitch through all layers using contrasting thread.

**Sample 3.** Arrange petals and leaves to create an individual flower. Secure with a satin-stitched center.

**Sample 2.** Gather petals with a running stitch to make three-dimensional blossoms, and attach them to a satin ribbon.

# Swing Time

The leaves and petals of silk flowers can be configured to create butterflies, hummingbirds, and even fairies.

## Materials

- photo
- one 12" x 12" (30.5 cm x 30.5 cm) sheet yellow paper
- one 8 1/2" x 11" (21.5 cm x 28 cm) sheet gray paper
- one 8 1/2" x 11" (21.5 cm x 28 cm) sheet cream patterned paper
- one 2" x 4" (5 cm x 10 cm) scrap gold moiré fabric
- one 4" x 5" (10 cm x 12.5 cm) scrap light blue fabric
- one 3" x 3" (7.5 cm x 7.5 cm) scrap medium blue fabric
- gold felt
- one pair small silk leaves, approximately 1" (2.5 cm) from tip to tip—Note: All leaf pairs are connected in the center.
- two pair medium silk leaves, approximately 2 1/2" (6.5 cm) from tip to tip
- one pair large silk leaves, approximately 3" (7.5 cm) from tip to tip
- one yellow silk flower, 1" (2.5 cm) in diameter
- four blue silk flowers, 1" (2.5 cm) in diameter
- two pink silk flowers, 2" (5 cm) in diameter
- blue thread
- blue embroidery floss
- gray embroidery floss
- one tan 1/10" (0.3 cm) chenille stem
- archival-quality adhesive spray
- black fine-tip marker (optional)

## Tools

- metal-edged ruler
- craft knife
- tracing paper
- needle
- scissors

## Instructions

1. Using the ruler and knife, trim the photo to 6 3/4" x 7 3/4" (17 cm x 20 cm). Coat the back with adhesive spray. Place on the gray paper; press to adhere. Center the photo, and trim the gray paper to 7 1/4" x 8 1/4" (18.5 cm x 21 cm). Place the mounted photo 1/2" (1 cm) from the right edge and 3/8" (1 cm) from the top edge of the yellow paper. With a pencil mark the yellow paper at the corners for placement. Coat the back with adhesive spray. Press in place.

2. Use the marker or a computer to print the poem on the cream patterned paper. Center the poem, and trim the paper to 6 7/8" x 2 3/8" (17.5 cm x 6 cm). Trim a separate strip of paper and print the author's name on it. Place the poem 7/8" (2 cm) from the left edge and 7/8" (2 cm) from the bottom edge of the yellow paper. Mark the yellow paper at the corners for placement. Coat the back with adhesive spray. Press in place. Coat the back of the author's name; press in place.

3. From the gold moiré fabric, cut one 1 3/4" x 3 1/2" (4.5 cm x 9 cm) rectangle. Referring to the photo for placement, layer one pair

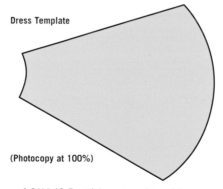

**Dress Template**

**(Photocopy at 100%)**

of 2 1/2" (6.5 cm) leaves and two blue flowers on the rectangle. With blue thread, stitch through the flower centers to secure. Repeat for the second flower. Place the fabric 1 3/4" (4.5 cm) from the right edge and 3/4" (2 cm) from the top edge of the yellow paper. Mark the yellow paper at the corners for placement. Coat the back with adhesive spray. Press in place.

4. From the light blue fabric, cut one 3 1/2" x 4 3/4" (9 cm x 12 cm) rectangle. Use the tracing paper to make the dress template. From the medium blue fabric, cut one dress shape. From the gold felt, cut one circle, 7/8" (2 cm) in diameter. Referring to Diagram A and the light blue rectangle,

layer the large leaves, stems, and dress. With blue thread, stitch around the outer edge of the dress to secure. Layer the small leaves, flower, and face. Stitch around the outer edge of the face to secure. Fold the top third of the pink flowers over to create a ruffled skirt. Place them side-by-side at the bottom of the dress; stitch through all layers to secure. Using two strands of gray embroidery floss, stitch the eyes, nose, and mouth. Using three strands of blue embroidery floss, stitch shoes. Place the fabric 1/4" (0.6 cm) from the right edge and 1/4" (6 cm) from the bottom edge of the yellow paper. Mark the yellow paper at the corners for placement. Coat the back with adhesive spray. Press in place. Use the eraser to remove pencil marks.

**Diagram A**

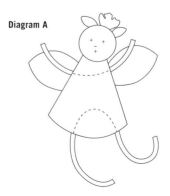

# '50s Kids

The versatility of silk flowers is demonstrated on this page. The same blue petals and small leaves are used for both the framed vignette and the bookmark.

## Materials

- photo
- one 12" x 12" (30.5 cm x 30.5 cm) sheet black embossed paper
- one 8 1/2" x 11" (21.5 cm x 28 cm) sheet handmade paper
- one 8 1/2" x 11" (21.5 cm x 28 cm) sheet silver paper
- one 8 1/2" x 11" (21.5 cm x 28 cm) sheet black paper
- two pair medium silk leaves, approximately 2 1/2"" (6.5 cm) from tip to tip
- one pair large silk leaves, approximately 3" (7.5 cm) from tip to tip
- one yellow silk flower, 1 1/2" (4 cm) in diameter
- seven blue silk flowers, 1" (2.5 cm) in diameter
- seven individual leaves, 1" (2.5 cm) in length
- 3/4" (2 cm)-wide green velvet ribbon, 6" (15 cm) long
- 1 1/2" (3.8 cm)-wide cream sheer ribbon, 6" (15 cm) long
- double-sided adhesive sheet, such as Peel-N-Stick
- archival-quality adhesive spray
- archival-quality tape
- green thread
- white pencil

## Tools

- metal-edged ruler
- craft knife
- scissors
- white craft glue
- sewing machine

## Instructions

1. Using the ruler and knife, trim the silver paper to 4 1/2" x 6" (11.5 cm x 15 cm). Center the rectangle, and use the knife to cut a 3 1/4" x 4 3/4" (8 cm x 12 cm) window to make a mat. Place the mat 3/4" (0.6 cm) from the right edge and 1/2" (1 cm) from the bottom edge of the black paper. Use the pencil to lightly mark the black paper at the corners of the mat for placement. Following the manufacturer's directions, coat the back of the mat with the adhesive spray. Press in place.

2. Using a silk leaf as a template, cut three leaves from the double-sided adhesive sheet. Peel off the protective paper, and attach the adhesive sheet to the backs of three silk leaves. Refer to the photo for placement of the leaves and the blossoms within the silver mat. Remove the remaining protective paper, and attach the leaves to the black paper. Repeat this process for the yellow flower and three blue flowers. From the silver paper, cut 1/8" (0.3 cm) strips. Trim the strips to make the stems.

Coat the backs of the stems with adhesive spray. Press in place. Trim small pieces from the strip to make the flower centers. Apply a small amount of white craft glue to the backs of the flower centers. Press them in place.

3. Trim the photo to 7 1/4" x 5 1/4" (18.5 cm x 13.5 cm). Trim the handmade paper to 7 3/4" x 5 3/4" (20 cm x 14.5 cm). Center and cut a 6 1/4" x 4 1/4" (16 cm x 11 cm) window to make a mat. Use the archival-quality tape to attach the photo to the back of the mat. Place the matted photo 1" (2.5 cm) from the left edge and 1/2" (1 cm) from the edge of the black paper. Use the pencil to mark the black paper at the corners of the matted photo for placement. Coat the back of the matted photo with the adhesive spray. Press in place.

4. Center and layer the ribbons, leaves, and flowers in the following order: sheer ribbon, leaves, velvet ribbon, and two layers of flowers. Pin in place. Machine-stitch through all layers down the center of the

layered ribbon. Referring to the photo, trim the top and bottom of the stitched ribbon. From the double-sided adhesive, cut one 1/2" x 3" (1 cm x 7.5 cm) strip. Peel off the protective paper, and attach the adhesive sheet to the back of the stitched ribbon. Remove the remaining protective paper, and attach the stitched ribbon to the black paper, along the right edge of the matted photo.

5. Using the white pencil, write the caption on the black paper. Center the caption box, and trim it to the desired size. Coat the back of the caption box with the adhesive spray, and press in place beneath the photo.

6. Use the kneaded rubber eraser to remove all pencil marks.

# Shaped Wire

Papercrafters have discovered that they can draw and write with malleable wire, almost as easily as they can with a pencil or pen. Become familiar with the tractability of wire, and let your imagination run wild. Drawing with wire is similar to drawing on an Etch-A-Sketch—the best designs consist of one continuous line. Wire messages or images add a particular attitude of whimsy to any scrapbook project. The downside to attaching shaped wire to paper is that the contact area is small and craft glues don't hold well. A better solution is to back the wire with thin strips of double-sided adhesive or to anchor the wire with strips of paper. Also, note that fragile papers or photos on a facing page may be scratched by the wire, so position your wire embellishments strategically.

**Sample 1.** Thread wooden fish buttons onto 24-gauge green wire. Then use needle-nose pliers to shape the wire to simulate the movement of ocean waves.

**Sample 2.** Bundle wire together to form a body. Then turn and twist yellow and purple 24-gauge wire to fashion this butterfly.

**Sample 3.** Shape a short holiday message from shiny 20-gauge copper wire. The wire is anchored with paper strips, which have been drawn through slits to the back of the page.

# Cooking

These playful spoons feature centers that are coiled tightly. The more wire that is used in fashioning an object, the more solid that object will appear.

**Materials**

- photo
- one 12" x 12" (30.5 cm x 30.5 cm) sheet brown paper
- one 8 1/2" x 11" (21.5 cm x 28 cm) sheet peach patterned paper
- one 8 1/2" x 11" (21.5 cm x 28 cm) sheet gold patterned paper
- one 8 1/2" x 11" (21.5 cm x 28 cm) sheet ivory paper
- archival-quality adhesive spray
- red 20-gauge coated wire
- blue 24-gauge coated wire
- black acrylic craft paint
- double-sided adhesive sheet, such as Peel-N-Stick

**Tools**

- craft knife
- metal-edged ruler
- pencil
- tracing paper
- fine paintbrush
- needle-nose pliers
- wire cutters
- scissors

## Instructions

1. Using the ruler and knife, trim the large photo to 5 1/2" x 4 1/4" (14 cm x 11 cm). Following the manufacturer's directions, coat the back of the photo with the adhesive spray. Place the photo on the peach patterned paper, and press to adhere. Center the photo, and trim the peach paper to 6" x 4 3/4" (15 cm x 12 cm). Center and place the mounted photo at an angle on the brown paper, with the left corner 1 3/4" (4.5 cm) and the right corner 1 1/4" (3.5 cm) from the top edge of the paper. Use the pencil to lightly mark the brown paper at the corners of the photo for placement. Coat the back of the mounted photo with adhesive spray. Press in place.

2. Use the tracing paper to make the hat template. From the ivory paper, cut the desired number of chef's hats. (See Hat template on page 284. Hat size may have to be adjusted, depending on the size of the people in the chosen photo.) Coat the backs of the hats with the adhesive spray.

Place the hats on the photo, and press to adhere.

3. Use the tracing paper to make the arch template. (See Arch template on page 286.) From the gold patterned paper, make one arch. Use the fine paintbrush to paint the title on the arch. Let dry. Coat the back of the arch with the adhesive spray. Referring to the photo for placement, set the arch approximately two-thirds of the way down from the top of the paper. Press in place.

4. Trim the small photo to 2 3/4" x 2 3/4" (7 cm x 7 cm). Place the photo 3" (7.5 cm) from the right edge and flush with the bottom edge of the brown paper. Use the pencil to mark the brown paper at the corners for placement. Coat the back of the photo with adhesive spray. Press in place.

5. Grip one end of the red wire with the needle-nose pliers, and make a coil 3/4" (2 cm) in diameter. Remove the pliers, and using

the spoon template as a guide, continue shaping the wire into a spoon. (See template on page 287.) Cut the end of the wire with the wire cutters. Make two more spoons. From the blue wire, cut one 2" (5 cm) length. Twist the blue wire three times around the neck of one of the red spoons. Use the wire cutters to trim the ends of the wire. Use the pliers to fold the ends in. Repeat for the remaining spoons.

6. From the double-sided adhesive sheet, cut six to nine 1/16" x 1" (0.2 cm x 2.5 cm) strips. Peel off the protective paper, and, following the contours of the red wire, carefully attach the strips to the backsides of the spoons. Remove the remaining protective paper from the strips. Referring to the photo for placement, set the spoons on the brown paper. Press to adhere.

7. Use the kneaded rubber eraser to remove all pencil marks.

# Favorite Books

This fine-gauge wire does double duty: it illustrates a love of reading, and it binds the paper books together.

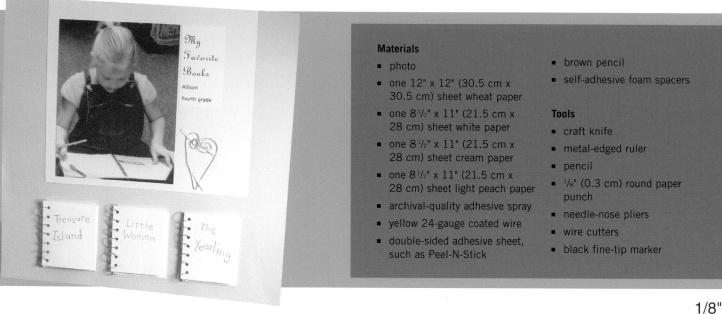

**Materials**

- photo
- one 12" x 12" (30.5 cm x 30.5 cm) sheet wheat paper
- one 8¹/₂" x 11" (21.5 cm x 28 cm) sheet white paper
- one 8¹/₂" x 11" (21.5 cm x 28 cm) sheet cream paper
- one 8¹/₂" x 11" (21.5 cm x 28 cm) sheet light peach paper
- archival-quality adhesive spray
- yellow 24-gauge coated wire
- double-sided adhesive sheet, such as Peel-N-Stick
- brown pencil
- self-adhesive foam spacers

**Tools**

- craft knife
- metal-edged ruler
- pencil
- ¹/₈" (0.3 cm) round paper punch
- needle-nose pliers
- wire cutters
- black fine-tip marker

**Instructions**

1. Using the ruler and knife, trim the peach paper to 8¹/₂" x 7³/₄" (21.5 cm x 20 cm). Trim the photo to 4⁷/₈" x 6⁵/₈" (12.5 cm x 17 cm). Place the photo ¹/₂" (1 cm) from the left edge and ¹/₄" (0.6 cm) from the bottom edge of the peach paper. Mark the peach paper at the corners for placement. Coat the back of the photo with the adhesive spray. Press in place. Use the marker to print the title on the white paper (or do this on a computer). Center the title, and trim the white paper to 1³/₄" x 3¹/₄" (4.5 cm x 8.5 cm). Coat the back with adhesive spray. Referring to the photo for placement, press the title box in place next to the photo.

2. Place the peach paper 1³/₄" (4.5 cm) from the left edge, flush with the top edge of the wheat paper. Mark the wheat paper at the corners for placement. Coat the back of the peach paper with adhesive spray. Press in place.

3. Cut one 10" (25.5 cm) length of the wire. Grip one end of the wire with the pliers, and make a coil ¹/₂" (1 cm) in diameter. Remove the pliers. Using the heart template as a guide, shape the wire into a heart. (See Small Heart template on page 284.) After forming the bottom half of the

heart, grip the opposite end of the wire and make a second coil to complete the shape. Cut the end of the wire with the wire cutters. Referring to the photo for placement, set the heart on the peach paper. From the double-sided adhesive sheet, cut one ³/₁₆" x 2¹/₂" (0.2 cm x 6.5 cm) strip. Peel off the protective paper, and attach the strip to a larger strip of peach paper. Trim the paper to match the adhesive. Cut the strip into thirds. Remove the remaining protective paper, and secure it to the paper with adhesive strip.

4. From the cream paper, cut three 2¹/₄" x 2³/₄" (6 cm x 7 cm) rectangles. Using the brown pencil, write one book title on each rectangle. From the white paper, cut three 2¹/₄" x 2³/₄" (6 cm x 7 cm) rectangles. Place one cream rectangle on one white rectangle. Referring to Diagram A, offset the rectangles. Using the hole punch, punch seven holes through both layers of the paper, ¹/₄" (0.6 cm) from the left edge of the cream rectangle. Remove the protective paper from the foam spacers, and attach one spacer on each corner of the white rectangle. Align the punched holes; attach the cream rectangle to the white rectangle. Repeat for the remaining books. From the yellow wire, cut three 10"

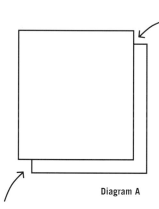

**1/8"**

**Diagram A**

**1/8"**

(25.5 cm) lengths. Wrap one length around the pencil eight times to create a spiral. Remove the pencil. Thread the spiraled wire through both sets of holes of one book. Using the wire cutters, trim the ends. Use the pliers to bend the ends toward the spiral. Place the book on the work surface, and carefully flatten the wire spiral. Repeat with the remaining books.

5. Place one book 1³/₄" (4.5 cm) from the left edge and ³/₄" (2 cm) from the bottom edge of the wheat paper. Align horizontally. Place the remaining books on the wheat paper, allowing ⁵/₈" (1.5 cm) between each book. Mark the wheat paper at the corners for placement. Coat the backs with adhesive spray. Press in place. Use the eraser to remove pencil marks.

# Quilling

This art form got its name from 14th-century artists who rolled paper strips on the end of a quill to curl them. These lacy papers were then used to decorate Bible pages. Coiled papers can be shaped through pinching and folding into all sorts of recognizable images, such as people, snowflakes, and insects. Quilling is also called paper filigree.

The following instructions call for a quilling tool. A quilling tool is a short metal rod with a narrow tip. The tip is split to accommodate the end of the paper strip. If a quilling tool is not available, the paper strips can be coiled onto a toothpick or a hat pin. The quilling tool, however, creates a more uniform coil because the end of the paper strip is held securely in its tip.

**Sample 2.** Add pizzazz to a flat tag with crazy-quilled curlicues.

**Sample 3.** Create swirling, quilled snowflakes to cover a simple snowman silhouette.

**Sample 1.** Adhere fanciful curls to the top of a window frame to make a perfect focal point for a Victorian house.

# Flower Girls

Little girls sporting curly hair and frilly dresses are fixtures at weddings and summer parties. In fact, these tresses look as if they were curled with a bird quill. Coiled paper flowers are the perfect complement to this angelic photo.

**Materials**

- photo
- one 12" x 12" (30.5 cm x 30.5 cm) sheet cream paper
- one 8 1/2" x 11" (21.5 cm x 28 cm) sheet pink patterned paper
- one 8 1/2" x 11" (21.5 cm x 28 cm) sheet light green patterned paper
- pink quilling paper
- green quilling paper
- white craft glue
- brown pencil
- brown acrylic paint
- archival-quality adhesive spray

**Tools**

- metal-edged ruler
- craft knife
- pencil
- quilling tool
- scissors
- toothpick
- flat paintbrush, 3/4" (2 cm) wide
- paper towel
- kneaded rubber eraser

**Instructions**

1. Using the ruler and knife, trim the pink patterned paper to 7 3/4" x 11" (20 cm x 28 cm). Place the pink paper 1" (2.5 cm) from the left edge and 1/2" (1 cm) from the top edge of the cream paper. Use the pencil to lightly mark the cream paper at the corners of the pink paper for placement. Following the manufacturer's directions, coat the back of the pink paper with the adhesive spray. Press in place. Trim the photo to 5" x 7" (12.5 cm x 18 cm). Place the photo 2 3/4" (7 cm) from the left edge and 1 3/4" (4.5 cm) from the top edge of the cream paper. Use the pencil to mark the pink paper at the corners of the photo for placement. Coat the back of the photo with adhesive spray. Press in place.

2. From the pink quilling paper, cut one 4" (10 cm) length. Insert one end of the paper into the quilling tool, and coil the paper to make a flower. Remove the curled paper from the tool. Repeat to make 11 more flowers. From the green quilling paper, cut one 6" (15 cm) length. Fold the strip in half lengthwise. Insert one end into the quilling tool, and coil the paper to within 1/2" (1 cm) of the fold to make a leaf. Insert the other end in the quilling tool and coil the paper to within 1/2" (1 cm) of the fold to make a second leaf. Use the toothpick to apply a small amount of craft glue, 1/2" (1 cm) from one side of the fold. Press the leaves together to make a stem. Repeat to make 11 more stems with leaves.

3. From the green paper, cut three 3 1/8" (8 cm) squares. Overlapping the pink paper, place one square 1/4" (0.6 cm) from the right edge and 3/4" (2 cm) from the top edge of the cream paper. Allowing 3/8" (1.5 cm) between squares, place the remaining two squares below the top square. Use the pencil to mark the pink and cream papers at the corners of the squares for placement. Coat the backs of the squares with adhesive spray. Press them in place to adhere. Use the toothpick to apply a small amount of craft glue to the back of one flower. Referring to the photo for placement, press the flower in place in the top-left corner of the top square. Apply a small amount of glue to the back of one stem with leaves. Press in place below the flower. Repeat to attach remaining flowers and stems with leaves.

4. Use the brown pencil to write the title. Dilute the brown acrylic paint to approximately three parts water to one part paint. Using two continuous, horizontal strokes, paint over the title. Blot the paint with a paper towel, if necessary.

5. Use the kneaded rubber eraser to remove all pencil marks.

# Live, Laugh, Love

These quilled papers look great on the stamped-wallpaper background. The simple title prompts further inspection of the candid and light-hearted photos.

**Materials**

- One 12" x 12" (30.5 cm x 30.5 cm) sheet ivory paper
- three floral stamps, with image size 1½" (4 cm) to 3" (7.5 cm)
- pink ink
- brown acrylic paint
- white quilling paper
- white craft glue
- archival-quality adhesive spray

**Tools**

- tracing paper
- pencil
- metal-edged ruler
- craft knife
- quilling tool
- scissors
- toothpick
- round-tip liner brush
- kneaded rubber eraser

**Instructions**

1. Lay the tracing paper over the bottom 5" (12.5 cm) of the ivory paper. Using the stamps and the ink, stamp the top 7" (18 cm) of the ivory paper in a random pattern. Let dry.

2. Use the pencil to mark light horizontal lines at 2" (5 cm), 4¼" (11 cm), and 6½" (16.5 cm) from the top edge of the ivory paper. Paint the title on the marked lines using the round-tip liner brush and brown acrylic paint. Let dry. Use the kneaded rubber eraser to remove the pencil lines. Mark a second set of horizontal lines with the pencil at 2¼" (6 cm), 4½" (11.5 cm), and 6¾" (17 cm) from the top edge of the cream paper.

3. From the quilling paper, cut one 8" (20.5 cm) length. Insert one end of the paper in the quilling tool, and coil 4" (10 cm) of the paper. Remove the paper from the tool. Insert the opposite end of the paper in the quilling tool, and coil the remaining 4" (10 cm) in the opposite direction to make an "S" shape. Repeat to make 23 more "S" shapes. Use the toothpick to apply a small amount of craft glue to the back of one "S" shape. Referring to the photo for placement and using the top pencil line as a guide, press the "S" shape in place. Repeat, gluing a total of 8 "S" shapes per line. Let dry.

4. Using the ruler and knife, trim the photos to the following sizes, from left to right: 2⅝" x 2¾" (6.5 cm x 7 cm), 3⅜" x 2¾" (8.5 cm x 7 cm), and 3⅛" x 2¾" (8 cm x 7 cm). Place the left photo 1" (2.5 cm) from the left edge and 1" (2.5 cm) from the bottom edge of the ivory paper. Aligning the top and bottom edges and allowing ⅜" (1 cm) between the photos, place the remaining two photos on the ivory paper. Use the pencil to mark the ivory paper at the corners of the photos for placement. Coat the backs of the photos with adhesive spray. Press in place.

5. With the kneaded rubber eraser, remove all pencil marks.

# Pencil Shadowing

This treatment was adapted from charcoal rubbing, an activity of genealogists and curiosity seekers. For charcoal rubbing, a sheet of blank paper is placed on a tombstone or a monument and then rubbed with charcoal. The stone's or monument's texture and design are transferred to the paper. Other soft mediums, such as colored pencils, chalk, and pastel sticks, also create designs when rubbed on raised textures. The patterns made with colored pencils are subtle and nonsmearing. Those made with chalk and pastel sticks are more dramatic because there is greater contrast between the dark and the light values. Paper rubbed with chalk and pastel sticks should be sprayed with fixative before being placed in an album.

**Sample 1.** Rub a pencil over nine round-top buttons. Then rub the paper on corrugated paper. Rotate and repeat to make a border design.

**Sample 2.** Rub the pencil over a needlepoint canvas to make this texture. The design can be used to suggest a screen door or a lacy tablecloth.

**Sample 3.** Rub the surface of corrugated paper to create the waves; a sticker floats in the foreground.

# Leaf Shadows

This treatment provides a quick and subtle way to enhance solid paper. It also enables your hole punches to do double duty.

**Materials**

- photo
- one 12" x 12" (30.5 cm x 30.5 cm) sheet sage paper
- one 8 1/2" x 11" (21.5 cm x 28 cm) sheet taupe paper
- one 8 1/2" x 11" (21.5 cm x 28 cm) sheet handmade paper with embedded leaves
- one 8 1/2" x 11" (21.5 cm x 28 cm) sheet pink vellum
- scrap of cardstock (any color)
- printed announcement
- black photo corners
- archival-quality adhesive spray
- taupe pencil

**Tools**

- leaf punch
- craft knife
- metal-edged ruler
- pencil
- tracing paper
- scissors
- kneaded rubber eraser
- black fine-tip marker (optional)

## Instructions

1. Use the leaf punch to punch a leaf shape in the cardstock. Place the vellum on the punched card stock. Using the flat side of the taupe pencil's tip, gently color over the punched-out leaf to create a leaf image. Move the cardstock around, repeat to make 10 more leaves along the right edge of the vellum. Referring to the photo for placement, punch two leaf shapes on the right side of vellum. Place the vellum sheet 5/8" (1.5 cm) from the right edge and 3/8" (1 cm) from the top edge of the sage paper. Use the pencil to lightly mark the sage paper at the corners of the vellum for placement. Following the manufacturer's directions, coat the back of the vellum with adhesive spray. Press in place.

2. Referring to the photo for placement, punch three leaf shapes on the left side and the bottom of the handmade paper. Place the handmade paper 2 1/2" (6.5 cm) from the right edge and 5/8" (1.5 cm) from the top edge of the sage paper. Use the

pencil to mark the pink vellum and the sage paper at the corners of the handmade paper for placement. Coat the back of the handmade paper with adhesive spray. Press in place.

3. Using the ruler and knife, trim the photo to 4 1/4" x 5 1/2" (11 cm x 14 cm). Place the photo 3 1/2" (9 cm) from the right edge and 1 1/4" (4 cm) from the top edge of the sage paper. Use the pencil to mark the handmade paper at the corners of the photo for placement. Following the manufacturer's directions, attach the photo to the handmade paper with the photo corners.

4. With the text centered, use the knife to trim the announcement to 4 1/4" x 2 1/2" (11 cm x 6.5 cm). Place the announcement 3" (7.5 cm) from the right edge, and 2 3/8" (6 cm) from the bottom edge of the sage paper. Use the pencil to mark the handmade paper at the corners of the announcement for placement. Coat the

back of the announcement with adhesive spray. Press in place.

5. Use the tracing paper to make the leaf template. From the taupe paper, cut one leaf shape. Coat the back of the leaf shape with adhesive spray. Refer to the photo for placement. Press the leaf shape on the handmade paper, overlapping the announcement.

6. Use the kneaded rubber eraser to erase all pencil marks.

**Leaf Template**

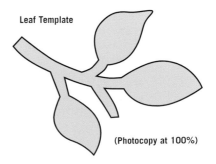

(Photocopy at 100%)

# Travel Textures

Collecting items to feature is as much fun as revealing the patterns. Group small items such as buttons, and overlap flat items such as coins.

**Materials**

- photos
- one 12" x 12" (30.5 cm x 30.5 cm) sheet brown paper
- one 8 1/2" x 11" (21.5 cm x 28 cm) sheet black paper
- one 8 1/2" x 11" (21.5 cm x 28 cm) sheet yellow paper
- one 8 1/2" x 11" (21.5 cm x 28 cm) sheet corrugated paper (any color)
- embossed tin
- white pencil
- archival-quality adhesive spray

**Tools**

- 3-D items with articulated textures, such as keys, coins, jewelry, and silverware
- craft knife
- metal-edged ruler
- pencil
- kneaded rubber eraser
- black fine-tip marker (optional)

**Instructions**

1. Place the three-dimensional items on the work surface. Place the black paper over the items. Use the flat side of the tip of the white pencil, and gently color over the raised surfaces of the items to create the images. After reproducing the desired number of images, fill in the negative spaces by repeating the process over the corrugated paper and the tin. Using the ruler and the knife, trim the decorated paper to 6 1/4" x 5 1/2" (16 cm x 14 cm). Following the manufacturer's directions, coat the back of the black paper with adhesive spray. Press the paper in the top-right corner of the brown paper to adhere.

2. Using the ruler and knife, trim the photos to the following sizes, clockwise from left: 5 1/8" x 5 1/8" (13 cm x 13 cm), 2 1/4" x 2 1/4" (6 cm x 6 cm), 5 1/2" x 6 1/2" (14 cm x 16.5 cm), and 4 1/2" x 5 1/4" (11.5 cm x 13.5 cm). Referring to the photo for placement, arrange the large photos on the brown paper. Place the top-right photo 3" (7.5 cm) from the right edge and 1/4" (0.6 cm) from the top edge of the black paper. Use the pencil to lightly mark the brown paper and the black paper at the corners of the photos for placement. Coat the backs of the photos with adhesive spray. Press the photos in place.

3. Use the marker to print the title on the yellow paper (or do this on a computer). With the title centered, trim the paper to 4" x 1" (10 cm x 2.5 cm). Coat the back of the title box with adhesive spray. Referring to the photo for placement, press the title box along the bottom edge of the black paper.

4. Use the kneaded rubber eraser to remove all pencil marks.

# Eyelets

Eyelets are small embellishments that pack a big punch. They not only are intrinsically attractive but also enable you to attach die-cuts to a page and layer paper without using adhesives. You can use them to reinforce holes from which you can hang, connect, or attach 3-D accents. They are available in a wide variety of sizes, colors, and shapes—literally from A to Z: alligators to zinnias. The tools required to inset eyelets are a hole punch (match the diameter of the punch with the diameter of the eyelets), an eyelet setter, and a hammer. Be sure to work on a cutting mat or other protective surface.

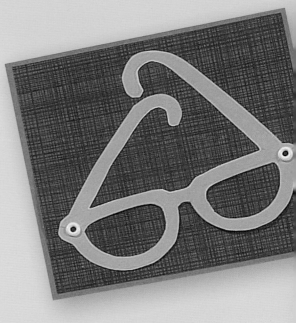

**Sample 2.** Use eyelets for decoration only. Eyelet hinges add flash to a pair of paper sunglasses.

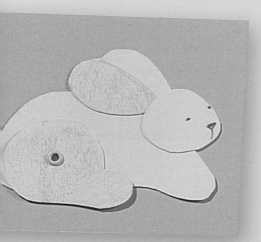

**Sample 1.** Make the hind leg of this rabbit movable by using an eyelet that acts as a joint.

**Sample 3.** Use eyelets and laces to add realism to an ordinary work boot.

# Make Believe

This page highlights the versatility of eyelets. They are used to suspend swingy strands of beads and also to hold a vellum screen in place over a dreamy butterfly.

## Materials

- one 12" x 12" (30.5 cm x 30.5 cm) sheet white paper
- one 12" x 12" (30.5 cm x 30.5 cm) sheet turquoise patterned paper
- one 8 1/2" x 11" (21.5 cm x 28 cm) sheet purple paper
- one 8 1/2" x 11" (21.5 cm x 28 cm) sheet pink paper
- one 8 1/2" x 11" (21.5 cm x 28 cm) sheet cream paper
- one 8 1/2" x 11" (21.5 cm x 28 cm) sheet violet paper
- one 8 1/2" x 11" (21.5 cm x 28 cm) sheet white vellum
- one 8 1/2" x 11" (21.5 cm x 28 cm) sheet white-and-yellow stripe paper
- one 8 1/2" x 11" (21.5 cm x 28 cm) sheet green patterned paper
- one 8" (20.5 cm) green border sticker
- purple eyelets
- peach eyelets
- white thread
- assorted seed and bugle beads: gold, silver, opaque white, and clear
- archival-quality adhesive spray
- archival-quality tape
- double-sided adhesive sheet, such as Peel-N-Stick

## Tools

- tracing paper
- metal-edged ruler
- craft knife
- scissors
- pencil
- beading needle
- hole punch
- eyelet setter
- hammer
- kneaded rubber eraser
- black fine-tip marker (optional)

## Instructions

1. Using the ruler and knife, trim the turquoise paper to an 11 1/2" x 11 1/2" (29 cm x 29 cm) square. Coat the back with adhesive spray. Center on the white paper, and press in place.

2. Use the tracing paper to make the templates for the feather and the mask. (See Feather template on page 286 and Mask template on page 287.) Referring to the photo, cut the shapes from the corresponding colors. Tape the pink trim piece to the back of the purple mask piece. From the double-sided adhesive sheet, cut 1/8" (0.3 cm)-wide strips. Trim the strips to fit the back of the feather. Peel off the protective paper, and attach the adhesive shape to the back of the feather. Remove the remaining protective paper, and press the feather in place on the mask.

3. Punch holes on the mask where indicated. Inset the purple eyelets in the holes. Using the needle, string one gold bead on the thread. Tie the end of the thread around the bead to secure. Continue threading to make a 1 1/2" (4 cm) strand. Insert the opposite end of thread through the left eyelet, and use the tape to secure the thread to the back of the mask. Trim the thread.

Repeat for the remaining eyelets. Note: Center strands measure 1 3/4" (4.5 cm).

4. Attach the border sticker 1 1/2" (4 cm) from the left edge and 2" (5 cm) from the top edge of the white paper. Place the mask 1 1/4" (4 cm) from the left edge and 1/4" (0.6 cm) from the top edge of the white paper. Mark the turquoise paper at the top and the bottom for placement. Coat the back with adhesive spray. Press in place.

5. Use the tracing paper to make the templates for the butterfly. (See Butterfly template on page 286.) Referring to the photo, cut the shapes from the corresponding colors. Coat the back of the pink wings with adhesive spray. Center and press to adhere the cream wings. From the double-sided adhesive sheet, cut one 1/8" x 1" (0.3 cm x 2.5 cm) strip. Peel off the protective paper, and attach the adhesive to the back of the body. Remove the remaining protective paper, and attach the body to the wings. Place the butterfly 1 3/8" (3.5 cm) from the right edge and 1 1/4" (4 cm) from the bottom edge of the white paper. Mark the turquoise paper for placement. Coat the back of the butterfly with adhesive spray. Press in place. Use the eraser to remove pencil marks.

6. From the white vellum, cut one 3 3/8" x 3 3/8" (8.5 cm x 8.5 cm) square. Center and place the square over the butterfly. Use the hole punch to punch holes through all the layers, at each corner of the vellum. Using the eyelet setter and hammer, inset the peach eyelets in the holes.

7. Trim the photo to a 5" x 5" (12.5 cm x 12.5 cm) square. Place the photo 2 1/4" (6 cm) from the left edge and 7/8" (2 cm) from the bottom edge of the white paper. Mark the turquoise paper for placement. Coat the back with adhesive spray. Press in place. From the white-and-yellow striped paper, cut one 4 1/2" x 1 1/2" (11 cm x 4 cm) rectangle. Coat the back with adhesive spray. Referring to the photo for placement, press in place, with the top edge 1/4" (0.6 cm) above the top edge of the photo. Use the marker to print the title on the green patterned paper (or do this on a computer). Trim the title box to 5" x 7/8" (12.5 cm x 2 cm). Coat the back with adhesive spray. Referring to the photo for placement, press in place.

8. Use the eraser to remove pencil marks.

# Winter Wind

Eyelets help suspend these ornamental tags so that they can move back and forth according to the weather.

## Materials

- photo
- one 12" x 12" (30.5 cm x 30.5 cm) sheet black paper
- one 8 ½" x 11" (21.5 cm x 28 cm) sheet wheat paper
- one 8 ½" x 11" (21.5 cm x 28 cm) sheet white paper
- two 2" x 3" (5 cm x 7.5 cm) tags with string
- one 1 ½" x 2" (4 cm x 5 cm) tag with string
- peach eyelets
- snowflake eyelets
- white milky pen
- archival-quality adhesive spray
- archival-quality tape
- double-sided adhesive sheet, such as Peel-N-Stick

## Tools

- tracing paper
- metal-edged ruler
- craft knife
- scissors
- pencil
- hole punch
- eyelet setter
- hammer
- kneaded rubber eraser
- black fine-tip marker (optional)

## Instructions

1. Use the tracing paper to make the templates for the wind. (See Wind template on page 285.) From the cream paper, cut the wind shapes. Following the manufacturer's directions, coat the backs of the wind pieces with adhesive spray. Press the pieces in the top-right corner of the black paper to adhere.

2. On the white paper, use the marker to print the letters for "winter" in various sizes and styles (or do this on a computer using various fonts). Using the scissors, cut each letter from the white paper. From the double-sided adhesive sheet, cut one ¼" x 3" (0.6 cm x 7.5 cm) strip. Trim the strip to fit the backs of the letters. Peel off the protective paper, and attach the adhesive sheet to the backs of the letters. Remove the remaining protective paper, and press the letters in place on the tags.

Use the hole punch to punch holes in the black paper at 3⅞" (10 cm) from the left edge and 1⅜" (3.5 cm) from the top edge, and at 6" (15 cm) from the left edge and 2" (5 cm) from the top edge. Punch a hole in the wind where indicated. Following the manufacturer's directions, inset the peach eyelets in the holes. Thread the tag strings through the corresponding eyelets. Use the archival-quality tape to secure the strings to the back of the black paper. Trim ends. Arrange the tags at the desired angle. Use the pencil to lightly mark the black paper at the corners of the tags for placement. From the double-sided adhesive sheet, cut three ¾" (2 cm) squares. Peel off the protective paper, and attach the adhesive to the backs of the tags. Remove the remaining protective paper, and press the tags in place to adhere.

3. Using the ruler and pencil, mark a line of five horizontal dots 1⅝" (4 cm) from the bottom edge of the black paper and spaced 1⅞" (5 cm) apart. Use the hole punch to punch holes over the dots. Use the eyelet setter and hammer to inset the snowflake eyelets in the holes.

4. Using the ruler and knife, trim the photo to 5" x 3½" (12.5 cm x 9 cm). Place the photo on the black paper 3" (7.5 cm) from the left edge and 2¾" (7 cm) from the bottom edge of the black paper. Use the pencil to mark the black paper at the corners of the photo for placement. Coat the back of the photo with adhesive spray. Press in place.

5. Write the caption using the milky pen.

6. Use the kneaded rubber eraser to remove all pencil marks.

# Sequins

Thumb through any clothing or home-decorating catalog, and you will see '60s fashion reborn, complete with exotic '60s embellishments, including glistening sequins. A few well-placed sequins can add sizzle and sophistication to a page layout because the shiny surface of the sequins provides the perfect complement to the matte finish of the paper. Placing sequins on a page creates a shimmering surface texture that resembles water or snow. Sequins come in all shapes and sizes and can be glued or stitched to the paper. You can also stitch them to a separate swatch of fabric, which you can then glue to the paper.

**Sample 1.** Combine $^2/_5$" (1 cm) sequins with twisted wire for this attractive trim.

**Sample 2.** Alternate $^1/_5$" (0.2 cm) sequins and tiny beads on a wire wreath for a charming baby accent.

**Sample 3.** Surround novelty snowflake sequins with ultra-thin gold wire, which is embedded in the dark teal fabric.

# Vegas Vacation

These pastel sequins bring to mind both neon lights and celestial stars.
They serve as the perfect finishing touch for a well-dressed page.

**Materials**

- photo
- one 12" x 12" (30.5 cm x 30.5 cm) sheet purple paper
- one 8 1/2" x 11" (21.5 cm x 28 cm) glossy blue paper
- one 8 1/2" x 11" (21.5 cm x 28 cm) glossy yellow paper
- one flat postcard
- one folded postcard
- 1/5" (0.2 cm) sequins in assorted colors
- pastel beads, size 10/0
- light blue thread
- archival-quality adhesive spray
- archival-quality tape
- white milky pen

**Tools**

- craft knife
- metal-edged ruler
- pencil
- needle
- scissors
- kneaded rubber eraser

**Instructions**

1. Using the ruler and knife, trim the flat postcard to 5 1/4" x 4 3/8" (13.5 cm x 11 cm). Place several sequins on the postcard. Use the pencil to mark the chosen points for the sequins. Thread the needle, and insert the needle from the back of the postcard at one of the marked points. Working from back to front, thread one sequin on the needle. Then thread one bead on the needle. Reinsert the needle through the top of the sequin and down through the postcard. Repeating this process, stitch the remaining sequins and beads to the postcard at the marked points. Use the archival-quality tape to secure the ends of the thread to the back of the postcard. Trim ends.

2. Place the postcard 3/8" (1 cm) from the right edge and 3/8" (1 cm) from the top edge of the purple paper. Use the pencil to mark the purple paper at the corners of the postcard for placement. Following the manufacturer's directions, coat the back of the postcard with adhesive spray. Press in place.

3. Place the folded postcard 1 3/8" (3.5 cm) from the left edge and 2" (5 cm) from the top edge of the purple paper. Use the pencil to mark the purple paper at the corners of the postcard for placement. Coat the back of the postcard with adhesive spray. Press in place.

4. Trim the photo to 5 1/2" x 4" (14 cm x 10 cm). Overlapping the bottom inside corner of the folded postcard, place the photo 2 3/4" (7 cm) from the right edge and 2 1/4" (6 cm) from the bottom edge of the purple paper. Use the pencil to mark the purple paper at the corners of the photo for placement. Coat the back of the photo with adhesive spray. Press in place.

5. Cut one 5 1/4" x 5/8" (13.5 cm x 1.5 cm) strip from the blue paper. Center the strip, and use the pencil to mark nine dots 1/2" (1 cm) apart on the strip. Referring to Diagram A, stitch the sequins and the beads on the strip. Place the strip 1 1/4" (4 cm) from the left edge and 1" (2.5 cm) from the bottom edge of the purple paper. Use the pencil to mark the purple paper at

the corners of the postcard for placement. Coat the back of the strip with adhesive spray. Press in place.

6. Cut one 4" x 3/8" (10 cm x 1 cm) strip from the yellow paper. Coat the back of the strip with adhesive spray. Center and place the yellow strip beneath the blue strip. Press to adhere.

7. Write the caption using the milky pen.

8. Use the kneaded rubber eraser to remove all pencil marks.

# Wishing For

The ripples created by a tossed penny extend beyond this photo, thanks to five meandering strands of sequins. The white sequins represent both light and movement.

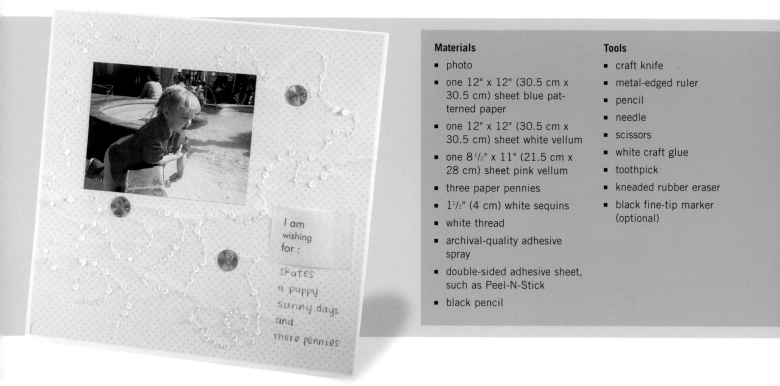

**Materials**

- photo
- one 12" x 12" (30.5 cm x 30.5 cm) sheet blue patterned paper
- one 12" x 12" (30.5 cm x 30.5 cm) sheet white vellum
- one 8 1/2" x 11" (21.5 cm x 28 cm) sheet pink vellum
- three paper pennies
- 1 1/2" (4 cm) white sequins
- white thread
- archival-quality adhesive spray
- double-sided adhesive sheet, such as Peel-N-Stick
- black pencil

**Tools**

- craft knife
- metal-edged ruler
- pencil
- needle
- scissors
- white craft glue
- toothpick
- kneaded rubber eraser
- black fine-tip marker (optional)

## Instructions

1. Using the ruler and the knife, trim the photo to 6" x 4 1/2" (15 cm x 11.5 cm). Place the photo 1 5/8" (4 cm) from the left edge and 1 3/4" (4.5 cm) from the top edge of the white vellum. Use the pencil to lightly mark the white vellum at the corners of the photo for placement. Referring to the photo for placement, set the paper pennies on the white vellum. Use the pencil to mark the placement for the center of each penny. With the craft knife, cut circles 1" (2.5 cm) in diameter around each mark.

2. Following the manufacturer's directions, coat the back of the white vellum with adhesive spray. Place the vellum on the blue patterned paper, and press to adhere. Coat the back of the photo with adhesive spray. Press in place. From the double-sided adhesive sheet, cut three circles, 3/4" (2 cm) in diameter. Peel off the protective paper, and attach the adhesive sheet to the backs of the pennies. Remove the remaining protective paper, and press the pennies in place inside the circles.

3. Use the marker to print the title on the pink vellum (or do this on a computer). Trim the pink vellum to 3" x 2" (7.5 cm x 5 cm). Place the title box 1/2" (1 cm) from the right edge and 3 3/4" (9.5 cm) from the bottom edge of the white vellum. Use the pencil to mark the white vellum at the corners of the title box for placement. From the double-sided adhesive sheet, cut four small triangles. Peel off the protective paper, and attach the triangles to the corners of the message box. Remove the remaining protective paper, and press in place.

4. Use the black pencil to write the captions below the title box.

5. Cut one 20" (51 cm) length of thread, and insert the thread in the needle. String a sequin on the thread, and choose a point on the page at which to begin a sequin strand. Use the toothpick to apply a small dot of white glue on the white vellum. Place the first sequin, convex side down, on the glue, and hold it in place for a moment to secure. Working in small sections with three or four sequins at a time, continue stringing sequins on the thread and gluing them in place. Refer to the photo for spacing between sequins and for free-form shapes of strands. After completing one strand, trim the thread and repeat with four more strands. Completed strands are between 10" (25.5 cm) and 18" (45.5 cm) long.

6. Use the kneaded rubber eraser to remove all pencil marks.

# Lace-Ups

Remember lace-up books? Generations of children were kept quiet on car trips, in waiting rooms, and in church services by drawing colored shoelaces through holes in chunky storybooks. The accents in these projects are punched with a small hole punch so that the component parts can be layered and laced together. Most hole punches don't reach to the interior of the page, so borders are a natural area for incorporating this technique. Relive your youth and, at the same time, add interest to your compositions. Try lacing with additional soft materials, such as yarn, twine, or bias-cut fabric strips. You can also use fine wire, but regular wire is not recommended because it may tear the paper.

**Sample 1.** Lace up a paper basket with nubby twine.

**Sample 2.** Lace an edging onto a photo frame with soft ribbon.

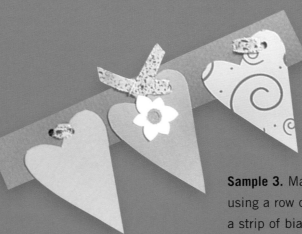

**Sample 3.** Make a great page topper using a row of hearts connected with a strip of bias-cut fabric.

# Desert Flowers

Re-create the drama of a desert flower with these graphic, lace-up flowers. The torn edges of the paper flowers resemble the ruffled edge of the real ones.

**Materials**

- photos
- one 12" x 12" (30.5 cm x 30.5 cm) sheet tan paper
- one 8 1/2" x 11" (21.5 cm x 28 cm) sheet tan patterned paper
- one 8 1/2" x 11" (21.5 cm x 28 cm) sheet dark pink paper
- one 8 1/2" x 11" (21.5 cm x 28 cm) sheet light pink paper
- 12" (30.5 cm) length cream plastic raffia
- archival-quality adhesive spray
- archival-quality tape
- black fine-tip marker

**Tools**

- craft knife
- metal-edged ruler
- pencil
- 1/8" (0.3 cm) round paper punch
- kneaded rubber eraser

## Instructions

1. Using the ruler and the knife, cut one 1 3/8" x 9 1/4" (3.5 cm x 23.5 cm) strip from the tan patterned paper. From the dark pink paper, tear two flower shapes, 2" (5 cm) in diameter. Place one flower on the tan print strip, with the center of the flower at 1 3/8" (3.5 cm) from the bottom edge of the strip. Using the hole punch, punch four holes through both layers, approximately 1/2" (1 cm) apart. With the center of the flower at 4 1/4" (11 cm) from the bottom edge of the strip, place the remaining flower on the strip. Punch four holes through both layers. From the light pink paper, tear two circles for flower centers, 3/4" (2 cm) in diameter. Place one flower center on one flower. Working from the back to the front of the strip, thread the raffia up through one hole and down through the opposite diagonal hole. Repeat to create an X. Secure the ends of raffia to back of strip using the archival-quality tape. Repeat for the remaining flower.

2. Place the strip 5/8" (1.5 cm) from right edge and 1/4" (0.6 cm) from bottom edge of the tan paper. Use the pencil to lightly mark the tan paper at the corners of the strip for placement. Following the manufacturer's directions, coat the back of the strip with adhesive spray. Place in place.

3. Trim the photos to the following sizes, clockwise from left: 4" x 6" (10 cm x 15 cm), 3 1/4" x 5 1/2" (8.5 cm x 14 cm), and 5 3/4" x 4" (14.5 cm x 10 cm). Referring to the photo for placement, arrange the photos on the tan paper. Use the pencil to lightly mark the tan paper at the corners of the photos for placement. Coat the back of the photos with adhesive spray. Press in place.

4. Write the captions using the black marker.

5. Use the kneaded rubber eraser to remove all pencil marks.

# Silver Celebration

A glitzy metallic-chenille stem is easily secured to this page with lacing. Because the chenille stem is sturdy enough to hold its shape, only a few stitches are needed.

**Materials**

- photo
- one 12" x 12" (30.5 cm x 30.5 cm) sheet blue paper
- one 8½" x 11" (21.5 cm x 28 cm) sheet light blue paper
- one 8½" x 11" (21.5 cm x 28 cm) sheet light gray paper
- one 12" (30.5 cm) silver metallic chenille stem
- 9" (23 cm) length gray embroidery floss
- letter stickers
- archival-quality adhesive spray
- archival-quality tape

**Tools**

- craft knife
- metal-edged ruler
- pencil
- ⅛" (0.3 cm) round paper punch
- wire cutter
- scissors
- kneaded rubber eraser

## Instructions

1. Using the ruler and knife, trim the photo to 5" x 6¾" (12.5 cm x 17 cm). Following the manufacturer's directions, coat the back of the photo with adhesive spray. Place the photo on the gray paper, and press to adhere. Center the photo, and trim the gray paper to 5¼" x 7" (13.5 cm x 18 cm).

2. Trim the light blue paper to 8" x 9½" (20.5 cm x 24 cm). Referring to Diagram A, punch six holes in the paper using the hole punch. Center the holes between the right and left edges of the paper and ¾" (2 cm) from the bottom edge of the paper. Referring to Diagram B, bend the chenille stem. Use the wire cutter to trim the ends of chenille stem. Referring to Diagram C, place the shaped chenille stem on the paper. Working from back to front and from right to left, thread embroidery floss through the holes to secure chenille stem in place. Secure the ends of floss to back

of the paper using the archival-quality tape. Trim ends.

3. Referring to the photo for placement, place the mounted photo ⅜" (1 cm) from the top edge of the gray paper. Use the pencil to mark lightly the light blue paper at the corners of the mounted photo for placement. Coat the back of the gray paper with adhesive spray. Press in place.

4. Place the light blue paper on the blue paper ¾" (2 cm) from the right edge and ⅜" (1 cm) from the top edge of the blue paper. Use the pencil to lightly mark the blue paper at the corners of the light blue paper for placement. Coat the back of the light blue paper with adhesive spray. Press in place.

5. Attach the stickers.

6. Use the kneaded rubber eraser to remove all pencil marks.

**Diagram A**

1¼" (3 cm)    7/16" (1 cm)

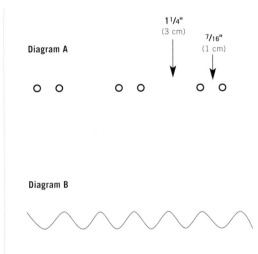

**Diagram B**

**Diagram C**

# Weaving

One kindergarten memory that we all share is weaving red and green paper strips to make a holiday place mat. Use this latent skill to create artistic page accents. Weaving is a straightforward technique, which can transform solid areas into intriguing patterns and configurations. For scrapbook layouts, use woven paper to make borders, shapes, backgrounds, and title boxes. It can naturally represent baskets, clothing, and rugs, and a simple tone-on-tone woven square looks great behind a journal message or a title box. Best of all, it is a great way to use your paper scraps.

**Sample 1.** After mastering the over-one-and-under-one weaving sequence, try weaving over one and under two.

**Sample 2.** Introduce floss or yarn into the weaving to add interest and change the texture.

**Sample 3.** Paper flower petals serve as spokes through which to weave. Weave in a circular pattern by starting in the center and working out.

# Happy Birthday Heart

Meandering strands of yarn are worked into this expressive heart.

**Materials**

- photos
- one 12" x 12" (30.5 cm x 30.5 cm) sheet gold patterned paper
- one 8½" x 11" (21.5 cm x 28 cm) sheet red patterned paper
- one 8½" x 11" (21.5 cm x 28 cm) sheet black paper
- one 8½" x 11" (21.5 cm x 28 cm) sheet tan paper
- one 8½" x 11" (21.5 cm x 28 cm) sheet burgundy paper
- birthday card
- pink yarn
- letter stickers
- brown pencil
- archival-quality adhesive spray
- double-sided adhesive sheet, such as Peel-N-Stick

**Tools**

- craft knife
- scissors
- tracing paper
- metal-edged ruler
- pencil
- kneaded rubber eraser

## Instructions

1. Place the birthday card 3½" (9 cm) from the right edge and ⅜" (1 cm) from the bottom edge of the gold patterned paper. Use the pencil to lightly mark the gold paper at the corners of the card for placement. Following the manufacturer's directions, coat the back of the card with adhesive spray. Place the card on the gold paper, and press to adhere.

2. Using the ruler and knife, trim the photos to 2½" x 3½" (6.5 cm x 9 cm). Referring to the photo for placement, set the photos diagonally inside the card. Use the pencil to mark the gold paper at the corners of the photos for placement. Coat the backs of the photos with the adhesive spray. Place the photos inside the card, and press to adhere.

3. From the red patterned paper, tear two 1½" x 11" (4 cm x 28 cm) strips. From the black paper, tear one 2" x 11" (5 cm x 28 cm) strip. Overlapping the left edge of gold paper, layer the strips on the left side of the gold paper. Coat the backs of the strips with adhesive spray. Place the strips on the gold paper, and press to adhere. Using the ruler and knife, trim the overlapping edges of the strips.

4. From the tan paper, cut one 4" x 4" (10 cm x 10 cm) square. Referring to Diagram A, cut ¼" (0.6 cm)- to ⅜" (1 cm)- wide vertical strips to within ½" (1 cm) of the top of the square. From the burgundy paper, cut two 3" x ¼" (7.5 cm x 0.6 cm) strips, and one 3" x ⅜" (7.5 cm x 1 cm) strip. From the pink yarn, cut two 8" (20.5 cm) lengths. Weave one narrow burgundy paper strip horizontally between strips of vertical tan paper. Weave one length of pink yarn horizontally between strips of brown paper. Note: Paper strips are woven with a basic over-under repeat. Yarn lengths are woven free-form, combining over-under repeats with loops that wrap completely around selected strips. Weave wide burgundy paper strip, followed by the remaining narrow burgundy paper strip, and finish with the remaining yarn length.

5. From the double-sided adhesive sheet, cut one 4" x 4" (10 cm x 10 cm) square. Peel off the protective paper, and attach the adhesive to the back of the woven heart. Use the tracing paper to make the heart template. (See Large Heart template on page 287.) Center and draw the heart on the front of the woven square. Cut the heart shape from the woven paper, but do not cut the ends of the yarn lengths or the ends of the paper strips. Referring to the photo for placement, remove the remaining protective paper, and attach the heart to the gold paper. Manipulate and arrange the ends of the yarn as desired. From the double-sided adhesive sheet, cut four 1/16" x 1/2" (0.2 cm x 1 cm) strips. Peel off the protective paper, and attach the adhesive sheet to the paper beneath the yarn ends. Remove the remaining protective paper, and press the yarn on the exposed adhesive. Trim the ends of the yarn and the ends of the paper strips, as desired.

6. Attach the stickers. Write the names and the date using the brown pencil.

7. Use the kneaded rubber eraser to remove all pencil marks.

**Diagram A**

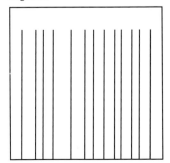

# Moiré Border

Woven paper doesn't have to be confined to rigid right angles. Inserting curved strips into this border makes it flow.

## Materials

- photo
- one 12" x 12" (30.5 cm x 30.5 cm) sheet dark brown paper
- one 12" x 12" (30.5 cm x 30.5 cm) sheet dark red paper
- one 8¹/₂" x 11" (21.5 cm x 28 cm) sheet blue patterned paper
- one 8¹/₂" x 11" (21.5 cm x 28 cm) sheet lavender paper
- one 8¹/₂" x 11" (21.5 cm x 28 cm) sheet dark gray paper
- one 8¹/₂" x 11" (21.5 cm x 28 cm) sheet light gray paper
- one 8¹/₂" x 11" (21.5 cm x 28 cm) sheet blue paper
- one 8¹/₂" x 11" (21.5 cm x 28 cm) sheet burgundy paper
- one 8¹/₂" x 11" (21.5 cm x 28 cm) sheet black paper
- gold pencil
- archival-quality adhesive spray
- double-sided adhesive sheet, such as Peel-N-Stick

## Tools

- craft knife
- tracing paper
- scissors
- metal-edged ruler
- pencil
- kneaded rubber eraser

## Instructions

1. Using the ruler and knife, trim 1" (2.5 cm) from the top edge of the dark red paper. Following the manufacturer's directions, coat the back of the dark red paper. Exposing ¹/₂" (1 cm) on both the top and the bottom of the dark brown paper, attach the dark red paper to the dark brown paper. Press to adhere.

2. Using the ruler and knife, trim the photo to 4³/₄" x 7⁵/₈" (12 cm x 19.5 cm). Coat the back of the photo with the adhesive spray. Place the photo on the black paper, and press to adhere. Center the photo, and trim the black paper to 5¹/₈" x 8" (13 cm x 20.5 cm). Place the mounted photo 1¹/₄" (3 cm) from the top edge, and 1³/₄" (4.5 cm) from the left edge of the dark red paper. Use the pencil to lightly mark the dark red paper at the corners of the mounted photo for placement. Coat the back of the mounted photo with adhesive spray. Press in place.

3. Use the tracing paper to make the border template. (See Curvy Border template on page 287.) From the blue patterned paper, cut one border shape. Cut the curved strips to within ¹/₄" (0.6 cm) of the left edge of the border. From the following papers, cut curved strips of various lengths and widths: lavender, dark gray, light gray, blue, and burgundy. Weave the strips in an over-under pattern. Note: Experiment with the length of strips and the direction in which they are woven. To obtain a random and fluid look, taper the ends of some of the strips. Complete the weaving.

4. From the double-sided adhesive sheet, cut 5¹/₂" x 11" (14 cm x 28 cm) rectangle. Peel off the protective paper, and attach the adhesive to the back of the woven border. Referring to the broken line on the border template, trim the long sides of the border. Remove the remaining protective paper, and attach the border on the right edge of the dark red paper.

5. Write the caption using the gold pencil.

6. Use the kneaded rubber eraser to remove all pencil marks.

# Ribbon Embroidery

You don't need to confine embroidered silk flowers to the corner of a collar or the edge of a handkerchief. These delicate blooms make a lovely addition to a romantic scrapbook page. And don't be intimidated by the elegance and intricacy of silk ribbon embroidery. Even a novice embroiderer can create beautiful flowers and borders by mastering a few simple stitches. To achieve the desired fullness characteristic of this technique, practice the stitches on a paper scrap.

**Sample 1.** Determine the desired rose size, and, with the pencil, lightly draw a circle on the paper.

**Sample 2.** Use the needle and thread to make five spokes in the center of the marked circle. Tape the ends of the thread to the back of the paper to secure.

**Sample 3.** Bring the ribbon from the back of the paper through the center, and, working from the center out, weave the ribbon over and under the spokes. End by inserting the needle through the paper at the outer edge of the rose. Tape the ends of the ribbon to the back of the paper to secure.

# Happy Birthday Window

Combine a running stitch and a Y stitch to create a playful border. The three-dimensional ribbon accent is as shiny as the dewy grass in the photo.

**Materials**

- photos
- one 12" x 12" (30.5 cm x 30.5 cm) sheet blue pinstripe paper
- one 8½" x 11" (21.5 cm x 28 cm) sheet green patterned paper
- one 8½" x 11" (21.5 cm x 28 cm) sheet emerald paper
- one 8½" x 11" (21.5 cm x 28 cm) sheet yellow paper
- one 8½" x 11" (21.5 cm x 28 cm) sheet mint patterned paper
- one 8½" x 11" (21.5 cm x 28 cm) sheet blue paper
- archival-quality tape
- archival-quality adhesive spray
- double-sided adhesive sheet such as Peel-N-Stick
- ⅕" (0.2 cm) light green silk ribbon
- ⅕" (0.2 cm) lavender silk ribbon
- ⅝" (1.5 cm) blue paper blossoms

**Tools**

- scissors
- needle
- craft knife
- metal-edged ruler
- pencil
- kneaded rubber eraser
- black fine-tip marker (optional)

## Instructions

1. Using the ruler and knife, trim the green patterned paper to a 7⅞" x 7⅞" (20 cm x 20 cm) square. Center and cut four 3" x 3" (7.5 cm x 7.5 cm) squares in the 7⅞" x 7⅞" (20 cm x 20 cm) square to make a mat. Use the marker to print the title on the blue paper. Center the title, and, using the ruler and knife, trim the blue paper to 3½" x 3½" (9 cm x 9 cm). Trim the emerald, yellow, and mint patterned papers to 3½" x 3½" (9 cm x 9 cm). Referring to the photo for placement, tape the papers to the back of the mat.

2. Cut the photos in circles 2⅞" (7.5 cm) in diameter. Following the manufacturer's directions, coat the backs of the photos with adhesive spray. Center and press the photos in the centers of the three blank windows. Place the matted photos 1¼" (3 cm) from the right edge and 1½" (4 cm) from the top edge of the pinstripe paper. Use the pencil to mark lightly the pinstripe paper at the corners of the mat for placement. Coat the back of the matted photos with adhesive spray. Press in place.

3. Using the ruler and the pencil, mark a line of 22 horizontal dots ⅝" (1.5 cm) below the bottom edge of the mat, and spaced ⅜" (1 cm) apart. Use the needle to slightly pierce the paper at each dot. Thread the needle with the light green ribbon. Insert the needle at the back of the paper through the far-right hole. Working right to left, stitch over-under (running stitch) through the paper at the pierced holes. Stitch loosely enough to create dimension with the ribbon. Use the archival-quality tape to secure the ends of the ribbon to the back of paper. Trim ends.

4. Refer to Diagram A for the Y stitch pattern. Mark the dots for the Y stitches between the running stitches. Using the needle, slightly pierce the paper at each dot. Bring the needle from the back to the front at A. Insert the needle at B. Pull the ribbon to the back until it forms a loose V shape. Bring the needle up at C and down at D to make a Y shape. Repeat to make four more Y stitches. Use the archival-quality tape to secure the ends of the ribbon to the back of the paper. Trim ends.

5. From the double-sided adhesive sheet, cut five circles, ⅜" (1 cm) in diameter. Peel off the protective paper, and attach the adhesive sheet to the backs of the blue blossoms. Remove the protective remaining paper, and attach the blossoms on the bottom of the mat.

6. Use the kneaded rubber eraser to remove all pencil marks.

**Diagram A**

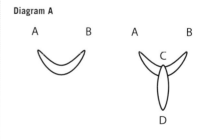

# Wedding Flowers

Special occasions call for special page treatments. Join the ribbon renaissance, and create exquisite roses of subtle color and rich texture to mark a special day.

### Materials

- photo
- printed announcement
- one 12" x 12" (30.5 cm x 30.5 cm) sheet plum paper
- one 12" x 12" (30.5 cm x 30.5 cm) sheet gray patterned paper
- one 8 1/2" x 11 (21.5 cm x 28 cm) sheet gray paper
- one 8 1/2" x 11 (21.5 cm x 28 cm) sheet pink pearlescent paper
- 1/5" (0.2 cm) pink silk ribbon
- 1/5" (0.2 cm) mauve silk ribbon
- 1/5" (0.2 cm) olive silk ribbon
- pink thread
- archival-quality tape
- archival-quality adhesive spray

### Tools

- scissors
- needle
- craft knife
- metal-edged ruler
- pencil
- kneaded rubber eraser

## Instructions

1. Referring to Diagram A, lightly mark the top-right corner of the gray paper with a pencil for stitch placement. (See Stitch Placement diagram on page 284.) Using the needle, slightly pierce the paper at each dot. Referring to Diagram B for the spiderweb rose stitch, stitch three roses as indicated, using the pink ribbon. Use the needle and thread to make five spokes in the center of the marked circles. Use the archival-quality tape to secure the ends of the thread to the back of the paper. Bring the needle from the back to the front at the center of the circle. Referring to Diagram C, insert the needle through the front of the paper at the outer edge of the rose, and come up again at the center. Continue weaving the ribbon over and under each spoke until the rose is complete, stitching loosely enough to create dimension with the ribbon. Tape the ends of the ribbon to the back of the paper to secure. Trim ends. Stitch two roses, as indicated, using the mauve ribbon. Referring to Diagram D for the leaves and with olive ribbon, stitch the leaves as indicated. Bring the needle from the back to the front at A. Insert the needle through the center of the ribbon at B. Pull the ribbon to the back until it forms a point at B. Tape the ends of the ribbon to the back of the paper to secure. Trim ends.

2. Referring to the photo, place the gray patterned paper diagonally, with the top right corner 1 1/4" (3 cm) from the right edge and 1 1/4" (3 cm) from the top edge of the plum paper. Use the pencil to lightly mark the plum paper at the corner and the sides of the gray patterned paper for placement. Following the manufacturer's directions, coat the back of the gray patterned paper with adhesive spray. Press in place. Using the ruler and knife, trim the overlapping top, left, and bottom edges of gray patterned paper.

3. Referring to the photo above, place the gray paper diagonally on the gray patterned paper. Use the pencil to mark the gray patterned paper at the corners of the gray paper for placement. Coat the back of the gray paper with adhesive spray. Press in place. Trim the overlapping edge.

4. Trim the photo to 7" x 5" (18 cm x 12.5 cm). Place the photo diagonally on the gray paper. Use the pencil to mark the gray paper at the corners of the photo for placement. Coat the back of the photo with adhesive spray. Press in place. Trim the announcement to 6 1/2" x 4 1/2" (16.5 cm x 11.5 cm). Coat the back of the announcement with adhesive spray. Overlap 1 1/4" (3 cm) of the bottom edge of the photo, and press in place to adhere.

From the pink pearlescent paper, cut one 3" x 2" x 2 1/4" (7.5 cm x 5 cm x 5.5 cm) triangle. Coat the back of the triangle with the adhesive spray. Overlap the gray paper, and place the triangle in the top-right corner of the plum paper. Press to adhere.

5. Use the kneaded rubber eraser to erase all pencil marks.

**Diagram B**

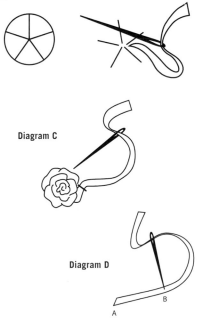

**Diagram C**

**Diagram D**

# Shrink Plastic

Shrink plastic is made from plastic stock that is heated and stretched in two directions until a thin sheet is formed. This thin sheet can be decorated in a variety of ways. When it's heated again, the plastic returns to its original dimensions and overall thickness. It's a great material for creative scrapbook pages because the final product is sturdy but flat enough to integrate easily into a page layout. You can design the plastic sheet using a wide variety of art supplies, including stamping inks, paint, markers, pastel crayons, colored pencils, and metallic, rub-on highlighting products. You can also use scissors to trim and shape it and using ordinary paper punches to punch holes in it. Finished designs are then baked. The plastic shrinks to approximately 45 percent of its original size with a thickness of $1/16$" (0.2 cm). During the shrinking process, most art materials are permanently bonded to the surface. The shrinking process has a wonderful effect on the designs and colors that are applied before baking. Simple designs become crisper, elaborate designs look amazingly detailed, and colors appear rich and vibrant.

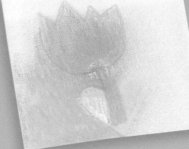

**Sample 1.** Begin to color a shrink-plastic tile with pencils before baking it.

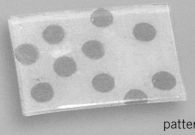

**Sample 2.** Here is a finished shrink-plastic tile featuring an orange background with purple dots.

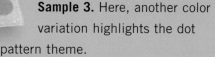

**Sample 3.** Here, another color variation highlights the dot pattern theme.

# Mother's Day Card

Use shrink plastic to create tiles that play off the motifs in a child's artwork. Use the tiles to create a colorful picture frame to house a photo of the artist.

## Materials

- photo
- one 12" x 12" (30.5 cm x 30.5 cm) sheet dark brown paper
- two or three 9" x 12" (23 cm x 30.5 cm) sheets shrink plastic
- colored pencils, including white (Prisma Colors work best)
- double-sided adhesive sheet, such as Peel-N-Stick
- archival-quality adhesive spray

## Tools

- craft knife
- metal-edged ruler
- pinking shears
- pencil
- kneaded rubber eraser

## Instructions

1. Refer to the manufacturer's directions to calculate the desired size of shrink plastic after baking. Enlarge your designs accordingly. Using your chosen artwork as inspiration, trace or draw the designs on the rough side of the shrink plastic with a pencil. Color in the designs with the colored pencils. Using the ruler and knife, cut the squares that will surround the artwork from the plastic. Calculate the finished size for the frame. Use the pencil to trace the frame outline on the rough side of the shrink plastic, and color in the frame area with the colored pencils. Cut the window from the frame. Using the pinking shears, cut around the outside edge of the frame. Following the manufacturer's directions, bake the shrink plastic. Let cool.

2. Using the ruler and knife, trim the artwork, if necessary. Trim the photo to fit the finished plastic frame.

3. Place the artwork, the tiles, and the frame on the brown paper in your desired arrangement. Refer to the photo in the book for placement. Use the pencil to lightly mark the brown paper at the corners of the artwork, the tiles, and the frame. Following the manufacturer's directions, coat the backs of the artwork and the photo with adhesive spray. Press them in place to adhere. From the double-sided adhesive sheet, cut squares that are slightly smaller than the tiles. Peel off the protective paper, and attach the adhesive to the rough side of the tiles. Remove the remaining protective paper, and press the tiles in place to adhere.

4. From the double-sided adhesive sheet, cut strips slightly narrower than the finished frame. Peel off the protective paper, and attach the adhesive to the rough side of the frame. Trim the ends of the adhesive strips to fit. Remove the remaining protective paper, and press the frame in place to adhere.

5. Using the pencil and ruler, mark a horizontal line for the caption. Write the caption using the white pencil.

6. Use the kneaded rubber eraser to erase all pencil marks.

# They Lived Happily Ever After

Create elegant photo corners from shrink-plastic tiles. A simple rubber stamp in a floral motif is used to create the delicate pattern.

## Materials

- photo
- one 12" x 12" (30.5 cm x 30.5 cm) sheet pink paper
- one 9" x 12" (23 cm x 30.5 cm) sheet straw paper
- one 9" x 12" (23 cm x 30.5 cm) sheet cream textured paper
- one 9" x 12"(23 cm x 30.5 cm) sheet shrink plastic
- two or three floral rubber stamps
- black inkpad
- double-sided adhesive sheet, such as Peel-N-Stick
- archival-quality adhesive spray
- archival-quality tape
- colored pencils in the following colors: white, cream, and pink (Prisma Colors work best)

## Tools

- tracing paper
- metal-edged ruler
- craft knife
- scissors
- pencil
- kneaded rubber eraser
- black fine-tip marker

## Instructions

1. Use the tracing paper to make the template for the corner piece. From the shrink plastic, make four corner pieces. With the black ink, stamp the floral designs in a random pattern on the rough side of the corner pieces. Let dry. Leaving some spaces open, color in the remaining spaces with the colored pencils. Following the manufacturer's directions, bake the shrink plastic. Let cool.

2. Using the ruler and knife, trim the straw paper to 7¹/₂" x 9¹/₂" (19 cm x 24 cm). Cut a 5¹/₄" x 7¹/₄" (13.5 cm x 18.5 cm) window in the center of the trimmed paper to make a mat. Trim the photo to 6" x 8" (15 cm x 20.5 cm). Tape the photo to the back of the mat using the archival-quality tape. Place the matted photo ³/₄" (2 cm) from the top edge, and 1³/₈" (3.5 cm) from the left edge of the pink paper. Use the pencil to lightly mark the pink paper at the corners of the matted photo for placement. Following the manufacturer's directions, coat the back of the matted photo with adhesive spray. Press in place.

3. Print a title or a personal sentiment on the cream textured paper using the pencil. Center the title, and trim the cream paper to 2¹/₂" x 5¹/₂" (6.5 cm x 14 cm). Tear the right edge of the title box. Coat the back of the title box with adhesive spray. Referring to the photo for placement, press in place next to the photo.

4. Use the marker to write the names and date.

5. Use the kneaded rubber eraser to remove all pencil marks.

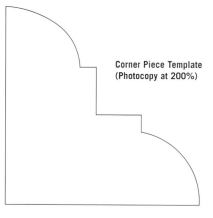

**Corner Piece Template (Photocopy at 200%)**

6. Using a finished plastic corner as a pattern, cut four corner pieces from the double-sided adhesive sheet. Peel off the protective paper, and attach the adhesive sheet to the shiny side of the corners. Remove the remaining protective paper, and overlapping the mat approximately ¹/₂" (1 cm), press the corners in place.

# Yarn Painting

Remember reading *Pat the Bunny*? Half the fun was in touching the soft accents added to the book's shiny pages. Add tactile elements to your pages with soft yarn. Mexican folk artists use colorful strands of yarn as paint. They embed it into beeswax to illustrate enchanting stories and to record historical events. Now you can paint with twisted, turned, and coiled yarn. Because the yarn is secured with double-sided adhesive rather than with beeswax, small yarn accents work best. Take advantage of the beautiful color selection and the inviting texture of yarn.

**Sample 1.** Cut a wavy horizontal line from the double-sided adhesive. Remove the protective paper to expose the adhesive, and cover it with similar types of yarn.

**Sample 2.** Add paper leaves and stems.

**Sample 3.** Top the stems with blossoms of coiled yarn.

# Summer Fun

Warm-colored yarn trim makes this affectionate sun even warmer.
Easy coils make all the difference.

## Materials

- photos
- one 12" x 12" (30.5 cm x 30.5 cm) sheet khaki paper
- one 8¹/₂" x 11" (21.5 cm x 28 cm) sheet yellow paper
- one 8¹/₂" x 11" (21.5 cm x 28 cm) sheet orange paper
- double-sided adhesive sheet, such as Peel-N-Stick
- white craft glue
- archival-quality adhesive spray
- light blue, brown, and pink pencils
- yellow yarn
- purple chisel-tip marker
- black fine-tip marker

## Tools

- scissors
- toothpick
- craft knife
- metal-edged ruler
- pencil
- tracing paper
- kneaded rubber eraser

## Instructions

1. Using the ruler and knife, trim all photos to 3¹/₄" x 4³/₄" (8.5 cm x 12 cm). Place the top photo 1¹/₂" (4 cm) from the right edge and 1³/₈" (3.5 cm) from the top edge of the khaki paper. Place the bottom-right photo 1¹/₂" (4 cm) from the right edge and ³/₄" (2 cm) from the bottom edge of the khaki paper. Aligning the top and the bottom edges, place the bottom-left photo ³/₈" (1 cm) from the bottom-right photo. Use the pencil to lightly mark the khaki paper at the corners of the photos for placement. Following the manufacturer's directions, coat the backs of the photos with adhesive spray. Press the photos in place.

2. On the double-sided adhesive sheet, draw 12 circles, each ⁵/₈" (1.5 cm) in diameter. Peel off the protective paper from the circles, and, allowing at least ¹/₂" (1 cm) between each circle, attach them to the yellow paper. Remove the remaining protective paper from one circle to expose the adhesive. Cut one 8" (20.5 cm) length of yarn. Place one end of the yarn in the center of the circle, and using the toothpick or knife, press to adhere. Working from the center out, coil the yarn to match the adhesive circle, and press to adhere. When complete, trim the end of the yarn. Use the toothpick to apply a small amount of white craft glue to the end of the yarn, and attach it to coiled circle. Hold the end in place until glue is dry. Repeat for remaining the circles. Trim the yellow paper around the circles.

3. Use the tracing paper to make the templates for the sun face. (See Sun template on page 288.) Cut the shapes from the corresponding colors of paper. Coat the back of the scalloped edge with adhesive spray, and press it in place on the sun face. Use the colored pencils to draw the face on the sun. Referring to the photo for shading, shade the eyelids, the nose, and the cheeks. Place the sun face 2³/₄" (7 cm) from the left edge and 1⁷/₈" (5 cm) from the top edge of the khaki paper. Use the pencil to mark the khaki paper at the top and the bottom of the sun face for placement. Coat the back of the sun face with adhesive spray. Press in place. Coat the backs of the yarn circles with adhesive spray. Place the yarn circles around the sun face, and press to adhere.

4. Write the title using the purple chisel-tip marker. Use the black fine-tip marker to write the captions under the photos.

5. Use the kneaded rubber eraser to remove all pencil marks.

# Tropical Retreat

This versatile medium can suggest grass, bark, and even coconuts.

## Materials

- photos
- one 12" x 12" (30.5 cm x 30.5 cm) sheet tan paper
- one 8 1/2" x 11" (21.5 cm x 28 cm) sheet gray paper
- one 8 1/2" x 11" (21.5 cm x 28 cm) sheet green paper
- one 8 1/2" x 11" (21.5 cm x 28 cm) sheet green patterned paper
- one 8 1/2" x 11" (21.5 cm x 28 cm) sheet rust paper
- double-sided adhesive sheet, such as Peel-N-Stick
- white craft glue
- archival-quality adhesive spray
- brown, tan, and pale green yarn
- green broad-tip marker

## Tools

- scissors
- toothpick
- craft knife
- metal-edged ruler
- pencil
- tracing paper
- kneaded rubber eraser

## Instructions

1. Using the ruler and knife, trim the photos to the following sizes, from the top down: 5" x 3 1/2" (12.5 cm x 9 cm), 5 3/4" x 3 1/2" (14.5 cm x 9 cm), and 5 3/4" x 3 1/2" (14.5 cm x 9 cm). Referring to the photo for placement, arrange the photos on the tan paper. Use the pencil to lightly mark the tan paper at the corners of the photos for placement. Following the manufacturer's directions, coat the backs of the photos with adhesive spray. Press the photos in place.

2. Use the tracing paper to make the palm tree templates. (See Palm Tree template on page 288.) Cut the shapes from the corresponding colors.

3. Referring to the broken lines on the palm tree pattern, draw three trunk stripes on the double-sided adhesive sheet. Peel off the protective paper, and attach the adhesive shapes to the large trunk shape, where indicated. Remove the remaining protective paper from the stripes to expose the adhesive. Cut 1 1/2" (4 cm) lengths of tan yarn. Center and place the yarn lengths side by side on the adhesive sheet until it is covered. Use the scissors to trim the ends of the yarn flush with the sides of the trunk. Place the large trunk shape

1" (2.5 cm) from the bottom edge and 2 3/4" (7 cm) from the right edge of the tan paper. Referring to the photo, place the remaining pattern pieces on the tan paper. Use the pencil to mark the tan paper at chosen reference points on the tree for placement. Coat the backs of the pattern pieces with adhesive spray. Press the pieces in place.

4. Draw three circles 5/8" (1.5 cm) in diameter on the double-sided adhesive sheet. Peel off the protective paper from the circles, and attach them to the rust paper, allowing at least 1/2" (1 cm) between each circle. Remove the remaining protective paper from one circle to expose the adhesive. Cut one 8" (20.5 cm) length of yarn. Place one end of the yarn in the center of the circle, and press with a toothpick to adhere. Working from the center out, coil the yarn around the adhesive circle, then press to adhere. When complete, trim the end of the yarn. Use the toothpick to apply a small amount of white craft glue to the end of the yarn, and attach it to the coiled circle. Hold the end in place until glue is dry. Repeat for the remaining circles. Trim the rust paper around the circles. Coat the backs of the circles with the adhesive

spray. Referring to the photo for placement, press the yarn circles in place.

5. From the double-sided adhesive sheet, cut eight 1/16" (0.2 cm)-wide strips of varying lengths. Peel off the protective paper from the strips. Referring to the photo, attach the strips to the tan paper. Remove the remaining protective paper from the strips to expose the adhesive. From the pale green yarn, cut eight 2 1/2" (6.5 cm) lengths. Place the yarn lengths on the adhesive strips, and press to adhere. Use the scissors to cut the ends of the yarn lengths to match the adhesive strips. From the double-sided adhesive sheet, cut two 1/16" (0.2 cm)-wide curved strips, 2" (5 cm) and 2 1/2" (6.5 cm) in length. Peel off the protective paper from the strips. Referring to the photo, attach strips to the palm fronds. Remove the remaining protective paper from the strips to expose the adhesive. From pale green yarn, cut two 4" (10 cm) lengths. Place the yarn lengths on the adhesive strips, and press to adhere. Use the scissors to cut ends of yarn lengths to match the adhesive strips.

6. Use the marker to write the title.

7. Use the kneaded rubber eraser to remove all pencil marks.

# Cross-Stitch

It is hard to believe that beautiful and complex samplers are made by repeating a simple cross-stitch. This basic building block can also be used to adorn scrapbook pages.

To complete a single cross-stitch, bring the needle from the back to the front at the lower-left corner of a cross (a set of four holes). Then insert the needle in the top-right corner of the cross. Refer to Diagram A. Repeat this process, going from the bottom-right corner to the top-left corner to form an X. Each square on the chart represents one complete stitch. Start with 12" to 15" (30.5 cm to 38 cm) lengths of floss. Longer lengths of floss may twist or knot. Use only the number of strands called for in step one. To secure the ends, hold 1" (2.5 cm) of floss at the back of the paper or fabric, and complete the first few cross-stitches over it, securing it in the stitches. To finish, insert the needle through several completed stitches on the back of the paper or fabric. Draw the floss through the stitches, and trim the end. Carry the floss by weaving it into previously completed stitches on the back of the paper or fabric. Remember that any loose threads on the back will show through to the front of the paper or fabric.

**Diagram A**

**Sample 1.** After stitching on the perforated paper, carefully cut around the image to create a delicate appliqué.

**Sample 2.** Secure small individual paper shapes to the page with cross-stitches.

**Sample 3.** This mesh sticks to paper and creates an instant grid on which to stitch. Adhesive mesh is available at scrapbook stores.

# By the Bay

For stitching, perforated paper is a great alternative to even-weave cross-stitch fabric. It is made from heavy paper stock and resists crinkling or tearing. And because it won't unravel like fabric, you don't have to finish the edges.

## Materials

- photos
- one 12" x 12" (30.5 cm x 30.5 cm) sheet blue polka-dot paper
- one 8½" x 11" (21.5 cm x 28 cm) sheet burgundy patterned paper
- cable-car ticket or postcard
- ticket stub
- 14-count white perforated paper
- embroidery floss in the following colors: light blue, brown, pink, and white
- brown chisel-tip marker
- archival-quality adhesive spray

## Tools

- scissors
- #10 sharp crewel needle
- craft knife
- metal-edged ruler
- line-art alphabet
- pencil
- tracing paper
- embroidery needle
- kneaded rubber eraser

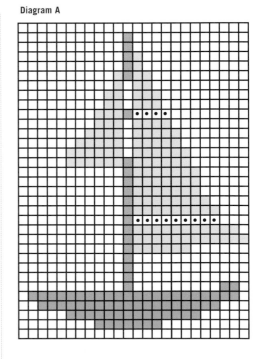

## Instructions

1. Using three strands of embroidery floss and referring to Diagram A, cross-stitch the sailboat on the perforated paper. Using the ruler and knife, trim the perforated paper to 2¼" x 4¾" (6 cm x 12 cm).

2. Trim the large photo to 6¾" x 4¼" (17 cm x 11 cm) and the small photo to 4⅛" x 3⅜" (10.5 cm x 8.5 cm). Place the large photo 1" (2.5 cm) from the bottom edge and ¾" (2 cm) from the left edge of the polka-dot paper. Overlapping the top corner of large photo, place the small photo 1½" (4 cm) from the right edge and 3¾" (9.5 cm) from the bottom edge of the polka-dot paper. Referring to the photo for placement, set the ticket, the ticket stub, and the cross-stitch sailboat on the polka-dot paper. Note: Because sizes may vary, adjust as needed, keeping all items at right angles. Use the pencil to lightly mark the polka-dot paper at the corners of the photos, the ticket, the ticket stub, and the cross-stitch sailboat for placement. Following the manufacturer's directions, coat the backs of all items with adhesive. Place them on the polka-dot paper, and press to adhere.

3. From line-art alphabet, enlarge an upper-case letter to 2¾" (7 cm) tall. Make a pattern for the letter on tracing paper. From the burgundy patterned paper, cut out the letter. Place the letter 1¼" (3 cm) from the left edge and 2¾" (7 cm) from the top edge of the polka-dot paper. Use the pencil to mark the polka-dot paper at the corners of the letter for placement. Coat the back of the letter with adhesive spray. Press in place.

4. Use the brown chisel-tip marker to write the title.

5. Use the kneaded rubber eraser to remove all pencil marks.

**Diagram A**

# Graduation Day, 1922

Waste canvas is even-weave canvas basted onto non-even-weave fabric to provide a grid for cross-stitching. After stitching, gently remove the waste canvas threads with tweezers.

### Materials

- photo
- 12" x 12" (30.5 cm x 30.5 cm) sheet mauve patterned paper
- 8 1/2" x 11" (21.5 cm x 28 cm) sheet light pink paper
- 8 1/2" x 11" (21.5 cm x 28 cm) sheet pink patterned paper
- 8 1/2" x 11" (21.5 cm x 28 cm) sheet green paper
- 6" x 12" (15 cm x 30.5 cm) rectangle pink print fabric
- 28" (71 cm) length 3/8" (1 cm)-wide green satin ribbon
- 14-count waste canvas
- antique postcard
- embroidery floss in light pink, medium pink, dark pink, and green
- spray starch
- archival-quality adhesive spray
- black fine-tip marker

### Tools

- tracing paper
- scissors
- #9 embroidery needle
- small embroidery hoop (optional)
- tweezers
- iron
- craft knife
- metal-edged ruler
- kneaded rubber eraser

### Instructions

1. Photocopy Diagram A, and make a template using the tracing paper. Center the pattern on the right side of the fabric, and use the pencil to trace lightly around the pattern.

2. From the waste canvas, cut five 4" (10 cm) squares. Referring to the photo for placement, center and baste one square on the top of the fabric strip. Place the fabric in the embroidery hoop, if desired. Using two strands of embroidery floss and stitching through both the fabric and the waste canvas, cross-stitch one flower (refer to Diagram B). Use the tweezers to carefully remove the waste canvas one thread at a time from behind the stitching. Pull out the threads parallel to the fabric. Do not pull at an angle, or you may loosen the cross-stitches. Repeat for the remaining flowers. Rotate the waste canvas squares before basting to change the direction of the flowers. (Three flowers are stitched with only the bottom leaf.)

3. Coat the back with spray starch. Use an iron to press the fabric. Use the scissors to trim the fabric strip along the marked lines. Coat the back of the fabric with adhesive spray. Align the right edge of fabric strip to the short side of the light pink paper, and press to adhere. From the green

paper, make a 3/8" x 5 1/2" (1 cm x 14 cm) strip with one torn side. Coat the back with adhesive spray. Referring to the photo for placement, set the straight side next to the fabric strip. Press to adhere. Using the ruler and knife, trim the overlapping strip. From the pink patterned paper, make one 1 1/2" x 4" x 4" (4 cm x 10 cm x 10 cm) triangle. Coat the back with adhesive spray. Referring to the photo for placement, press the triangle next to the fabric strip.

4. Trim the photo to 4 5/8" x 3 5/8" (11.5 cm x 9 cm). Place the photo diagonally, with the lower-left corner 1" (2.5 cm) from the bottom edge and the lower-right corner 1 7/8" (5 cm) from the bottom edge of the pink paper. Mark the pink paper at the corners for placement. Coat the back with adhesive spray. Press in place. Place the pink paper 1/4" (0.6 cm) from the right edge and 3" (7.5 cm) from the top edge of the mauve patterned paper. Mark the mauve paper at the corners for placement. Coat the back with adhesive spray. Press in place. Referring to the photo for placement, set the bottom edge of the postcard parallel to the top edge of the photo. Mark the pink and mauve papers at the corners for placement. Coat the back with adhesive spray. Press in place.

5. Coat the back of the ribbon with adhesive spray. Overlap the photo and keep the ribbon parallel to the fabric border; press in place. Wrap the ribbon around the back of the mauve paper; press in place. Bring the ribbon to the front of the pink paper, press the end of ribbon parallel to the photo. Fold the end of the ribbon in a loop, and press in place on the pink paper. Use the scissors to trim the ends.

6. Use the black marker to write the caption. Use the eraser to remove pencil marks.

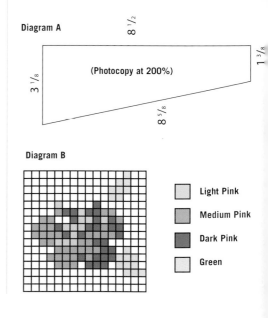

Diagram A

8 1/2

3 1/8    (Photocopy at 200%)    1 3/8

8 5/8

Diagram B

Light Pink

Medium Pink

Dark Pink

Green

# Quilting

Papercrafters have discovered the age-old art of quilting. Everybody loves quilts, and now you can sew a soft block to smooth paper or stitch up a quilted vignette. If you can use scissors and thread a needle, then you can add a puffy fabric design to a page. Browse through quilt books for inspiration, and choose from hundreds of traditional block designs. By introducing the patterns and textures of fabric, you can make any page layout more interesting and more inviting.

**Sample 2.** Pin the templates to the selected fabrics, and cut out the shapes.

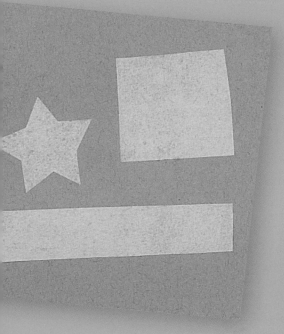

**Sample 1.** Begin by making templates using tracing paper.

**Sample 3.** Using a running stitch, stitch the fabric shapes to the paper.

# County Fair

Mom, apple pie, county fairs, and quilts.

## Materials

- photos
- one 12" x 12" (30.5 cm x 30.5 cm) sheet wheat paper
- archival-quality adhesive spray
- archival-quality tape
- scraps of fabric in the following colors: tan, tan print, gold print, red print, brown print, blue, light blue print, medium blue print, and dark blue print
- red thread
- polyester batting
- blue pencil
- letter stickers

## Tools

- craft knife
- metal-edged ruler
- pencil
- tracing paper
- scissors
- needle
- kneaded rubber eraser

## Instructions

1. Using the ruler and knife, trim the photos to 4$\frac{1}{2}$" x 3$\frac{1}{2}$" (11.5 cm x 9 cm). Place the top photo 1" (2.5 cm) from the right edge and 1" (2.5 cm) from the top edge of the wheat paper. Overlapping the corner of the top photo, place the bottom photo 2$\frac{3}{4}$" (7 cm) from the left edge and 4" (10 cm) from the top edge of the wheat paper. Use the pencil to lightly mark the wheat paper at the corners of the photos for placement. Following the manufacturer's directions, coat the backs of the photos with adhesive spray. Press the photos in place to adhere.

2. From the red fabric, cut one 5$\frac{1}{4}$" x $\frac{7}{8}$" (13.5 cm x 2 cm) strip. Use the tracing paper to make the template for the zigzag border. (See Zigzag Border template on page 286.) From the tan print fabric, cut one zigzag shape. Place the red strip 1" (2.5 cm) from the right edge and 1" (2.5 cm) from the top edge of the wheat paper. Place the zigzag strip over the red strip. Stitch over and under (running stitch) through the paper and the fabric along the top of the strip. Secure the ends of the thread to the back of the paper using the archival-quality tape. Trim the ends. Repeat along the center of the zigzag shape.

3. Make the templates for Block A. (See Block A template on page 289.) Cut the shapes from the corresponding fabrics. Using a running stitch, stitch the small squares to the large square. From the batting, cut one 3$\frac{1}{4}$" (8.5 cm) square. Aligning the right side of batting with the right side of the top photo, place the batting below the photo. Center and place Block A on the batting. Stitch through all of the layers around the outside edge of the block. Secure the ends of the thread to the back of the paper with the archival-quality tape. Trim the ends.

4. Make the templates for Block B. (See Block B template on page 289.) Cut the shapes from the corresponding fabrics. Note: A $\frac{1}{4}$" (0.6 cm) seam allowance should be added to the center pieces because they overlap each other slightly. Stitch the small strips to the center square. Stitch the large strips to the small strips. Place Block B 2$\frac{1}{4}$" (6 cm) from the right edge and 1$\frac{1}{2}$" (4 cm) from the bottom edge of the wheat paper. Stitch through all of the layers around the outside edge of the block. Secure the ends of the thread to the back of the paper with archival-quality tape. Trim the ends.

5. Attach the stickers. Write the captions using the blue pencil.

6. Use the kneaded rubber eraser to remove all pencil marks.

# Sweet Dreams

When introducing large areas of color, try sewing on a scrap of fabric instead of paper. Also try securing design elements with a few well-placed quilting stitches instead of adhesives.

**Materials**

- photo
- one 12" x 12" (30.5 cm x 30.5 cm) sheet blue paper
- 8½" x 11" (21.5 cm x 28 cm) sheet cream paper
- archival-quality adhesive spray
- archival-quality tape
- scrap of yellow fabric
- 9" (23 cm) dark blue fabric
- white thread
- polyester fiber fill
- white craft glue
- blue broad-tip marker
- black fine-tip marker

**Tools**

- pencil
- tracing paper
- scissors
- metal-edged ruler
- needle
- craft knife
- toothpick
- kneaded rubber eraser

**Instructions**

1. Using the tracing paper, make the templates for the star and the moon. (See Moon and Star templates on page 290.) Cut the shapes from the corresponding fabrics. Place the sky ³/₄" (2 cm) from the right edge and ¼" (0.6 cm) from the top edge of the blue paper. Separate the fiberfill into two small clumps. Referring to the photo for placement, set one clump in the center of the sky and one clump in the corner of the sky. Place the moon shape over the center clump of the fiberfill. Stitch over and under (running stitch) through all layers around the moon shape. Secure the ends of the thread to the back of the paper using the archival-quality tape. Trim the ends. Above the moon shape, stitch free-form, horizontal lines in the sky, securing the second clump of fiberfill in the stitching. Below the moon shape, stitch a free-form, horizontal line in the sky. Secure the ends of the thread to the back of the paper using the archival-quality tape. Trim the ends. Use the toothpick to apply a small amount of craft glue to the wrong side of the fabric at the edges of the sky. Hold in place until the glue dries.

2. Trim the cream paper to 5³/₄" x 4³/₄" (14.5 cm x 12 cm). Center and cut a 4¼" x 3¼" (11 cm x 8.5 cm) window in the cream rectangle to make a mat. Using the ruler and the knife, trim the photo to 4³/₄" x 3³/₄" (12 cm x 9.5 cm). Tape the photo to the back of the mat. Place the matted photo 1" (2.5 cm) from the right edge and 1" (2.5 cm) from the bottom edge of the blue paper. Use the pencil to lightly mark the blue paper at the corners of the matted photo for placement. Coat the back of the matted photo with adhesive spray. Press in place.

3. From the cream paper cut one star. Coat the back of the star with adhesive spray. Referring to the photo for placement, press the star in place above the top-right corner of the mat.

4. Write the title using the blue marker. Use the black marker to write the caption.

5. Use the kneaded rubber eraser to remove all pencil marks.

# Machine-Stitching

This technique is part decoration and all fun. You can use machine-stitching to join layers of paper or to attach embellishments, but the real excitement is with the design possibilities. Use lines of stitching to outline and to contour. So dust off your sewing machine, and use it to enhance your paper art.

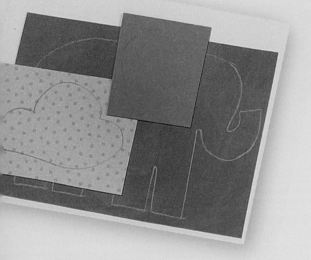

**Sample 1.** To machine-stitch a small paper design to the page, begin by tracing the shapes onto the selected papers.

**Sample 2.** Cut out the shapes.

**Sample 3.** Machine-stitch the large shape to the background paper. Attach the small pieces with double-sided adhesive or with adhesive spray.

# Birthday Cake

This page illustration is paper-piecing with a twist. The paper shapes are enhanced by machine-stitching. Review your favorite paper-pieced designs, and enhance them with this decorative application.

## Materials

- photos
- one 12" x 12" (30.5 cm x 30.5 cm) sheet tan paper
- one 8 1/2" x 11" (21.5 cm x 28 cm) sheet dark pink paper
- one 8 1/2" x 11" (21.5 cm x 28 cm) sheet light pink paper
- one 8 1/2" x 11" (21.5 cm x 28 cm) sheet purple paper
- one 8 1/2" x 11" (21.5 cm x 28 cm) sheet white-and-yellow striped paper
- one 8 1/2" x 11" (21.5 cm x 28 cm) sheet yellow paper
- one 8 1/2" x 11" (21.5 cm x 28 cm) sheet blue patterned paper
- magenta cellophane streamer

- white thread
- purple pencil
- black fine-tip marker
- archival-quality adhesive spray
- archival-quality tape
- double-sided adhesive sheet, such as Peel-N-Stick

## Tools

- scissors
- sewing machine
- metal-edged ruler
- craft knife
- pencil
- tracing paper
- kneaded rubber eraser

## Instructions

1. Use the tracing paper to make the templates for the cake, plate, and candles. (See Cake, Plate, and Candles template on page 290.) Although areas of the scalloping are covered by layering, make it one piece. Cut the shapes from the corresponding colors. Referring to the photo for placement, arrange the plate and the base of the cake on the tan paper. Machine-stitch around the sides and the bottom of the base of the cake. Place the scalloping on the base of the cake, and place the top of the cake on the scallop. Machine-stitch around the top of the cake. Carefully pull the ends of the thread to the back of the paper, and secure them with archival-quality tape. Trim the ends. Place the candles and the flames on the cake. Use the pencil to mark lightly the tan paper at the tops of the flames for placement. From the double-sided adhesive sheet, cut 1/8" (0.3 cm)-wide strips. Trim the strips to fit the backs of the candles and the flames. Peel off the protective paper, and attach the adhesive to the backs of the candles and the flames. Remove the remaining protective paper, and press the candles and the flames in place to adhere.

2. Referring to the photo for placement, arrange the streamer on the top-left corner of the tan paper. Machine-stitch over the streamer to secure it. Pull the ends of the thread to the back of the paper, and secure them with tape. Trim the ends.

3. Using the ruler and knife, trim the right photo to 3 1/8" x 4 5/8" (8 cm x 11.5 cm). Place the photo 1 1/2" (4 cm) from the right edge and 2 3/4" (7 cm) from the bottom edge of the tan paper. Use the pencil to mark the tan paper at the corners of the photo for placement. Following the manufacturer's directions, coat the back of the photo with adhesive spray. Press in place. Trim the left photo to 5 1/4" x 3 1/2" (13.5 cm x 9 cm). Overlapping the right photo, place the photo 2 1/4" (6 cm) from the left edge and 1 1/2" (4 cm) from the bottom edge of the tan paper. Use the pencil to mark the tan paper at the corners of the photo for placement. Coat the back of the photo with adhesive spray. Press in place.

4. Use the purple pencil to write Happy Birthday on the cake plate. Use the marker to write the caption.

5. Use the kneaded rubber eraser to remove all pencil marks.

# Paper Horizon

All of the paper edges in this arrangement, with the exception of the trimmed edge of the mat, are torn. Tearing the shapes makes them soft and irregular. Machine-stitching enhances the meandering nature of the paper shapes.

## Materials

- photo
- one 12" x 12" (30.5 cm x 30.5 cm) sheet ivory paper
- one 12" x 12" (30.5 cm x 30.5 cm) sheet blue print vellum
- one 8½" x 11" (21.5 cm x 28 cm) sheet blue patterned paper
- one 8½" x 11" (21.5 cm x 28 cm) sheet silver paper
- one 8½" x 11" (21.5 cm x 28 cm) sheet cream paper
- one 8½" x 11" (21.5 cm x 28 cm) sheet white paper
- one brown paper sack
- white tissue paper
- 12" x 6" (30.5 cm x 15 cm) piece purple sheer fabric
- white thread
- navy blue thread
- archival-quality adhesive spray
- archival-quality tape

## Tools

- scissors
- sewing machine
- metal-edged ruler
- craft knife
- pencil

## Instructions

1. With the pencil, print the title on the blue patterned paper.

2. From the tissue paper, the silver paper, and the cream paper, tear several hill shapes. From the paper sack, tear a road shape. From the blue print fabric, tear two small cloud shapes. Tear a large cloud shape around the title printed on the blue patterned paper.

3. Place the fabric on the top half of the vellum. Referring to the photo for placement, arrange the torn shapes on the vellum. Using the white thread and straight and zigzag stitches, machine-stitch over the shapes to secure them to the vellum. Using the navy thread and a zigzag stitch, stitch a broken line in the center of the road.

4. Using the ruler and knife, trim the photo to 3¾" x 5¼" (9.5 cm x 13.5 cm). Trim the white paper to 4½" x 6" (11.5 cm x 15 cm). Center and cut a 3¼" x 4¾" (8.5 cm x 12 cm) window in the white rectangle to make a mat. Tape the photo to the back of the mat. Place the matted photo 1" (2.5 cm) from the right edge and ¾" (2 cm) from the bottom edge of the vellum paper. Using the white thread and a straight and a zigzag stitch, stitch the mat to the vellum. Carefully pull the ends of the thread to the back of the paper, and secure them with archival-quality tape. Trim the ends.

5. Following the manufacturer's directions, coat the back of the vellum. Place the vellum on the ivory paper, and press to adhere.

# Found-Object Collage

Bits of lace, luggage tags, feathers, old jewelry, paper labels, shoelaces, matchbooks, and chop sticks. Why include this curious list in a scrapbook recipe? One of these things may be the perfect accent to add to your scrapbook page. The fun of found-object art is incorporating something quirky or unexpected into a composition of otherwise flat component parts. So before your next scrapping session begins, hunt through your sewing box or your junk drawer. You will be surprised at what you will find.

**Sample 1.** A transparent shrink-wrap label works great as a sticker.

**Sample 2.** Pin a romantic message to a special page using a gold safety pin.

THE EVENING PROMISES
ROMANTIC INTERESTS
02 06 10 14 20 27

**Sample 3.** Fashion cotton swabs into a unique frame for baby. Use a spot of white craft glue under each cotton-wrapped end.

# Nature's Canopy

Gather a handful of colorful leaves, and press them between the pages of a heavy book. Dried leaves look great bordering artwork or outdoor photos.

## Materials

- artwork
- 12" x 12" (30.5 cm x 30.5 cm) sheet green patterned paper
- scraps of rust paper
- award ribbon
- dried leaves
- twigs
- white milky pen
- archival-quality adhesive spray
- double-sided adhesive sheet

## Tools

- craft knife
- metal-edged ruler
- pencil
- kneaded rubber eraser

## Instructions

1. Using the ruler and knife, trim the artwork to 8 1/2" x 10 1/2" (21.5 cm x 26.5 cm). Place the artwork diagonally with the top left corner 1" (2.5 cm) and the top right corner 1/4" (0.6 cm) from the top edge of the green paper. Use the pencil to mark lightly the green paper at the corners of the artwork for placement. Following the manufacturer's directions, coat the back of the art work with adhesive spray. Place the artwork on the green paper, and press to adhere.

2. From the double-sided adhesive sheet, cut 1" x 2" (2.5 cm x 5 cm) rectangle. Peel off the protective paper, and attach the adhesive lengthwise to the back of the ribbon, directly below the eyelet. Remove the remaining protective paper; referring to the photo for placement, press the ribbon in place.

3. Coat the backs of the dried leaves with adhesive spray. Arrange them on and around the artwork as desired. From the double-sided adhesive sheet, cut one

3/16" x 7" (0.5 cm x 18 cm) strip. Peel the protective paper, and attach the strip to the back of the rust paper. Trim the paper to match the adhesive. Cut the strip into seven lengths. Peel the remaining protective paper from the adhesive strips. Place the strips over the twigs at selected points to secure the twigs to the artwork.

4. Write the caption using the white milky pen.

5. Use the kneaded rubber eraser to remove all pencil marks.

# Little Boy Collage

Empty the contents of your 9-year-old's pockets, and you will have the makings for a great page layout. This is a case in which art definitely imitates life.

### Materials

- photo
- one 12" x 12" (30.5 cm x 30.5 cm) sheet oatmeal paper
- one 8½" x 11 (21.5 cm x 28 cm) sheet blue patterned paper
- assorted flat objects
- archival-quality adhesive spray
- double-sided adhesive sheet, such as Peel-N-Stick

### Tools

- craft knife
- metal-edged ruler
- pencil
- kneaded rubber eraser
- black fine-tip marker (optional)

### Instructions

1. On the blue patterned paper, use the marker to print the title (or do this on a computer). Using the ruler and the knife, center the title and trim the blue patterned paper to 3" x 10" (7.5 cm x 25.5 cm). Place the title box ⅛" (0.3 cm) from the right edge and ⅜" (1 cm) from the top edge of the oatmeal paper. Use the pencil to lightly mark the oatmeal paper at the corners of the title box for placement. Following the manufacturer's directions, coat the back of the title box with adhesive spray. Press in place.

2. Trim the photo to 5" x 6½" (12.5 cm x 16.5 cm). Place it diagonally with the top-left corner 1¾" (4.5 cm) and the top right corner ¾" (2 cm) from the top edge of the oatmeal paper. Use the pencil to mark the oatmeal paper at the corners of the photo for placement. Coat the back of the photo with adhesive spray. Press in place.

3. Referring to the photo, arrange selected items on the page as desired. Mark the oatmeal paper at desired points on the items for placement. Attach the items to oatmeal paper. Paper items can be attached with adhesive spray, and plastic or fiber items can be attached with the double-sided adhesive sheet.

4. Use the kneaded rubber eraser to remove all pencil marks.

# Paper-Piecing

Paper-piecing consists of cutting shapes from colored paper and arranging the individual shapes to make a complete design. It is usually done in one of two ways. One version requires that some pieces in the composition overlap each other. It is necessary to allow for excess paper along the edges that will be covered by another layer of paper. When layering, remember to overlap when making the templates. With the second version, the pieces fit together like the pieces of a puzzle, with no overlap. These pieces are usually simple geometric shapes, such as squares and rectangles. Because the pieces fit together snugly, care should be taken to cut the pieces as accurately as possible.

The finished compositions are made of flat areas of color, so paper-piecing resembles silk screening done by fine artists or appliqué done by quilters. In fact, many paper-piecing patterns are borrowed from line art intended for iron-on or needle-turned appliqué.

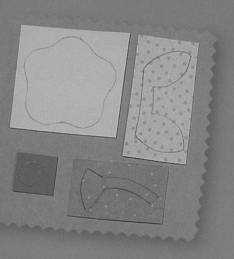

**Sample 1.** Make the patterns for the design, and trace the shapes onto the selected papers.

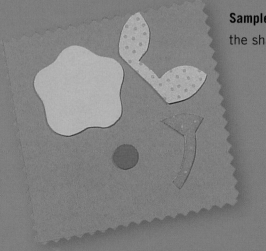

**Sample 2.** Cut out the shapes.

**Sample 3.** Layer the shapes, and attach them to the page with adhesive.

# Housewarming House

This warm and welcoming house tag is made from simple geometric shapes. The finished tag could be used as a greeting card or as a gift tag.

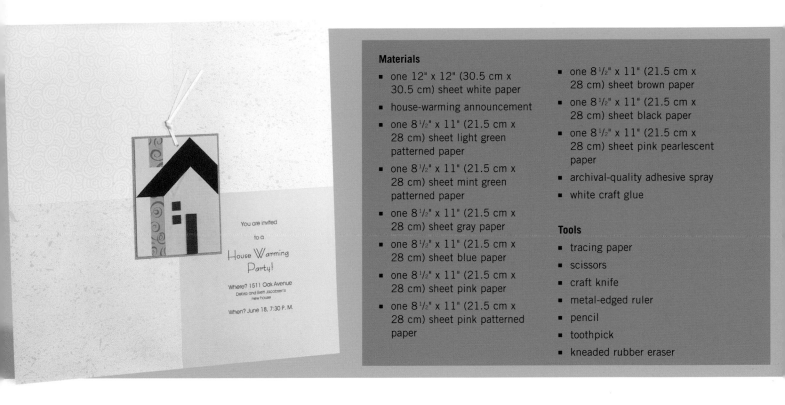

## Materials

- one 12" x 12" (30.5 cm x 30.5 cm) sheet white paper
- house-warming announcement
- one 8 1/2" x 11" (21.5 cm x 28 cm) sheet light green patterned paper
- one 8 1/2" x 11" (21.5 cm x 28 cm) sheet mint green patterned paper
- one 8 1/2" x 11" (21.5 cm x 28 cm) sheet gray paper
- one 8 1/2" x 11" (21.5 cm x 28 cm) sheet blue paper
- one 8 1/2" x 11" (21.5 cm x 28 cm) sheet pink paper
- one 8 1/2" x 11" (21.5 cm x 28 cm) sheet pink patterned paper
- one 8 1/2" x 11" (21.5 cm x 28 cm) sheet brown paper
- one 8 1/2" x 11" (21.5 cm x 28 cm) sheet black paper
- one 8 1/2" x 11" (21.5 cm x 28 cm) sheet pink pearlescent paper
- archival-quality adhesive spray
- white craft glue

## Tools

- tracing paper
- scissors
- craft knife
- metal-edged ruler
- pencil
- toothpick
- kneaded rubber eraser

## Instructions

1. Use the tracing paper to make the templates for the house. (See House template on page 289.) Note: The windows and the door are the only overlapping pieces. The remaining pieces fit together with the sides flat against each other. Therefore, cut these pieces as accurately as possible. Cut the shapes from the corresponding papers. Following the manufacturer's directions, coat the backs of the pieces with adhesive spray. Referring to the template, press all the pieces in place on the gray paper. Center the house design. Using the ruler and knife, trim the gray paper to 3 1/4" x 4 1/4" (8.5 cm x 11 cm). Center the hole punch 3/8" (1 cm) from the top edge of the gray paper, and punch a hole in the sky. From the pink pearlescent paper, cut one 1/4" x 9" (0.6 cm x 23 cm) strip. Thread the strip through the hole, and carefully knot the ends together. Trim the ends, if necessary.

2. Trim the announcement to 6" x 6" (15 cm x 15 cm). From the light green patterned paper, make one 6" (15 cm) square. From the mint green paper, make two 6" (15 cm) squares. Coat the backs of the squares with adhesive spray. Referring to the photo for placement, press the squares into place on the white paper.

3. Coat the back of the house tag with adhesive spray. Center it on the intersecting corners, and press in place to adhere. Press the knotted strip flat. Use the toothpick to apply a small amount of white craft glue to the back of the strip, and press in place.

# Lily of the Valley

This pair of flower sprigs serves as the perfect symmetrical embellishment for an oval mat.

## Materials

- photo
- one 12" x 12" (30.5 cm x 30.5 cm) sheet light blue paper
- one 8½" x 11" (21.5 cm x 28 cm) khaki mat with 4½" x 6½" (11 cm x 17 cm) oval window
- one 8½" x 11" (21.5 cm x 28 cm) sheet pink paper
- one 8½" x 11" (21.5 cm x 28 cm) sheet cream paper
- one 8½" x 11" (21.5 cm x 28 cm) sheet mint paper
- one 8½" x 11" (21.5 cm x 28 cm) sheet olive patterned paper
- four ⅛" (0.3 cm)-wide pink sticker borders
- purple pencil
- black fine-tip marker
- archival-quality tape
- archival-quality adhesive spray

## Tools

- pencil
- tracing paper
- scissors
- craft knife
- metal-edged ruler
- kneaded rubber eraser

## Instructions

1. Using the ruler and knife, trim the photo to 5½" x 7½" (14 cm x 19 cm). Center the oval, and trim the mat to 7¾" x 9⅝" (20 cm x 24.5 cm). Tape the photo to the back of the mat. Place the matted photo 2⅛" (5.5 cm) from the right edge and 1" (2.5 cm) from the top edge of the light blue paper. Use the pencil to lightly mark the light blue paper at the corners of the mat for placement. Following the manufacturer's directions, coat the back of the matted photo with adhesive spray. Press in place.

2. Use the tracing paper to make the templates for the flowers and the leaves. (See Flowers and Leaves template on page 288.) Cut the shapes from the corresponding colors. Reverse the templates, and cut a second set of shapes in the mirror image of the first set. Referring to the photo for placement, arrange leaves and flowers on the bottom corners of the mat. Use the pencil to lightly mark the light blue paper at the chosen reference points on the flowers and the stems for placement. Coat the backs of the flowers and the leaves with adhesive spray. Press in place.

3. Use the colored pencil to draw the details on the mat, the flower centers, and the leaves. Attach the sticker border 1¼" (3 cm) from the outside edge of all four sides of the blue paper. Trim the border from the paper-piecing designs. Write the caption using the marker.

4. Use the kneaded rubber eraser to remove all pencil marks.

# Stenciling

An art form that is centuries old, stenciling has a novelty and a versatility all its own. The concept is an easy one: create a negative space, or stencil, and fill the space with color. Plastic stencils can be used again and again. Just clean them occasionally, and store them flat. A good stencil can become as indispensable to paper decoration as a good stamp. Stenciling requires no extraordinary skill and is a great way to decorate any flat surface, including scrapbook pages. The projects included in this chapter require hand-cut stencils, but many precut stencils are available at craft and paper stores. Using a precut stencil eliminates the steps of transferring the design to the stencil blank and cutting the stencil.

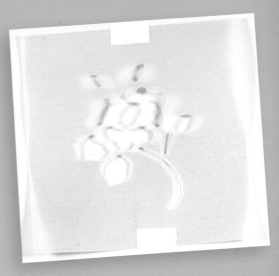

**Sample 1.** To create a stenciled flower, cut the design from the Ostencil blank. Place the stencil on the paper.

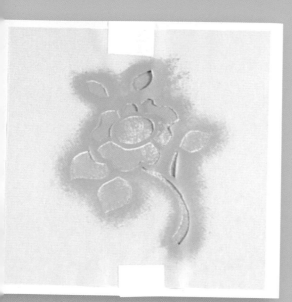

**Sample 2.** Use the stencil brush to apply a thin coat of paint.

**Sample 3.** Remove the stencil to reveal the finished flower.

# How Do I Love Thee?

A classic floral field serves as the perfect backdrop for a candid wedding photo. Although the difference in value between the paint and the paper is subtle, the pattern is still visible through the tulle sashing.

## Materials

- photo
- one 12" x 12" (30.5 cm x 30.5 cm) sheet cream paper
- one 8$\frac{1}{2}$" x 11" (21.5 cm x 28 cm) sheet cream vellum
- one 8$\frac{1}{2}$" x 11" (21.5 cm x 28 cm) sheet white paper
- one 18" x 7" (45.5 cm x 18 cm) strip white tulle
- one stencil blank, 6" x 6" (15 cm x 15 cm) or larger
- white acrylic craft paint
- black fine-tip marker
- archival-quality adhesive spray
- archival-quality tape

## Tools

- craft knife
- metal-edged ruler
- pencil
- kneaded rubber eraser
- stencil brush
- paper towel
- scissors
- black fine-tip marker (optional)

## Instructions

1. Use the marker to trace the floral stencil design on the stencil blank. (See Floral Motif template on page 289.) Place the stencil blank on a cutting surface, and use a craft knife to cut out each section. Position the stencil on the cream paper. Apply a small amount of the white paint to the tip of the stencil brush. Blot the tip of the brush on the paper towel. Hold the stencil firmly in place with one hand and the brush perpendicular to the paper surface with the other. Lightly touch the paper with the brush, applying the paint with short, pouncing strokes. Repeat this process until the exposed areas are covered with a thin coat of paint. Remove the stencil, and allow the paint to dry. Rotate the paper, stenciling the design in a random pattern until the paper is covered.

2. Using the ruler and knife, trim the photo to 7" x 4$\frac{3}{4}$" (18 cm x 12 cm). Center and place the photo at an angle on the cream paper, with the left corner 2$\frac{3}{4}$" (7 cm) and the right corner 1$\frac{3}{4}$" (4.5 cm) from the top edge of the paper. Use the pencil to lightly mark the cream paper at the corners of the photo for placement. Following the manufacturer's directions, coat the back of the photo with adhesive spray. Press in place.

3. Use the marker or a computer to print a poem or a personal sentiment on the white paper. Center the poem, and trim the white paper to 1$\frac{1}{8}$" x 3$\frac{1}{8}$" (3 cm x 8 cm). Coat the back of the poem box with adhesive spray. Place the poem box below the bottom-left edge of the photo, and press to adhere.

4. From the cream vellum, cut three $\frac{3}{8}$" x 4$\frac{1}{4}$" (1 cm x 11 cm) strips. Referring to the photo for placement, mark three pairs of parallel lines for slits on the cream paper. The slits are $\frac{1}{2}$" (1 cm) long and 1$\frac{1}{4}$" (3 cm) apart. Cut the slits with the craft knife.

5. Lightly coat the tulle with adhesive spray. (Spray only enough to make the fabric slightly tacky so that it will stick to itself when shaped. The spray does not adhere the fabric to the cream paper.) Place the tulle lengthwise on the work surface, and gather in the center and 6" (15 cm) from center on both sides. Manipulate the tulle to the desired shape, and place it on the cream paper. From back to front, thread the vellum strips through the slits and over the top of the gathered sections of tulle to secure it.

6. Working on the backside of the cream paper, pull the strips slightly, and secure the ends of the strips to the back of the paper using the archival-quality tape.

7. Use the scissors to trim the ends of the tulle so that they are flush with the sides of the cream paper.

8. Use the kneaded rubber eraser to remove all pencil marks.

# The Great Outdoors

Pay homage to nature and all things wild by adding this row of charming squirrels to your page. A thin coat of stencil paint allows for the faint shading of the tails.

**Materials**

- photos
- one 12" x 12" (30.5 cm x 30.5 cm) sheet olive patterned paper
- one 12" x 12" (30.5 cm x 30.5 cm) sheet sage patterned paper
- one stencil blank, 6" x 6" (15 cm x 15 cm) or larger
- black fine-tip marker
- brown pencil
- light brown acrylic paint
- medium brown acrylic paint
- archival-quality adhesive spray

**Tools**

- craft knife
- metal-edged ruler
- pencil
- kneaded rubber eraser
- stencil brush
- paper towel

**Instructions**

1. Use the marker to trace the squirrel stencil design on the stencil blank. (See Squirrel template on page 291.) Place the stencil blank on the cutting surface, and use a craft knife to cut out each section. Use the pencil to draw a light baseline ⁵/₈" (1.5 cm) from the bottom edge of the sage paper. Position the squirrel body section on the baseline 5" (12.5 cm) from the left edge of the sage paper. Apply a small amount of medium brown paint to the tip of the stencil brush. Blot the tip of the brush on the paper towel. Hold the stencil firmly in place with one hand and the brush perpendicular to the paper surface with the other. Lightly touch the paper with the brush, applying the paint with short, pouncing strokes. Cover the exposed area with a thin coat of paint. Remove the stencil, and allow the paint to dry. Working from right to left, repeat this process with a second and a third body section, allowing 1¹/₄" (3 cm) between each. Align the arms and back-leg section on one of the body sections. Using the medium brown paint, stencil and repeat for remaining bodies. Align the tail section on one of the body sections. Use the light brown acrylic paint to stencil the tail. Repeat to complete three squirrels.

2. Using the ruler and knife, trim the stenciled strip to 11¹/₄" x 3³/₄" (28.5 cm x 9.5 cm). Tear the top edge of the stenciled strip. Place the strip on the olive paper ¹/₄" (0.6 cm) from the bottom edge, and flush with the right edge of the paper. Use the pencil to lightly mark the olive paper at the corners of the stenciled strip for placement. Following the manufacturer's directions, coat the back of the strip with adhesive spray. Press in place.

3. Trim the photos to the following sizes, from left and moving clockwise: 3³/₄" x 5¹/₂" (9.5 cm x 14 cm), 4³/₄" x 4" (12 cm x 10 cm), and 4" x 3" (10 cm x 7.5 cm). Referring to the photo for placement, arrange the photos on the olive paper. Use the pencil to lightly mark the olive paper at the corners of the photos for placement. Coat the back of the photos with adhesive spray. Press the photos in place to adhere.

4. Write the text using the brown pencil.

5. Use the kneaded rubber eraser to remove all pencil marks.

# Wrapped Thread

Most scrapbook stores offer yarn, ribbon, twine, and other decorative fibers for use as embellishments. As an interesting alternative to stitching, these threads can be wrapped around frames and simple paper shapes. The enhancement is unique. When selecting materials, keep in mind that the finer the strand, the more subtle the effect. Other non-fiber materials, such as quilling paper, curling ribbon, and twinc, can be used for wrapping.

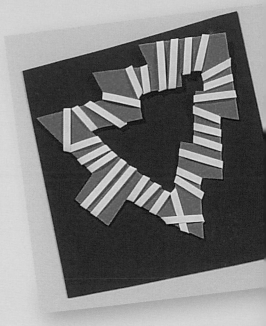

**Sample 1.** Try wrapping a simple shape with narrow quilling paper strips. Draw a hollow shape on the paper.

**Sample 2.** Cut out the shape.

**Sample 3.** Wrap the shape with the paper strips, and attach the wrapped shape to the background paper.

# Once-Upon-a-Time Babies

Pastel floss and metallic pearl cotton highlight the pitted texture of handmade paper.

### Materials

- photos
- one 12" x 12" (30.5 cm x 30.5 cm) sheet lavender paper
- one 8½" x 11" (21.5 cm x 28 cm) sheet pale yellow paper
- one small sheet lavender handmade paper
- one small sheet green handmade paper
- one precut blue patterned paper mat, 5⅓" x 6⅝" (13.5 cm x 17 cm) with a 3¼" x 4⅜" (8.5 cm x 11 cm) window
- one purple paper bow
- floral stamp with 1" x 1½" (2.5 cm x 4 cm) image size
- embroidery floss in yellow, green, and lavender
- cream pearl cotton; size 5
- metallic pearl cotton; size 5
- green ink
- brown pencil
- archival-quality adhesive spray
- archival-quality tape

### Tools

- craft knife
- metal-edged ruler
- pencil
- scissors
- kneaded rubber eraser

### Instructions

1. Using the ruler and knife, trim the yellow paper to 2⅞" x 3¾" (7.5 cm x 9.5 cm). Center and cut a 1⅞" x 2¾" (5 cm x 7 cm) window in the trimmed paper to make a mat. Referring to the photo for placement, set the mat diagonally on the lavender paper with the top-left corner 1⅛" (3 cm) and the top-right corner 1¾" (4.5 cm) from the top edge of the page. Trim the yellow paper to a 3" (7.5 cm) square. Center and cut a 2" (5 cm) square window in the trimmed paper to make a mat. Referring to the photo for placement, set the mat diagonally on the lavender paper with the bottom-left corner ¾" (2 cm) and the bottom-right corner 1¼" (3 cm) from the bottom edge of the page. Mark the lavender paper at the corners of the mats for placement. Following the manufacturer's directions, coat the backs of the mats with the adhesive spray. Place the mats on the lavender paper, and press to adhere.

2. Use the knife to cut a circle 2⅝" (6.5 cm) in diameter from the lavender handmade paper. Center and cut a round window 1¾" (4.5 cm) in diameter in the trimmed paper to make a mat. Cut a 26" (66 cm) length from both the lavender and green flosses. Secure the ends of both lengths to the back of the round mat using the archival-quality tape. Carefully wrap the floss around the mat. Secure the loose ends of the floss to the back of the mat with the

tape. Trim the ends of the floss. Referring to the photo for placement and overlapping the bottom-left corner, place the mat on the large yellow mat. Use the pencil to mark the lavender paper at the top and bottom of the mat for placement. Coat the back of the mat with adhesive spray. Place the mat on the lavender paper and the yellow mat, and press to adhere.

3. Trim the green handmade paper to a 3¼" (8.5 cm) square. Center and cut a 2½" (6.5 cm) square window in trimmed paper to make a mat. From the cream pearl cotton, cut one 20" (51 cm) length. Secure the end of the pearl cotton to the back of the mat with the tape, and carefully wrap it around the mat at selected areas. Secure the loose ends of the pearl cotton to the back of the mat with the tape. Trim the end. Overlapping the small yellow mat, place the green mat 3" (7.5 cm) from the right edge and ¾" (2 cm) from the bottom edge of the lavender paper. Use the pencil to mark the lavender paper at the corners of the mat for placement. Coat the back of the mat with adhesive spray. Place the mat on the lavender paper and press to adhere.

4. Trim the lavender handmade paper to 3⅝" x 2⅞" (9 cm x 7.5 cm). Center and cut a 2⅝" x 1⅞" (6.5 cm x 5 cm) window in the trimmed paper to make a mat. From the metallic pearl cotton, cut two 24" (61 cm) lengths. Secure the end of one length of the pearl cotton to the back

of the mat using tape, and carefully wrap the pearl cotton around the mat at selected areas. Secure the loose ends of the pearl cotton to the back of the mat with tape. Trim the end. Repeat with the second length. Place the lavender mat 1" (2.5 cm) from the left edge and 1¼" (3 cm) from the bottom edge of the lavender paper. Use the pencil to mark the lavender paper at the corners of the mat for placement. Coat the back of the mat with the adhesive spray. Place the mat on the lavender paper, and press to adhere.

5. Place the precut mat 1⅝" (4 cm) from the left edge and ½" (1 cm) from the top edge of the lavender paper. Use the pencil to mark the lavender paper at the corners of the mat for placement. Coat the back of the mat with adhesive spray. Place the mat on the lavender paper, and press to adhere. Coat the back of the paper ribbon with adhesive spray. Press in place above the green mat.

6. Trim the photos so that they are smaller than the mat windows. Coat the backs of the photos with adhesive spray, and press in place inside the mats. With the stamp and the ink, stamp a flower in the round mat. Let dry.

7. Write captions with the brown pencil.

8. Use the kneaded rubber eraser to remove all pencil marks.

# A Boy and His Dog

Contrasting fibers make a statement when wrapped around a large and colorful silhouette.

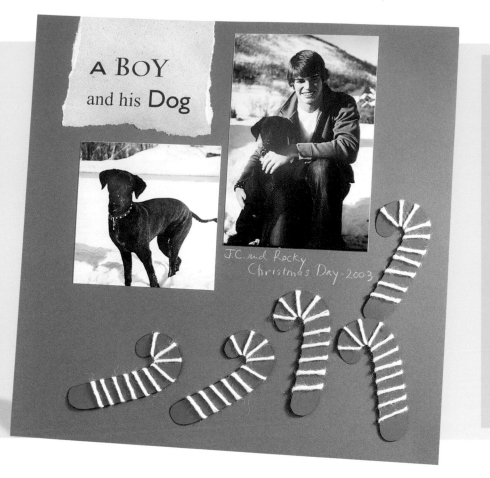

## Materials

- photos
- one 12" x 12" (30.5 cm x 30.5 cm) sheet dark green paper
- one 8 1/2" x 11" (21.5 cm x 28 cm) sheet green patterned paper
- one 8 1/2" x 11" (21.5 cm x 28 cm) sheet red paper
- cream yarn
- cream pencil
- archival-quality adhesive spray
- archival-quality tape

## Tools

- craft knife
- tracing paper
- metal-edged ruler
- pencil
- scissors
- kneaded rubber eraser
- black fine-tip marker (optional)

## Instructions

1. Using the ruler and knife, trim the left photo to 4" x 4" (10 cm x 10 cm). Place it 1 1/2" (4 cm) from the left edge and 3 1/2" (9 cm) from the top edge of the green paper. Trim the right photo to 4" x 6" (10 cm x 15 cm). Place it 2 1/4" (6 cm) from the right edge and 1/4" (0.6 cm) from the top edge of the green paper. Use the pencil to mark the green paper at the corners of the photos for placement. Following the manufacturer's directions, coat the backs of the photos with adhesive spray. Place them on the green paper, and press to adhere.

2. Print the title on the green patterned paper with the marker or on a computer. Tear left, bottom, and right edges of title box to measure 4" x 3" (10 cm x 7.5 cm). Align the title box with the top edge and 1" (2.5 cm) from the left edge of the green paper. Use the pencil to mark the green paper at the corners of the title box for placement. Coat the back of the title box with adhesive spray, and press in place.

3. Use the tracing paper to make the template for the candy cane. (See Candy Cane template on page 285.) From the red paper make five candy canes. From the yarn, cut one 18" (45.5 cm) length. Secure the end of one yarn length to the back of one candy cane using the tape. Wrap it diagonally around the candy cane. Secure the remaining end of the yarn to the back of the candy cane with tape. Trim the end. Wrap the remaining candy canes. Referring to the photo for placement, set the candy canes on the green paper. Use the pencil to mark the green paper at the top and the bottom of each candy cane for placement. Coat the backs of the candy canes with adhesive spray. Press in place.

4. Write the captions with the cream pencil.

5. Use the kneaded rubber eraser to remove all pencil marks.

# Gold Leafing

Animal, vegetable, or mineral? Definitely mineral! Gilded urns, picture frames, and statuary look as if they have been dipped in liquid gold. Actually, they have been covered with thinner-than-paper composition gold leaf. Use the same user-friendly material to add a splash of sophistication to a paper scrap. Available at craft or art supply stores, it serves as a quick and stunning accent. Because gold is inherently showy, cover only small areas. Remember that with this technique, less is more.

**Sample 2.** Create a royal background for small, stamped icons.

**Sample 1.** Remember the story about the goose that laid the golden egg? Illustrate a fairy tale with these impressive eggs.

**Sample 3.** Make a paper crown fit for a king.

# Moving On

This paper doily once served as a coaster at a farewell dinner party. What better way to preserve it, and all of the party memories, than in gold?

**Materials**

- photo
- one 12" x12" (30.5 cm x 30.5 cm) sheet embossed burgundy paper
- one sheet composition gold leaf
- gift card and envelope
- round paper doily, approximately 4¹/₂" (11.5 cm) in diameter
- white pencil
- archival-quality adhesive spray

**Tools**

- metal-edged ruler
- craft knife
- soft paintbrush with a blunt end, such as a stencil brush
- kneaded rubber eraser

**Instructions**

1. Tear the doily, removing the flat center and one-fourth of the remaining arc. Tear the arc into several sections. Following the manufacturer's directions, lightly coat the front of the doily sections with adhesive spray. Place the gold-leaf paper over the torn sections, and gently press to adhere. With the paintbrush, brush the gold leaf to remove any excess from around the edges and from the recesses of the doily sections.

2. Referring to the photo for placement, set the doily sections on the burgundy paper. Use the pencil to mark lightly the top and the bottom of the doily for placement. Coat the backs of the doily sections with adhesive spray. Press in place.

3. Overlapping the doily sections, place the envelope and the gift card on the burgundy paper. Use the pencil to mark the burgundy paper at the corners of the envelope for placement. Coat the back of the envelope with adhesive spray. Press in place. Coat the back of the greeting card with adhesive spray. Press in place.

4. Using the ruler and knife, trim the photo to 3¹/₄" x 5" (8.5 cm x 12.5 cm). Place the photo 2¹/₄" (6 cm) from the right edge and 2" (5 cm) from the bottom edge of the burgundy paper. Use the pencil to mark the burgundy paper at the corners of the photo for placement. Coat the back of the photo with adhesive spray. Press in place.

5. Write the caption with the white pencil.

6. Use the kneaded rubber eraser to remove all pencil marks.

# Then and Now

Squinting at the waves . . . a priceless pastime for generations. A touch of gold brings to mind reflected sunlight.

## Materials

- photos
- one 12" x 12" (30.5 cm x 30.5 cm) sheet gray paper
- one 12" x 12" (30.5 cm x 30.5 cm) sheet cream paper
- one sheet composition gold leaf
- three imitation wax seals
- black fine-tip marker
- archival-quality adhesive spray
- double-sided adhesive sheet, such as Peel-N-Stick

## Tools

- metal-edged ruler
- craft knife
- tracing paper.
- soft paintbrush with a blunt end, such as a stencil brush
- scissors
- kneaded rubber eraser

## Instructions

1. Using the ruler and knife, trim the large photo to 9 1/2" x 6 1/4" (24 cm x 16 cm). Place the photo 3/8" (1 cm) from the right edge and 1/8" (0.3 cm) from the top edge of the gray paper. Use the pencil to lightly mark the gray paper at the corners of the photo for placement. Following the manufacturer's directions, coat the back of the photo with adhesive spray. Press in place. Trim the small photo to 4 1/2" x 3" (11.5 cm x 7.5 cm). Overlapping the large photo, place the small photo 1 1/4" (3 cm) from the right edge and 3 3/4" (9.5 cm) from the bottom edge of the gray paper. Use the pencil to mark the gray paper at the corners of the photo for placement. Coat the back of the photo with adhesive spray. Press in place.

2. Trim the cream paper to 12" x 2 1/2" (30.5 cm x 6.5 cm). Tear the top edge of the cream strip. Place the tracing paper over the bottom 1 1/2" (4 cm) of the cream strip. Lightly coat the exposed area with adhesive spray. Place the gold-leaf paper over the adhesive, and gently press to adhere. Use the paintbrush to remove any excess gold leaf from the torn edge of the strip. Place the strip 1 3/8" (3.5 cm) from the bottom edge of the gray paper. Use a pencil to mark the gray paper below the strip for placement. Coat the back of the strip with adhesive spray. Press in place.

3. From the double-sided adhesive sheet, cut three circles slightly smaller in diameter than the wax seals. Peel off the protective paper, and attach the adhesive to the backs of the wax seals. Remove the remaining protective paper from the adhesive circles. Referring to the photo for placement, attach the wax seals to the bottom of the strip.

4. Write the title and captions with the fine-tip marker.

5. Use the kneaded rubber eraser to remove all pencil marks.

# Sand Painting

Not many materials can beat colored art sand for interesting visual effects. Its unique texture is fuzzy and shiny at the same time. With the help of double-sided adhesive, the sand is applied in one smooth and solid layer. The fine grains of the sand and the variety of available colors allow for detailed designs. Popular scrapbook themes that can be created with sand include hieroglyphics, geckos, sand dollars, sand castles, and egg timers. Note that sand is abrasive, and shiny photos or papers on a facing page may be scratched.

**Sample 1.** To make a sandy sun, mark the design on the double-sided adhesive. Cut the design from the sheet, and attach it to the paper.

**Sample 3.** The finished sand-painted sun warms the page.

**Sample 2.** Remove the protective paper, one section at a time, and sprinkle the exposed adhesive with the colored sand.

# Mayan Bird

Geometric bas-relief designs inspired by the ancients can be recreated with brightly colored sand.

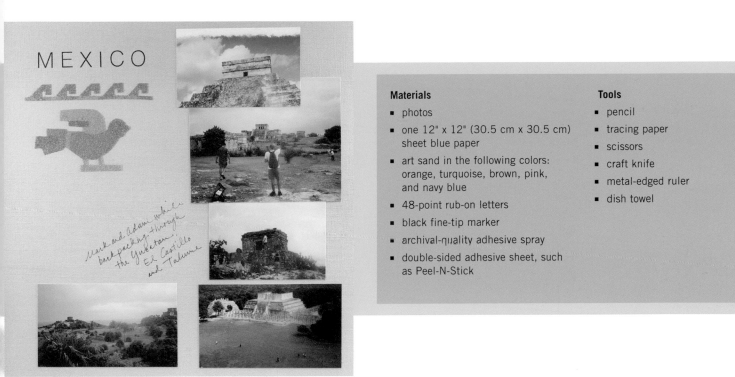

**Materials**

- photos
- one 12" x 12" (30.5 cm x 30.5 cm) sheet blue paper
- art sand in the following colors: orange, turquoise, brown, pink, and navy blue
- 48-point rub-on letters
- black fine-tip marker
- archival-quality adhesive spray
- double-sided adhesive sheet, such as Peel-N-Stick

**Tools**

- pencil
- tracing paper
- scissors
- craft knife
- metal-edged ruler
- dish towel

## Instructions

1. Use the tracing paper to make the border and the bird templates. (See Mayan Border template on page 288 and Mayan Bird template on page 285.) From the double-sided adhesive sheet, cut one border. Use the pencil to lightly mark the blue paper 1 1/8" (3 cm) from the left edge and 2 3/4" (7 cm) from the top edge for border placement. Peel off the protective paper, and attach the border to the blue paper. Remove the remaining protective paper to expose the adhesive. Lightly sprinkle several small areas along the bottom of the border with the turquoise sand. Remove any excess sand. Sprinkle the orange sand over the remaining area of the border. Remove any excess sand.

2. From the double-sided adhesive sheet, cut one bird. Use the pencil to mark the design on the top layer of the protective paper. Place the bird with the tail 1 1/2" (4 cm) from the left edge and the base

5" (12.5 cm) from the top edge of the blue paper. Peel the protective paper from the back of the bird, and, using your marks as guides, attach it to the blue paper. Use the craft knife to cut lightly along the marked lines, being careful to cut through only the protective layer of the adhesive. Remove the protective layer of paper from the wing, the vertical band on the tail, and the base. Sprinkle the turquoise sand over the exposed areas. Remove any excess sand. Continue this process, removing the protective paper for only one color at a time. The eye and beak are navy blue, the body and top tail feather are brown, the head and the bottom tail feather are orange, and the wing feather and the middle tail feather are pink. Gently wipe the blue paper with the dish towel because the rub-on letters and photos won't adhere well if there is any sand residue on the page.

3. Following the manufacturer's directions, apply the rub-on letters. To make the spacing easier, start with the center letter and work out in both directions.

4. Using the ruler and knife, trim the photos to the following sizes, from the top and moving clockwise: 4" x 2 1/2" (10 cm x 6.5 cm), 4 3/4" x 4" (12 cm x 10 cm), 3 3/4" x 2 3/4 (9.5 cm x 7 cm), 4 1/2" x 2 3/4" (11.5 cm x 7 cm), and 4 1/2" x 2 3/4" (11.5 cm x 7 cm). Note the overlaps. Referring to the photo for placement, arrange the photos on the blue paper. Use the pencil to mark the blue paper at the corners of the photos for placement. Following the manufacturer's directions, coat the backs of the photos with adhesive spray. Press in place.

5. Write the captions with the fine-tip marker.

6. Use the kneaded rubber eraser to remove all pencil marks.

# Falling Leaves

Falling leaves made from sand can catch the light almost as well as their botanical counterparts.

## Materials

- photo
- one 12" x 12" (30.5 cm x 30.5 cm) sheet tan patterned paper
- one 8 1/2" x 11" (21.5 cm x 28 cm) sheet tan vellum
- black photo corners
- brown art sand
- pink art sand
- brown chisel-tip marker
- double-sided adhesive sheet, such as Peel-N-Stick

## Tools

- tracing paper
- pencil
- scissors
- craft knife
- metal-edged ruler
- dish towel

## Instructions

1. Use the tracing paper to make the leaf template. (See Leaf template on page 286.) From the double-sided adhesive sheet, cut five leaves. Referring to the photo, arrange the leaves in a random pattern around the top and the sides of the tan paper. Use the pencil to mark the tan paper at chosen reference points on the leaves for placement. Peel off the protective paper, and attach the leaves to the tan paper. Remove the remaining protective paper from the leaves to expose the adhesive. Lightly sprinkle the bottom edge of the bottom leaves with the pink sand. Remove any excess sand. Sprinkle the brown sand over all of the leaves. Remove

any excess sand. Gently wipe the tan paper with the dish towel because the photo corners won't adhere well if there is any sand residue on the page.

2. From the tan vellum, cut two leaves. Fold the leaves in half, lengthwise. From the double-sided adhesive sheet, cut one leaf. Cut the leaf in half, lengthwise. Peel the protective paper from the back of one half, and attach it to the back of one of the folded leaves. Repeat with the remaining leaf. Use the pencil to mark the tan paper at chosen reference points on the leaves for placement. Remove the remaining protective paper, and press the leaves in place.

3. Using the ruler and knife, trim the photo to 6 1/4" x 4 1/2" (16 cm x 11.5 cm). Place the photo 1 1/2" (4 cm) from the right edge and 3 3/4" (9.5 cm) from the top edge of the tan paper. Use the pencil to mark the tan paper at the corners of the photo for placement. Following the manufacturer's directions, attach the photo to the paper with the photo corners.

4. Write the caption using the chisel-tip marker.

5. Use the kneaded rubber eraser to remove all pencil marks.

# Micro Beads

For a unique and shimmery 3-D effect, look to glass micro beads, sometimes called tiny marbles, holeless beads, or no-hole beads. This popular embellishment is easy to apply using strong, double-sided sheets, craft glue, or heat-activated liquid adhesives.

Micro beads work best on pages where you want to achieve a festive, glittery design, such as wedding pages or party and celebration pages. Micro beads are available in a wide array of colors, both single colored and multicolored; pearlescent and metallic finishes; and a number of specials shapes. Just apply the tape in the shape of the desired design, then sprinkle on the beads and gently press. Sprinkle a second time, if needed.

**Sample 2.** Cut a heart shape from an adhesive sheet. Peel off the protective paper, and attach the heart to the background paper. Using the craft knife, cut a curve through the protective paper only. Remove the paper from the small area to expose the adhesive. Place one large bead on the adhesive, and then fill in with micro beads. Remove the remaining protective paper, and apply multicolored micro beads.

**Sample 1.** To make a beaded frame, cut strips from an adhesive sheet. Peel off the protective paper, and, overlapping the edge of the photo, attach the strips to the background paper. Remove the remaining protective paper, and apply clear beads to the exposed adhesive.

**Sample 3.** Create a decorative border to accent initials or a page title. Cut curvy shapes from the adhesive sheet, peel off the protective paper, and position the shapes on the background above and below the lettering. Remove the remaining protective paper, and apply assorted beads on the exposed adhesive.

# Friends

Create festive micro-bead borders for a favorite photo. Accent the page further by adding some glistening stars.

**Materials**

- photo
- one 12" x 12" (30.5 cm x 30.5 cm) sheet pink paper
- one 9" x 12" (23 cm x 30.5 cm) sheet tan vellum
- one 9" x 12" (23 cm x 30.5 cm) sheet cream paper
- purple micro beads, mixed
- double-sided adhesive sheet, such as Peel-N-Stick
- archival-quality adhesive spray

**Tools**

- craft knife
- metal-edged ruler
- tracing paper
- scissors
- kneaded rubber eraser
- black fine-tip marker (optional)

**Instructions**

1. Using the ruler and knife, trim the vellum to 8 1/2" x 8 1/2" (21.5 cm x 21.5 cm). Place the trimmed vellum 1 1/8" (3 cm) from the right edge, and 1 3/8" (3.5 cm) from the bottom edge of the pink paper. Use the pencil to lightly mark the pink paper at the corners of the vellum for placement. Following the manufacturer's directions, coat the back of the vellum with adhesive spray. Press in place.

2. Use the marker to print a poem or a personal sentiment on the cream paper (or do this on a computer). Center the poem, and trim the cream paper to 5 1/4" x 6" (13.5 cm x 15 cm). Place the poem box 2 5/8" (6.5 cm) from the right edge and 2" (5 cm) from the bottom edge of the pink paper. Use the pencil to lightly mark the vellum at the corners of the trimmed cream paper for placement. Coat the back of the cream paper with adhesive spray. Press in place.

3. Trim the photo to 4 1/4" x 3 3/4" (11 cm x 9.5 cm). From the double-sided adhesive sheet, cut two 4 1/4" x 1/2" (11 cm x 1 cm) strips. Peel off the protective paper, and attach the adhesive strips to the top and bottom of the photo. Referring to the photo for placement and overlapping the cream paper, place the photo diagonally on the page. Use the pencil to lightly mark the pink paper and the vellum at the corners of the photo for placement. Coat the back of the photo with adhesive spray. Press in place.

4. Photocopy the Star template and use the tracing paper to make the template. From the double-sided adhesive sheet, cut two

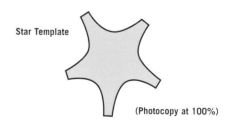

**Star Template**

**(Photocopy at 100%)**

stars. Peel off the protective paper, and, referring to the photo for placement, attach the stars to the pink paper.

5. Use the kneaded rubber eraser to remove all pencil marks.

6. Remove the remaining paper from the strips and the stars. Sprinkle the beads on the exposed adhesive. Remove any excess beads. Sprinkle again, if necessary.

# Wedding Streamers

Make a dazzling yet elegant wedding layout by adding curving, beaded strips that wind their way off the edges of the page.

**Materials**

- photos
- one 12" x 12" (30.5 cm x 30.5 cm) straw paper
- silver and white micro beads, mixed
- black photo corners
- double-sided adhesive sheet, such as Peel-N-Stick

**Tools**

- craft knife
- metal-edged ruler
- tracing paper
- scissors
- pencil
- kneaded rubber eraser

**Instructions**

1. Using the ruler and knife, trim the photos to 6" x 4½" (15 cm x 11.5 cm). Referring to the photo for placement, set the photos diagonally on the straw paper. Use the pencil to mark lightly the straw paper at the corners of the photos for placement. Slide the photo corners on the photos. Following the manufacturer's directions, attach the photos to the straw paper with the photo corners.

2. Use the kneaded rubber eraser to remove all pencil marks.

3. Use the tracing paper to make the streamer templates. (See Streamers templates on page 290.) From the double-sided adhesive sheet, cut the streamers. Peel off the protective paper; referring to the photo for placement, attach the streamers to the right corner of the straw paper.

4. Remove the remaining protective paper from the streamers. Sprinkle the beads on the exposed adhesive. Remove the excess beads. Sprinkle again, if necessary.

# Dip-Dyeing

Dip-dyeing is a simple technique for creating custom-dyed rice papers. To create a sheet of dip-dyed paper, fold a sheet of rice paper, then dip various corners in dyes made from watercolor paint. Open the paper, and let dry. The effect creates a softly mottled background with a lovely texture resulting from the folds. Tearing, rather than cutting, the edges of your rice paper pieces also creates a soft deckle effect.

The sheet can be used whole, or gently torn into smaller pieces that can be used as paper tiles, collage accents, or as background papers.

**Sample 1.** Originally white paper with gold threads, these pink- and orange-hued pieces of rice paper were dyed following the folding and dipping sequence explained in the first project. Burgundy and gold watercolor paints were used.

**Sample 2.** This sample, which also started with white rice paper, was created by accordion-folding the paper in two directions and dyeing one edge with lavender watercolor paint. The folds help spread the pigment into the creases.

# X-O-X-O

Use a soft lavender dip-dyed paper as the background for a simple page layout that features
a lovely black-and-white photo of a happy couple. Write the caption with a lavender pencil
to coordinate with the dyed background.

### Materials

- photo
- one 12" x 12" (30.5 cm x 30.5 cm) sheet white paper
- one sheet rice paper, available at art supply stores (embedded gold threads optional)
- one 9" x 12" (23 cm x 30.5 cm) sheet cream textured paper
- lavender watercolor paint
- purple pencil
- archival-quality adhesive spray

### Tools

- atomizer containing water
- saucer
- paper towels
- scissors
- craft knife
- metal-edged ruler
- pencil

### Instructions

1. From the rice paper, cut four 6¹/₂" (16.5 cm) squares. Use the atomizer to slightly mist both sides of each square. Referring to Diagram A, fold the squares. In the saucer, mix the lavender watercolor paint in approximately 6 tablespoons of water. Referring to Diagram B, dip the corners of the folded squares in the paint, allowing the paper to absorb the paint. Unfold the squares, and place them on the paper towels to dry. Do not overlap the squares, and do not blot them because blotting will remove the color.

2. Use the pencil to lightly mark a horizontal and a vertical line in the center of the white paper to divide it into quarters. Carefully tear the edges around each rice paper square. Following the manufacturer's directions, coat the backs of the squares with the adhesive spray. Align one rice paper square in each of the marked squares on the white paper. Press in place.

3. Using the ruler and knife, trim the photo to 6" x 4" (15 cm x 10 cm). Coat the back of the photo with adhesive spray. Place the photo on the cream textured paper, and press to adhere. Allowing ¹/₄" (0.6 cm) around the top and the sides and ³/₄" (2 cm) below the photo, trim the cream paper. Center and place the mounted photo 3¹/₄" (8.5 cm) from top edge of the white paper. Mark the rice paper at the corners of the mounted photo for placement. Coat the back of the mounted photo with adhesive spray. Press in place.

4. Write the names and caption using the purple pencil.

5. Use the kneaded rubber eraser to remove all exposed pencil marks.

**Diagram A**

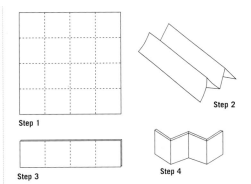

Step 1

Step 2

Step 3

Step 4

**Diagram B**

Dip each corner separately

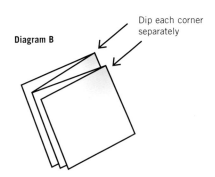

# Vintage Portrait

Use two colors in your dip-dyed paper to echo the muted tones of a vintage photo. You may even want to experiment with coloring your own black-and-white photos to coordinate with your custom dip-dyed papers.

### Materials

- photo
- one 12" x 12" (30.5 cm x 30.5 cm) sheet cream paper
- one 9" x 12" (23 cm x 30.5 cm) sheet white paper
- one 9" x 12" (23 cm x 30.5 cm) sheet pink patterned paper
- one sheet rice paper, available at art supply stores (embedded gold threads optional)
- one large bird sticker
- two small rose stickers
- decorative paper border
- gold and burgundy watercolor paint
- archival-quality adhesive spray

### Tools

- atomizer containing water
- two saucers
- craft knife
- metal-edged ruler
- pencil
- kneaded rubber eraser
- black fine-tip marker (optional)

### Instructions

1. From the rice paper, cut one 11$\frac{1}{2}$" (29 cm) square. Use the atomizer to slightly mist each side of the rice paper square. Referring to Diagram A, fold the square. In the saucers, mix each color of paint in approximately 6 tablespoons water. Referring to Diagram B, dip the sides of the folded square in the paint, allowing the paper to absorb the paint. Unfold the square, and place it on the paper towel to dry. Do not blot the square because blotting will remove the color.

2. Following the manufacturer's directions, coat the back of the rice paper square with adhesive spray. Center and place the square on the cream paper. Press to adhere. Referring to the photo for placement, attach the stickers to the rice paper. Using the ruler and knife, trim the edge of the overlapping sticker.

3. Using the ruler and knife, trim the photo to 4" x 6" (10 cm x 15 cm). Coat the back of photo with adhesive spray. Place the photo on the white paper, and press to adhere. Center the photo, and trim the white paper to 4$\frac{1}{2}$" x 6$\frac{1}{2}$" (11.5 cm x 16.5 cm). Place the mounted photo 1$\frac{3}{8}$" (3.5 cm) from the top edge, and 3$\frac{3}{4}$" (9.5 cm) from the right edge of the cream paper. Use the pencil to mark lightly the rice paper at the corners of the mounted photo for placement. Coat the back of the mounted photo with adhesive spray. Press the mounted photo in place to adhere.

4. Use the marker to print the names and date on the pink patterned paper. Center the names and date, and trim the pink paper to 5" x 1$\frac{1}{2}$" (12.5 cm x 4 cm). Place the caption box 2" (5 cm) from the right edge and 2" (5 cm) from the bottom edge of the cream paper. Use a pencil to mark the rice paper at the corners of the caption box for placement. Coat the back of the caption box with adhesive spray. Press in place. Trim the two border strips to 2$\frac{5}{8}$" x $\frac{5}{8}$" (6.5 cm x 1.5 cm). Coat the backs of the strips with adhesive spray. Center and overlap the strips on the top and bottom edges of the caption box. Press to adhere.

5. Use the kneaded rubber eraser to remove all pencil marks.

**Diagram A**

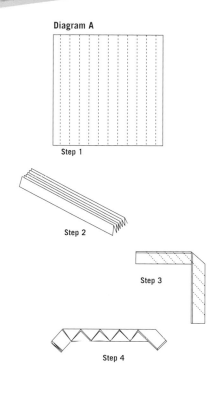

Step 1

Step 2

Step 3

Step 4

**Diagram B**

# Aged Paper

The essence of scrapbooking is preserving photos and mementos in a creative and personal fashion. Great care is taken to keep precious memorabilia looking new. Artificially aged paper, however, is the perfect complement to old photos or keepsakes. Old photos and documents are by their nature delicate and fragile, but this delicacy can be highlighted as a design element. Paper can be treated (or mistreated) to simulate aging by wrinkling, sanding, tearing, and painting. These treated papers can then be used as backdrops or accents for the real thing.

**Sample 1.** To emphasize wrinkles, crinkle the paper, apply diluted acrylic paint, and dry the paper in a microwave oven to set the wrinkles. Coat the back with adhesive spray. To enhance the three-dimensional effect, compress the paper slightly while pressing it to the page.

**Sample 2.** Carefully singe the edges of the paper over a candle flame or on a hot stove coil.

**Sample 3.** To highlight inherent irregularities in handmade paper, lightly coat the paper with spray paint. Let dry, and sand the surface of the paper with fine-grain sandpaper.

# Garden Party

This photo and mat board have been naturally aging for the past 90 years, but it took only a few minutes to transform these clip-art flowers from vibrant to vintage.

**Materials**

- photo
- one 12" x 12" (30.5 cm x 30.5 cm) sheet dark brown paper
- paper flowers cut from color clip art, greeting cards, or wrapping paper
- pages of text
- acrylic sealer
- dark gray acrylic paint
- archival-quality adhesive spray
- double-sided adhesive sheet such as Peel-N-Stick

**Tools**

- scissors
- sandpaper
- paintbrush
- paper towel
- metal-edged ruler
- craft knife
- kneaded rubber eraser

**Instructions**

1. From the clip art, cut seven flowers and stems. Apply one coat of sealer to the flowers. Let dry. Repeat with two more coats of sealer. Sand the surface of the flowers in several directions, being careful not to sand completely through the sealer. Dilute the gray acrylic paint to approximately three parts water to one part paint. Paint the flowers with the diluted paint. Blot the paint lightly, leaving some paint in the sanded recesses. Let dry. Repeat painting, if necessary.

2. Tear the pages of text into various lengths and sizes. Following manufacturer's directions, coat the backs of the pages with adhesive spray. Overlapping the pieces, press them in place along the bottom of the sheet of dark brown paper. Using the ruler and knife, trim the overlapping pieces.

3. Referring to the photo for placement, set the flowers around three sides of the brown paper. Use the pencil to lightly mark the brown paper at selected reference points on the flowers for placement. Coat the backs of the flowers. Press the flowers in place to adhere.

4. Referring to the photo for placement, set the photo on the brown paper. Use the pencil to mark the brown paper at the corners of the photo for placement. Cut three strips of double-sided adhesive approximately $1/2$" (1 cm) wide. Trim the strips $1/2$" (1 cm) shorter than the length of the photo. Peel off the protective paper, and attach the adhesive to the back of the photo. Remove the remaining protective paper, and attach the photo to the page.

5. Use the kneaded rubber eraser to remove all pencil marks.

# Letters from France

When are wrinkles attractive? When they complement the age and character of significant treasures.

## Materials

- photo
- one 12" x 12" (30.5 cm x 30.5 cm) sheet butterscotch patterned paper
- one 12" x 12" (30.5 cm x 30.5 cm) sheet pale green paper
- small paper memorabilia, such as letters, calendar pages, and maps
- postage stickers
- black fine-tip marker
- archival-quality adhesive spray
- double-sided adhesive sheet, such as Peel-N-Stick

## Tools

- metal-edged ruler
- craft knife
- pencil

## Instructions

1. Using the ruler and knife, trim the green paper to 11¼" x 2¾" (28.5 cm x 7 cm). Place with the right edge flush and 1" (2.5 cm) from the bottom edge of the butterscotch paper. Use the pencil to mark lightly the butterscotch paper along the top edge of the green paper. Arrange the paper items with their bottom edges overlapping the marked line. Trim the photo to 3¾" x 5¾" (9.5 cm x 14.5 cm). Place the photo 3¾" (9.5 cm) from the right edge and 2⅛" (5.5 cm) from the top edge of the butterscotch paper. Tuck the paper items behind the photo. Use the pencil to mark the butterscotch paper at the corners of the photo and of the paper items for placement. Use adhesive spray to attach lightweight items to the paper. Use the double-sided adhesive sheet to attach thicker or heavier items to the paper. Press in place. Coat the back of the green strip with adhesive spray. Press in place.

2. Place the remaining paper items on the strip. Use the pencil to mark the butterscotch paper at the corners the paper items for placement. Attach the remaining items to the paper.

3. Referring to the photo for placement, attach the stickers.

4. Write the title using the marker.

5. Use the kneaded rubber eraser to remove all pencil marks.

# Stamping

A rubber stamp and an inkpad are the most user-friendly tools available to paper artists. Stamping is versatile and nearly foolproof. With more enthusiasts shopping for more designs, an eclectic array of motifs is available to choose from. And techniques have become increasingly sophisticated. Stamps are now partnered with masks, bleach, pencils, and powders to create elegant paper projects. So avoid the humdrum, and start stamping with style.

**Sample 1.** This faded image brings to mind hand-tinted etchings and photographs. After stamping, lightly color in the areas with colored pencils.

**Sample 2.** Sprinkle metallic embossing powder on wet ink to add some sparkle.

**Sample 3.** Layers of stamped papers create a subtle echo of pattern.

# Little Hands

Stamped images stay within a confined space with the help of a paper stencil.

### Materials

- photo
- one 12" x 12" (30.5 cm x 30.5 cm) sheet ivory paper
- one 8½" x 11" (21.5 cm x 28 cm) sheet cream patterned paper
- one 8½" x 11" (21.5 cm x 28 cm) sheet melon patterned paper
- one 8½" x 11" (21.5 cm x 28 cm) sheet light green paper
- one 8½" x 11" (21.5 cm x 28 cm) sheet light green patterned paper
- one 8½" x 11" (21.5 cm x 28 cm) sheet tan patterned paper
- one 8½" x 11" (21.5 cm x 28 cm) sheet typing paper

- alphabet rubber stamps
- 4 to 6 small image rubber stamps
- brown ink
- black ink
- brown pencil
- brown crayon
- archival-quality tape
- archival-quality adhesive spray

### Tools

- craft knife
- scissors
- metal-edged ruler
- tracing paper
- pencil
- kneaded rubber eraser

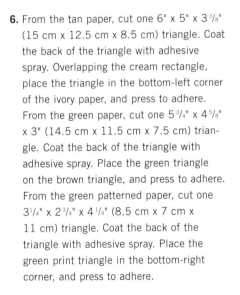

### Instructions

1. Use the tracing paper to make the mat template. (See Mat template on page 289.) Cut the photo into an oval shape slightly larger than the window in the template. From the typing paper, make one mat. From the melon patterned paper, cut two mat quadrants. From the cream paper, cut two mat quadrants. Following the manufacturer's directions, coat the backs of the mat quadrants. Place quadrants on the typing paper frame to form a complete oval. Press to adhere. Trim the typing paper, if necessary. Secure the photo to the back of the mat with tape.

2. Referring to the photo for placement, use the brown crayon to trace around the child's hands. Trace over crayon hands on tracing paper, and cut out the centers. Leave the paper around the hands complete to use as a stencil. Align both pairs of hands, and place the stencil on the ivory paper. Use the brown and the black ink to stamp the images in the spaces. Let dry. Remove the stencil.

3. Using the ruler and knife, trim the green patterned paper to 4¾" x 2¾" (12 cm x 7 cm). Place the green print rectangle diagonally in the top-right corner of the

ivory paper, with the left corner 2" (5 cm) and the right corner ½" (1 cm) from the top edge of the paper. Use the pencil to lightly mark the ivory paper at the corners of the green print rectangle for placement. Coat the back of the rectangle with adhesive spray. Press in place.

4. Referring to the photo for placement and overlapping the rectangle slightly, place the matted photo on the ivory paper. Use the pencil to mark the ivory paper at the top and the bottom of the oval mat for placement. Coat the back of the matted photo with the adhesive spray. Press in place.

5. Trim the cream paper to 11" x 4" (28 cm x 10 cm). Referring to the photo for placement, set the rectangle diagonally on the bottom of the ivory paper, with the top-right corner 4" (10 cm) from the bottom edge of the ivory paper and the top-left corner 1½" (4 cm) from the bottom edge of the ivory paper. Use the pencil to mark the ivory paper at the top edge of the cream rectangle. Coat the back of the cream rectangle with adhesive spray. Press in place. Use the ruler and the knife to trim the overlapping edges of the cream rectangle.

6. From the tan paper, cut one 6" x 5" x 3⅜" (15 cm x 12.5 cm x 8.5 cm) triangle. Coat the back of the triangle with adhesive spray. Overlapping the cream rectangle, place the triangle in the bottom-left corner of the ivory paper, and press to adhere. From the green paper, cut one 5¾" x 4⅝" x 3" (14.5 cm x 11.5 cm x 7.5 cm) triangle. Coat the back of the triangle with adhesive spray. Place the green triangle on the brown triangle, and press to adhere. From the green patterned paper, cut one 3¼" x 2¾" x 4¼" (8.5 cm x 7 cm x 11 cm) triangle. Coat the back of the triangle with adhesive spray. Place the green print triangle in the bottom-right corner, and press to adhere.

7. Use the brown ink to stamp the name on the green print rectangle. Let dry. Use the brown ink to stamp the alphabet on the cream rectangle. Let dry. Use the brown pencil to write caption on the green print rectangle below the stamped name.

8. Use the kneaded rubber eraser to remove all pencil marks.

# Golf Heaven

Lift the dye from colored paper with this clever technique. Each solid color of paper produces its own unique reverse-dye color. Swab small sample snippets with bleach to reveal the surprise results.

**Materials**

- photos
- one 12" x 12" (30.5 cm x 30.5 cm) sheet dark blue patterned paper
- one 12" x 12" (30.5 cm x 30.5 cm) sheet blue paper
- one 8 1/2" x 11" (21.5 cm x 28 cm) sheet maize paper
- one 8 1/2" x 11" (21.5 cm x 28 cm) sheet plum paper
- 48-point rub-on letters
- liquid bleach
- small cosmetic sponges
- brown ink
- sun rubber stamp
- archival-quality adhesive spray

**Tools**

- scissors
- small saucer
- paper towel
- craft knife
- metal-edged ruler
- pencil
- kneaded rubber eraser

## Instructions

1. From the cosmetic sponges, cut two or three cloud shapes measuring approximately 2" x 1" (5 cm x 2.5 cm). Tear several layers of paper towel, and place them in the saucer. Pour enough bleach into the saucer to saturate the paper towels. Dip the cloud sponges in the bleach, and stamp the top edge of the blue paper, overlapping shapes, if desired. Let dry. Note: Immediately after stamping, rinse the sponges and the rubber stamp thoroughly with running water. Continued exposure to the bleach will corrode them. Dip the sun stamp in the bleach, and stamp the top edge of the maize paper. Let dry. Rinse the stamp thoroughly with running water. Use the brown ink to stamp the top edge of the maize paper over the beached sun. Let dry.

2. Tear a 2 1/2" (6.5 cm)-wide strip from the blue paper. Make sure to include the bleached clouds in the section that you tear. Following the manufacturer's directions, coat the back of the strip with adhesive spray. Place the strip 1/4" (0.6 cm) from the top edge of the dark blue patterned paper. Press in place. Tear around the sides and bottom of sun, measuring 3 1/2" x 2 1/2" (9 cm x 6.5 cm). Consider the locations of the clouds on the blue strip, and place the sun rectangle on top of the cloud strip. Use the pencil to lightly mark the dark blue paper at the corners of the sun rectangle for placement. Coat the back of the sun rectangle with adhesive spray. Press in place.

3. Using the ruler and knife, trim the photos to the following sizes, clockwise from left: 6" x 4" (15 cm x 10 cm), 3 1/2" x 4 1/2" (9 cm x 11.5 cm), and 3 1/4" x 5 1/2" (8.5 cm x 14 cm). Referring to the photo for placement, arrange the photos on the dark blue paper with the top-right photo overlapping the cloud strip. Use the pencil to mark lightly the dark blue paper and the cloud strip at the corners of the photos for placement. Coat the backs of the photos with the adhesive spray. Press the photos in place.

4. Trim the plum paper to 6" x 1 3/8" (15 cm x 3.5 cm). Using the ruler and pencil, lightly draw a baseline for rub-on letters. Following the manufacturer's directions and using the marked line as a guide, apply the rub-on letters. To make the spacing easier, start with the center letters and work out in both directions. Place the title strip on the dark blue paper with the top edge of the strip 1/4" (0.6 cm) from the bottom edge of the left photo. Use the pencil to mark the dark blue paper at the corners of the strip for placement. Coat the back of the strip with adhesive spray. Press in place.

5. Use the kneaded rubber eraser to remove all pencil marks.

# Decoupage

Although this technique was developed in Venice, its name is derived from a French word, *découper*, which means "to cut out." Decoupage is a creative, step-by-step process of cutting, pasting, and varnishing. European artists used this process to transform plain surfaces to look as though they had been hand-painted. The traditional treatment has been simplified for scrapbook art. Because this adaptation requires no intricate cutting, it is actually decoupage without the découper. The varnishing is done with ordinary craft glue.

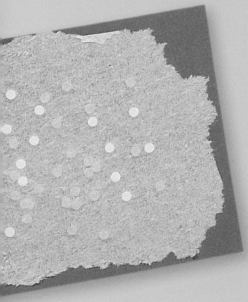

**Sample 1.** Use this technique to embed confetti in a paper appliqué. Place the confetti on plastic wrap, and cover it with a single layer of tissue.

**Sample 2.** Carefully coat the tissue with a layer of diluted white craft glue, and let dry. Repeat with a second coat of glue.

**Sample 3.** Carefully peel the tissue from the plastic wrap, and trim it into a fun shape. Attach it to the page with adhesive spray.

# Yankee Doodle Dandies

Transform bright paper napkins into opaque paper appliqués.

**Materials**

- photos
- one 12" x 12" (30.5 cm x 30.5 cm) sheet white paper
- one 8½" x 11" (21.5 cm x 28 cm) sheet of each of six different shades of blue paper
- one 8½" x 11" (21.5 cm x 28 cm) sheet of yellow paper
- printed napkins
- blue pencil
- black fine-tip marker
- white craft glue
- archival-quality adhesive spray

**Tools**

- metal-edged ruler
- craft knife
- pencil
- curved-corner paper punch
- plastic wrap
- paintbrush
- kneaded rubber eraser

## Instructions

1. Remove and discard the bottom ply from the print napkins. Tear three 4" (10 cm) squares from the napkins. Dilute the craft glue to approximately two parts water to one part glue. Place the torn squares on the plastic wrap. Use the paintbrush to carefully paint one coat of the diluted glue into the squares. Let dry. Repeat with one more coat of glue.

2. Use the pencil to draw light horizontal and vertical lines spaced 3" (7.5 cm) apart on the white paper. Using the ruler and the knife, cut one 5⅞" (15 cm) square from one sheet of blue paper. From each of the remaining blue papers, cut one 2⅞" (7.5 cm) square. From the yellow paper, cut one 2⅞" (7.5 cm) square. Referring to the photo for placement, set the colored squares on the corresponding white squares. Following the manufacturer's directions, coat the backs of the squares with the adhesive spray. Press the squares in place to adhere. Trim the coated napkin squares to 2⅞" (7.5 cm) squares. Place the napkin squares on the corresponding white squares. Coat the backs of the napkin squares with adhesive spray. Press the squares in place.

3. Trim the large photo to 4⅜" x 4" (11 cm x 10 cm). Use the corner punch to punch the corners of the photo. Place the photo in the center of the large blue square. Use the pencil to mark the blue paper at the corners of the photo for placement. Coat the back of the photo with adhesive spray. Press in place. Trim the small photo to a 2⅞" (7.5 cm) square. Coat the back of the photo with adhesive spray. Place in the corresponding square, and press to adhere.

4. Use the pencil and the ruler to draw light horizontal lines in the top white square to use as a baseline for the title. Use the blue pencil to write the title. Write the captions for the photos using the fine-tip marker.

5. Use the kneaded rubber eraser to remove all pencil marks.

# Wedding Wreath

Theses delicate tissue blossoms and berries weren't hand-painted, although they look as if they were. This labor of love took almost no time at all to complete.

## Materials
- photos
- one 12" x 12" (30.5 cm x 30.5 cm) sheet white enamel finish paper
- one 12" x 12" (30.5 cm x 30.5 cm) sheet pale green paper
- printed napkins
- black fine-tip marker
- white craft glue
- archival-quality adhesive spray

## Tools
- metal-edged ruler
- craft knife
- pencil
- plastic wrap
- paintbrush
- kneaded rubber eraser

## Instructions

1. Remove and discard the bottom ply from the printed napkins. Tear 12 to 15 small images from the napkins. Dilute the craft glue to approximately two parts water to one part glue. Place the torn squares on the plastic wrap. Use the paintbrush to carefully paint the squares with one coat of diluted glue. Let dry. Repeat with one more coat of glue.

2. Using the ruler and knife, trim the photo to 3$\frac{1}{2}$" x 5$\frac{1}{4}$" (9 cm x 13.5 cm). Place the photo 3$\frac{1}{4}$" (8.5 cm) from the left edge and 2" (5 cm) from the top edge of the white paper. Use the pencil to lightly mark the white paper at the corners of the photo for placement. Trim the green paper to 2$\frac{1}{4}$" x 12" (6 cm x 30.5 cm). Align the green strip with the right edge of the white paper. Use the pencil to mark the white paper along the left edge of the green strip for placement. Following the manufacturer's directions, coat the back of the photo and of the strip with adhesive spray. Press in place.

3. Referring to the photo for placement, arrange the images around the photo. Use the pencil to mark the white paper at the top and bottom of each image for placement. Coat the backs of the images with the adhesive spray. Press in place.

4. Write the title using the fine-tip marker.

5. Use the kneaded rubber eraser to remove all pencil marks.

# Marbling

Marbled paper is characterized by flowing, organic patterns that resemble ocean waves or striated rock. It is reproduced commercially for use as end papers and as wallpaper. To marble paper, colors are floated on a surface of thickened liquid. The colors can be manipulated to form specific patterns or left untouched to spread and co-mingle naturally. The paper is placed face-down on the surface to transfer the design. It is an instant-gratification art because the design appears as soon as the paper touches the paint. Like snowflakes, each individual print is unique.

Beginning marbling can be done on a gelatin surface. Simply drop the paint on the set gelatin, and let it spread. Then print. The sugar in the gelatin actually leaves a nice glaze on the paper. Then try floating the paint on a less stable surface, such as liquid starch or commercially prepared solutions such as carrageen. Liquid surfaces allow for more design variation. Remember to discard the gelatin after use.

**Sample 1.** Dress a paper doll in bold marbled papers. The doll's apron was made from paper that was marbled with liquid starch.

**Sample 2.** Make a declarative statement on a colorful and campy backdrop.

**Sample 3.** The organic pattern inside this envelope serves as a nice contrast to the button-down stripe of the outside. This paper was also marbled with liquid starch.

# You're Out of This World

For stellar results, keep silhouettes simple when working with fancy paper.

## Materials

- photo
- one 12" x 12" (30.5 cm x 30.5 cm) sheet black paper
- one 8½" x 11" (21.5 cm x 28 cm) sheet blue paper
- one 8½" x 11" (21.5 cm x 28 cm) sheet cream paper
- acrylic paint in the following colors: red, gray, gold, and blue (or alternate colors)
- gelatin
- white milky pen
- archival-quality adhesive spray

## Tools

- 9" x 12" (23 cm x 30.5 cm) glass or metal tray
- eye droppers (optional)
- feather or fork (optional)
- old newspaper torn into 3" (7.5 cm)-wide strips
- paper towel
- iron
- tracing paper
- scissors
- craft knife
- metal-edged ruler
- curved-corner paper punch
- kneaded rubber eraser

## Instructions

1. Following the manufacturer's directions, make the gelatin, and pour it into the pan. Allow it to set. Dilute each color of paint to approximately three parts water to one part paint. Use either eye droppers or plastic squirt bottles to drop a few drops of each selected color on the surface of the gelatin. Manipulate the paint with the feather or the fork, or let the colors spread naturally. Carefully place the blue paper on the gelatin. Remove the paper from the gelatin. Place the paper on the paper towel. With the newspaper strips, squeegee the excess gelatin from the paper. Let dry. Repeat with the cream paper.

2. Press the paper with an iron to flatten.

3. Use the tracing paper to make the star and planet templates. (See Star and Planet templates on page 291.) Cut the shapes from the corresponding colors. Referring to the photo for placement, set the stars and the planet on the black paper. Place the ring to overlap the right edge of the paper. Use the pencil to lightly mark the black paper at selected reference points on the planet and the stars for placement. Following the manufacturer's directions, coat the backs of the planet and the stars with adhesive. Press them in place. Use the ruler and knife to trim the overlapping piece.

4. Trim the photo to 3¼" x 3⅝" (8.3 cm x 9.2 cm). Using the corner punch, punch the corners of the photo. Referring to the photo for placement, set the photo on the black paper. Use the pencil to mark the black paper at the corners of the photo for placement. Coat the back of the photo with the adhesive spray. Press the photo in place to adhere.

5. Write the title and the caption using the milky pen.

6. Use the kneaded rubber eraser to remove all pencil marks.

# A Windy Day

Patchwork kites made from marbled paper are a high-flying success.

## Materials

- photo
- one 12" x 12" (30.5 cm x 30.5 cm) sheet blue paper
- one 8½" x 11" (21.5 cm x 28 cm) sheet blue paper
- one 8½" x 11" (21.5 cm x 28 cm) sheet cream paper
- one 8½" x 11" (21.5 cm x 28 cm) sheet yellow paper
- one 8½" x 11" (21.5 cm x 28 cm) sheet black paper
- blue print fabric
- alphabet stamps
- gelatin
- acrylic paint in the following colors; red, gray, gold, and blue (or alternate colors)
- blue ink
- archival-quality adhesive spray
- double-sided adhesive sheet, such as Peel-N-Stick

## Tools

- 9" x 12" (23 cm x 30.5 cm) glass or metal tray
- eye droppers (optional)
- feather or fork (optional)
- old newspaper torn into 3" (7.5 cm)-wide strips
- paper towel
- iron
- tracing paper
- scissors
- craft knife
- metal-edged ruler
- kneaded rubber eraser

## Instructions

1. Following the manufacturer's directions make the gelatin, and pour it into the pan. Allow it to set. Dilute each color of paint to approximately three parts water to one part paint. Use either eye droppers or plastic squirt bottles to drop a few drops of each selected color on the surface of the gelatin. Manipulate the paint with the feather or the fork, or let the colors spread naturally. Carefully place the blue paper on the gelatin. Remove the paper from the gelatin. Place the paper on the paper towel. With the newspaper strips, squeegee the excess gelatin from the paper. Let dry. Repeat with the cream paper and with the yellow paper.

2. Press the paper with the iron to flatten.

3. Use the tracing paper to make the kite template. (See Kite template on page 291.) Cut one kite from each color. Using the ruler and knife, cut each kite into four sections. Referring to the photo for placement, set the kites on the blue paper. Place the center kite to overlap the top edge of the paper. Use the pencil to lightly mark the blue paper at the corners of the kites for placement. Following the manufacturer's directions, coat the backs of the kite sections with adhesive spray. Press the sections in place. Using the ruler and knife, trim the overlapping pieces.

4. From the black paper, cut one ⅛" x 7½" (0.3 cm x 19 cm) strip. Place the strip below the right kite and 1¾" (4.5 cm) from the right edge of the blue paper. Use the pencil to mark the blue paper along the edge of the strip for placement. From the blue fabric cut four ⅜" x 3½" (1 cm x 9 cm) strips. Tie each strip around the black paper strip. From the double-sided adhesive, cut five ⅛" x ½" (0.3 cm x 1 cm) strips. Peel off the protective paper, and attach the adhesive to the back of the black paper strip at the top and bottom and between the ties. Remove the remaining protective paper, and attach the strip to the blue paper. From the double-sided adhesive sheet, cut eight ¼" (0.6 cm) squares. Peel off the protective paper, and attach the adhesive to the backs of the ties. Remove the remaining protective paper, and attach the ties to the blue paper. Trim the ends of the ties, if necessary.

5. Using the ruler and knife, trim the photo to 5" x 7" (12.5 cm x 18 cm). Place the photo 2½" (6.5 cm) from the left edge and ⅜" (1 cm) from the bottom edge of the blue paper. Use the pencil to mark the blue paper at the corners of the photo for placement. Coat the back of the photo with adhesive spray. Press the photo in place.

6. Use the blue ink to stamp the title above the photo.

7. Use the kneaded rubber eraser to remove all pencil marks.

# Mosaics

For centuries, individual tiles, bits of glass, and even small pebbles have been arranged to portray still lifes, landscapes, and borders. Mosaics made from glass and ceramic tile are durable enough to walk on, but mosaics made from craft foam and corrugated paper are light-weight enough to decorate a page. These mosaics have an intriguing, touchable quality, and they are fun to make.

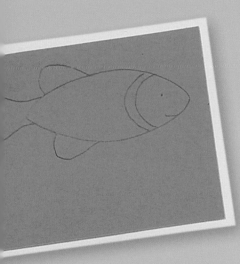

**Sample 1.** Begin by transferring the line art to the backing paper.

**Sample 2.** Cut out the silhouette, and attach it to the page over the line art.

**Sample 3.** Fill in the spaces with paper shapes and corrugated paper tiles.

# Teacher Tribute

A drawing is worth a thousand words. These small mosaic flowers are sprinkled on a well-deserved thank-you for a favorite teacher.

**Materials**

- artwork
- photo
- one 12" x 12" (30.5 cm x 30.5 cm) sheet purple paper
- one 8 1/2" x 11" (21.5 cm x 28 cm) sheet lavender patterned paper
- one 8 1/2" x 11" (21.5 cm x 28 cm) sheet burgundy paper
- 1/16" (0.2 cm) craft foam in light blue, purple, peach, tangerine, yellow, and pink.
- double-sided adhesive sheet, such as Peel-N-Stick
- archival-quality adhesive spray
- archival-quality tape

**Tools**

- tracing paper
- scissors
- metal-edged ruler
- pencil
- kneaded rubber eraser

## Instructions

1. Use the tracing paper to make the flower template. From the double-sided adhesive sheet, cut three flowers. Peel off the protective paper, and, allowing 1/2" (1 cm) between shapes, attach the adhesive to the burgundy paper. Remove the remaining protective paper to expose the adhesive. From the purple craft foam, cut two circles for the flower centers. From the light blue craft foam, cut one circle for the flower center. Place the circles on the adhesive in the centers of the flowers. Cut the remaining colors of foam into small tiles of various shapes. The tiles should range in size from 1/4" (0.6 cm) to 3/8" (1 cm). Working from the center out, carefully pick up each tile with the point of the craft knife, and place it on the adhesive. Refer to the photo for color shading. Leave enough space between each tile for the burgundy paper to show. Outer tiles may need to be trimmed slightly to conform to the curves of the flower petals.

2. Trim each flower, allowing 1/8" (0.3 cm) of paper around outside edge.

3. Using the ruler and the knife, trim the artwork to 8 1/2" x 11" (21.5 cm x 28 cm). Place the artwork 1/4" (0.6 cm) from the right edge and 3/4" (2 cm) from the top edge of the purple paper. Use the pencil to lightly mark the purple paper at the corners of the artwork for placement. Following the manufacturer's directions, coat the back of the artwork with adhesive spray. Press in place.

4. Trim the photo to 2 1/4" x 3" (6 cm x 7.5 cm). Trim the lavender patterned paper to 2 3/4" x 3 1/2" (7 cm x 9 cm). Center and cut a 1 7/8" x 2 5/8" (5 cm x 6.5 cm) window in the lavender rectangle to make a mat. Secure the photo to the back of the mat using the archival-quality tape. Overlapping the artwork, place the matted photo on the purple paper. Use the pencil to mark the purple paper and the artwork at the corners of the matted photo for placement. Coat the back of the matted photo with adhesive spray. Press in place.

5. Place the mosaic flowers on the paper at chosen spots. Use the pencil to mark the purple paper and the artwork at the flower tops for placement. Coat the backs of the mosaic flowers with adhesive spray. Press the flowers in place.

6. Use the kneaded rubber eraser to remove all pencil marks.

**Small Flower Template**

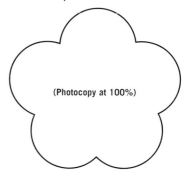

(Photocopy at 100%)

# Waves

The movement of watery ocean waves is portrayed with three-dimensional foam tiles. You can almost feel heat of the sun and taste the salty spray of the sea.

**Materials**

- photos
- one 12" x 12" (30.5 cm x 30.5 cm) sheet shaded pastel paper
- one 8¹/₂" x 11" (21.5 cm x 28 cm) sheet yellow patterned paper
- one 8¹/₂" x 11" (21.5 cm x 28 cm) sheet gold print paper
- ¹/₁₆" (0.2 cm) light blue craft foam
- ¹/₁₆" (0.2 cm) lavender craft foam
- black fine-tip marker
- double-sided adhesive sheet, such as Peel-N-Stick
- archival-quality adhesive spray
- archival-quality tape

**Tools**

- craft knife
- metal-edged ruler
- scissors
- tracing paper
- pencil
- kneaded rubber eraser

## Instructions

1. Using the ruler and knife, trim the yellow patterned paper to 9" x 5" (23 cm x 12.5 cm). Cut a 6¹/₂" x 4¹/₂" (16.5 cm x 11.5 cm) window offset to the right of the rectangle, to make a mat. Trim the large photo to 7" x 5" (18 cm x 12.5 cm). Secure the photo to the back of the mat using the tape. Place the matted photo diagonally on the pastel paper with the left corner 2" (5 cm) and the right corner ¹/₂" (1 cm) from the top edge of the paper. Use the pencil to mark lightly the pastel paper at the corners of the matted photo for placement. Following the manufacturer's directions, coat the back of the matted photo with adhesive spray. Press in place.

2. Trim the gold patterned paper to 8³/₄" x 3¹/₄" (22 cm x 8.5 cm). Center and cut three 2¹/₄" (6 cm) squares in the rectangle to make a mat. Trim the small photos to 2¹/₂" (6.5 cm) squares. Secure the photos to the back of the mat with tape. Place the matted photos diagonally on the pastel paper with the left corner 1" (2.5 cm) and the right corner ¹/₂" (1 cm) from the bottom edge of the paper. Use the pencil to mark the pastel paper at the corners of the matted photo for placement. Coat the back of the matted photo with the adhesive spray. Press in place.

3. Use the tracing paper to make the wave templates. (See Waves templates on page 287.) From the double-sided adhesive sheet, cut one of each wave shape. Referring to the photo for placement, peel the protective paper from the backs of the wave shapes, and attach them to the pastel paper. Remove the remaining protective paper to expose the adhesive. From the blue craft foam, cut one large wave shape.

Press it in place on a matching adhesive shape. Cut the lavender and the blue foam into small tiles of various shapes. Tiles should range in size from ¹/₄" (0.6 cm) to ³/₈" (1 cm). Carefully pick up each tile with point of craft knife, and place it on the remaining wave shapes. Refer to the photo for color shading. Leave enough space between each tile so that the pastel paper shows.

4. Write the caption and the names using the fine-tip marker.

5. Use the kneaded rubber eraser to remove all pencil marks.

# Layered Borders

Scrapbook enthusiasts of all skill levels know that the easiest solution to a successful page layout is an attention-grabbing border. You can't go wrong with a strong focal point in the center and an interesting graphic along the vertical margin. Build these snappy borders by layering simple geometric strips along the side of the page. No special skills are required—just elementary cutting and gluing.

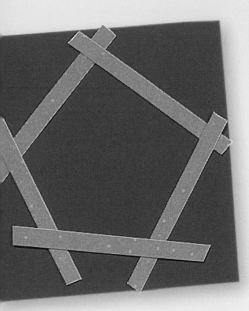

**Sample 1.** To layer shapes, attach the first layer of the design with double-sided adhesive or adhesive spray.

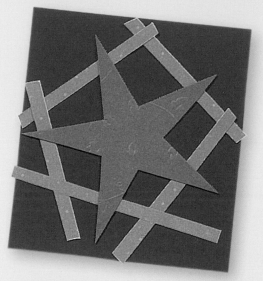

**Sample 2.** Attach the second layer of shapes.

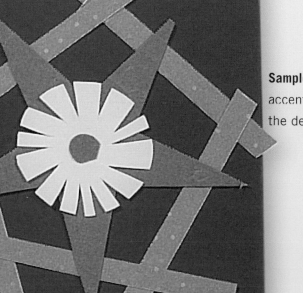

**Sample 3.** Attach the accents to complete the design.

# Nick

This basic border sports paper buttons of various colors and sizes. It can be adapted to resemble train tracks or a baby's growth chart.

**Materials**

- photos
- one 12" x 12" (30.5 cm x 30.5 cm) sheet green paper
- one 12" x 12" (30.5 cm x 30.5 cm) sheet light blue paper
- one 12" x 12" (30.5 cm x 30.5 cm) sheet cream paper
- one 8 1/2" x 11" (21.5 cm x 28 cm) sheet cream paper
- one 8 1/2" x 11" (21.5 cm x 28 cm) sheet cream patterned paper
- one 8 1/2" x 11" (21.5 cm x 28 cm) sheet medium blue paper
- paper buttons in assorted sizes and colors
- archival-quality adhesive spray
- archival-quality tape
- double-sided adhesive sheet

**Tools**

- craft knife
- metal-edged ruler
- pencil
- scissors
- kneaded rubber eraser

**Instructions**

1. Using the ruler and knife, cut a 1 3/8" x 12" (3.5 cm x 30.5 cm) strip from the light blue paper. Center and cut twelve 3/4" (2 cm) squares in the strip to make a ladder. From the ivory paper, cut one 1/4" x 12" (0.6 cm x 30.5 cm) strip. Weave the ivory strip through the center of the ladder. From the cream paper, cut three 1" (2.5 cm) squares. From the cream patterned paper, cut three 1" (2.5 cm) squares. Referring to the photo for sequence, tape the squares to the back of the ladder.

2. Place the ladder strip 1 1/4" (3 cm) from the right edge of the green paper. Use the pencil to lightly mark the green paper at the edge of the strip for placement. Following the manufacturer's directions, coat the back of the strip with adhesive spray. Press in place.

3. Referring to the photo for placement, set the buttons on the strip and on the green paper. From the double-sided adhesive sheet, cut circles slightly smaller in diameter than the paper buttons. Peel off the protective paper, and attach adhesive to the backs of the buttons. Remove the remaining protective paper, and attach the buttons to the strip and to the green paper.

4. Trim the photos to 4" x 6" (10 cm x 15 cm). Place the top photo 2 3/4" (7 cm) from the right edge and 1/2" (1 cm) from the top edge of the green paper. Place the bottom photo 2 3/4" (7 cm) from the right edge and 1 1/4" (3 cm) from the bottom edge of the green paper. Use the pencil to mark the green paper at the corners of the photos for placement. Coat the backs of the photos with adhesive spray. Press in place.

5. Use the pencil to draw the letters for the name on the blue paper, making uppercase letters and lowercase letters. Cut the letters for the name from the medium blue paper. Referring to the photo for placement, set the letters on the green paper. Use the pencil to mark the green paper at the top and bottom of each letter for placement. From the double-sided adhesive sheet, cut strips the same width as the letters. Trim the strips to fit the backs of the letters. Peel off the protective paper, and attach the adhesive to the backs of the letters. Remove the remaining protective paper, and press the letters in place.

6. Use the kneaded rubber eraser to remove all pencil marks.

# Play Ball

Combining two strands of rickrack to look like a complex braid is an old sewing trick that works even better with paper. By using narrow zigzag strips, a keyhole design appears.

Put me in coach

## Materials

- photo
- one 12" x 12" (30.5 cm x 30.5 cm) sheet blue paper
- one 12" x 12" (30.5 cm x 30.5 cm) sheet ivory paper
- one 12" x 12" (30.5 cm x 30.5 cm) sheet light green paper
- one 12" x 12" (30.5 cm x 30.5 cm) sheet rust paper
- one 8 1/2" x 11" (21.5 cm x 28 cm) sheet white paper
- one 8 1/2" x 11" (21.5 cm x 28 cm) sheet medium blue paper
- archival-quality adhesive spray
- archival-quality tape

## Tools

- metal-edged ruler
- craft knife
- tracing paper
- scissors
- pencil
- kneaded rubber eraser

## Instructions

1. Using the ruler and knife, trim the photo to 5" x 7" (12.5 cm x 18 cm). Place the photo 2 3/4" (7 cm) from the right edge and 2 1/8" (5.5 cm) from the top edge of the blue paper. Use the pencil to lightly mark the blue paper at the corners of the photo for placement. Following the manufacturer's directions, coat the back of the photo with adhesive spray. Press in place.

2. Trim the rust paper to 1 1/4" x 12" (3 cm x 30.5 cm). Coat the back of the strip with the adhesive spray. Align the top, the bottom, and the right edge of the strip with the blue paper, and press in place.

3. Use the tracing paper to make the zigzag template. (See Long Zag template on page 291.) Cut one zigzag strip from both the ivory paper and the light green paper. Hold the strips so that they are mirror images of each other, and wrap them around each other so that they are inter-twined from the top to the bottom of the strips. Referring to the photo, pull the strips apart enough to create negative spaces. Coat the back of the strip with adhesive spray. Press in place to cover the left edge of the rust strip.

4. Use the pencil to print the title on the white paper. Trim the title box to 4 3/4" x 5/8" (12 cm x 1.5 cm). Place the title box 2 1/2" (6.5 cm) from the right edge and 1/8" (0.3 cm) from the bottom edge of the blue paper. Use the pencil to mark the blue paper at the corners of the title box for placement. Coat the back of the title box with adhesive spray. Press in place. From the medium blue paper, cut one 3/4" (1.9 cm) square. Coat the back of the square with adhesive spray, and press in place over the right end of the title box.

5. Use the kneaded rubber eraser to remove all pencil marks.

# Tassels

Tassels have a modest beginning as loose threads, knotted together to prevent coarse fabrics from unraveling. Over the years they evolved into lovely, frivolous objects that decorate pillows and window shades. Tassels used for textile embellishment are borrowed to serve as exotic additions to these paper projects. They are made from ordinary cotton floss that is wrapped, knotted, and snipped to make swingy pendants.

**Sample 1.** Adorn a plain paper cuff with a bright cotton tassel.

**Sample 2.** No mortarboard is complete without a swinging tassel.

**Sample 3.** Brighten up a dreary page with a tassel-trimmed umbrella.

# Old-World Christmas Tree

Reminisce about romantic and formal Christmas scenes with a few well-placed tassels.

### Materials

- photos
- one 12" x 12" (30.5 cm x 30.5 cm) sheet taupe patterned paper
- one 8 1/2" 11 (21.5 cm x 28 cm) sheet green paper
- one 8 1/2" x 11" (21.5 cm x 28 cm) sheet gold-striped paper
- gold pearl cotton, size 5
- brown paper bow
- alphabet stickers
- archival-quality adhesive spray
- archival-quality tape

### Tools

- metal-edged ruler
- craft knife
- chipboard
- scissors
- pencil
- tracing paper
- round hole punch, 1/8" (0.3 cm) in diameter
- kneaded rubber eraser

### Instructions

1. Using the ruler and knife, trim the top photos to 3 1/4" (8.5 cm) squares. Trim the bottom photo to 4" x 5 1/4" (10 cm x 13.5 cm). Following the manufacturer's directions, coat the back of the bottom photo with adhesive spray. Place the photo on the gold-striped paper, and press. Center the photo and trim the gold-striped paper to 4 1/2" x 5 3/4" (11.5 cm x 14.5 cm).

2. Place the top photo 1 5/8" (4 cm) from the right edge and 1/4" (0.6 cm) from the top edge of the taupe paper. Overlapping the corner of the top photo, place the middle photo 4" (10 cm) from the right edge and 2 1/2" (6.5 cm) from the top edge of the taupe paper. Place the mounted photo 1 7/8" (5 cm) from the left edge and 1/4" (0.6 cm) from the bottom edge of the taupe paper. Mark the taupe paper at the corners of the photos for placement. Coat the backs of the photos with adhesive spray. Press them in place.

3. From the chipboard, cut one 3" x 1 3/4" (7.5 cm x 4.5 cm) rectangle. Wrap the pearl cotton around the short length of the rectangle 18 to 20 times. Cut two 5" (12.5 cm) lengths of pearl cotton. Thread one length under the wrapped pearl cotton, and knot at the top edge of the chipboard. Slide the wrapped pearl cotton from the chipboard. Referring to Diagram A, wrap the second length around the top of the wrapped bundle, and knot to secure. Trim the ends. Cut through the loops at the bottom of the bundle to create a tassel. Repeat to make four more tassels.

4. Use the tracing paper to make the Christmas tree template. (See Christmas Tree template on page 290.) From the green paper, cut one Christmas tree. Punch holes in the tree, where indicated. Thread the tassel ties through each hole, and secure the ties to the back of the tree with the tape. Coat the back of the tree with adhesive spray. Align the right edge of the tree with the right edge of the taupe paper. Press in place. Coat the back of the paper bow with adhesive spray. Center along the bottom of the trunk and press in place.

5. Attach the stickers to taupe paper.

6. Use the kneaded rubber eraser to remove all pencil marks.

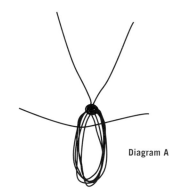

**Diagram A**

# Lunatic Fringe

This row of dancing tassels brings to mind fun combined with fashion.

## Materials

- photo
- one 12" x 12" (30.5 cm x 30.5 cm) sheet dark blue paper
- one 8½" x 11" (21.5 cm x 28 cm) sheet pink patterned paper
- party invitation
- paper tag with string
- paper button
- blue plastic nails for paper
- size 5 pearl cotton in variegated pink, variegated purple, variegated turquoise, and solid pink
- black fine-tip marker
- archival-quality adhesive spray

## Tools

- metal-edged ruler
- craft knife
- chipboard
- scissors
- pencil
- kneaded rubber eraser

## Instructions

1. Using the ruler and knife, trim the photo to 4" x 6" (10 cm x 15 cm). Place the photo 1⅞" (5 cm) from the right edge and 1¾" (4.4 cm) from the top edge of the blue paper. Use the pencil to lightly mark the blue paper at the corners of the photo for placement. Following the manufacturer's directions, coat the back of the photo with adhesive spray. Press in place. Referring to the photo for placement, set the invitation diagonally on the blue paper with the left corner 1¼" (3 cm) and the right corner ¾" (2 cm) from the top edge of the blue paper. Mark the blue paper at the corners of the invitation for placement. Coat the back of the invitation with adhesive spray. Coat the back of the paper button with adhesive spray. Press in place on blue paper, overlapping the top edge of the invitation. Coat the back of the tag with adhesive spray. Press in place on blue paper, overlapping left edge of invitation.

2. From the chipboard, cut one 3" x 1¾" (7.5 cm x 4.5 cm) rectangle. Wrap the variegated pink pearl cotton around the short length of the rectangle 18 to 20 times. Cut two 5" (12.5 cm) lengths of variegated pink pearl cotton. Thread one length under the wrapped pearl cotton, and knot at the top edge of the chipboard. Slide the wrapped pearl cotton from the chipboard. Referring to Diagram A, wrap the second length around the top of the wrapped bundle, and knot to secure. Trim the ends. Cut through the loops at the bottom of the bundle to create a tassel. Repeat to make one more variegated pink tassel, three variegated purple tassels, one variegated turquoise tassel, and one solid pink tassel.

3. From the pink patterned paper, cut one 11" x ⅝" (28 cm x 1.5 cm) strip. Center and place the strip 3¼" (8.5 cm) from the bottom edge of the blue paper. Mark the blue paper at the ends of the strip for placement. Trim the ends of the tassels as desired. Referring to the photo for placement, set the tassels in a horizontal row on the blue paper. Coat the back of the pink print strip with adhesive spray. Press in place over the tassel ties to adhere. Use the craft knife to cut small holes in the strip at each end and between tassels. Following the manufacturer's directions, insert nails in the holes and secure.

4. Write the caption on the tag using the fine-tip marker.

5. Use the kneaded rubber eraser to remove all pencil marks.

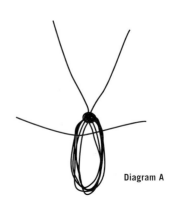

**Diagram A**

# chapter two

# Spring Break

## Multimedia layered border

Layering is what makes this project interesting. With the vellum on the paper, the tissue on the vellum, the netting on the tissue, and the trim on the netting, you can build an aquatic scene worthy of your favorite vacation photos.

### Instructions for the Water Borders

1. Coat the back of the vellum sheet with spray adhesive. Place the vellum on the white paper and press to adhere.

2. From the turquoise and lavender tissue paper, cut several 2" x 13" (5.1 cm x 33 cm) lengths. Trim two strips to create one wavy edge, leaving the remaining edge straight. Trim both sides of remaining lengths to make wavy strips. Coat the backs of the strips with spray adhesive. Press the narrow strips in place on the sides of the pages, overlapping where desired. Matching the straight edges of the wide strips with the sides of the pages, press in place. Trim the edges of the tissue.

3. From the netting, cut one 5" x 12" (12.7 cm x 30.5 cm) rectangle. Coat the back of the netting with spray adhesive. Place the netting on the right side of the right-hand page and press to adhere.

4. From the pastel trim, cut three lengths, 3" (7.6 cm), 4" (10.2 cm), and 7" (17.8 cm). Referring to the photo for placement, machine stitch the trim to the right-hand page.

### Instructions for Completing the Pages

1. Trim the photos.

2. Use the adhesive sheet to mount the selected photos on the tan and mint papers. Trim the colored papers to make narrow borders.

3. Use the tracing paper to make the fish template (see below). From the light turquoise paper, cut one 7" x 4" (17.8 cm x 10.2 cm) rectangle. Referring to the photo for colors, draw the desired letters on the assorted papers. Cut out the letters and fish.

4. Arrange the rectangle, photos, letters, and fish on the pages. Use adhesive to attach the components to the pages. Use the colored pencils to write captions.

*Fish Template*

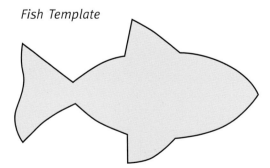

### MATERIALS

12" x 12" (30.5 cm x 30.5 cm) white paper

12" x 12" (30.5 cm x 30.5 cm) polka dot vellum

turquoise tissue paper

lavender tissue paper

turquoise polyester netting

pastel trim with matching sewing thread

paper in the following colors: pink, lavender, light turquoise, dark turquoise, mint, tan, gold

spray adhesive

double-sided adhesive sheet, such as Peel-N-Stick

### TOOLS

metal-edged ruler

craft knife

tracing paper

pencil

scissors

sewing machine

blue colored pencil

pink colored pencil

# Party Umbrellas

## Party favor border

It's a tropical party when you drop a paper umbrella into your glass. Combine these umbrellas and transform them from kitsch to chic by creating a beautiful abstract border. (If only you could do the same with your old grass skirt.)

### Instructions for the Umbrella Border

1. Open an umbrella and, with the scissors, carefully clip the supports that connect the paper ring to the ribs of the umbrella. Run the craft knife around the top of the umbrella to remove the paper from the center toothpick. Set the iron to a medium setting and press the paper circle flat. Repeat with the remaining umbrellas.

2. Coat the backs of all but one of the paper circles with spray adhesive. Note that one circle is attached to the page with the ribs exposed, which means you'll need to spray the front of one umbrella. Overlapping as desired, place the circles along the top edges of the pages and press to adhere. Trim the overhanging edges of the circles.

### Instructions for Completing the Pages

1. Trim the photos.

2. Use adhesive to mount the photos on the tan and blue papers. Trim the colored papers to make narrow borders.

3. Loop short lengths of the floss through the labels and trim the floss ends. Arrange the labels and photos on the pages. Use the double-sided adhesive to attach the components to the pages.

**MATERIALS**

12" x 12"
(30.5 cm x 30.5 cm)
brown paper

ten paper umbrellas
in assorted colors
(approximately
3¼" [8.2 cm] in
diameter)

tan paper

blue paper

spray adhesive

double-sided
adhesive sheet,
such as Peel-N-Stick

gray embroidery
floss

faux metal labels

**TOOLS**

metal-edged ruler

craft knife

scissors

iron

## MATERIALS

**12" x 12"
(30.5 cm x 30.5 cm)
print green paper**

**faux metal stickers**

**vintage postcard**

**printed
announcement**

**tan tissue paper**

**floral tissue paper**

**pink twine**

**spray adhesive**

**double-sided
adhesive sheet,
such as Peel-N-Stick**

## TOOLS

**metal-edged ruler**

**craft knife**

**scissors**

**black fine-tip
marker**

# An Engaging Couple

## Scalloped tissue paper border

Use floral tissue to bring up the curtain on your new life together.
Vintage papers and trendy stickers serve as the perfect accents.

### Instructions for the Curtain Border

1.  From the tan tissue paper, cut two 12½" x 3" (31.8 cm x 7.6 cm) strips. From the
    floral tissue paper, cut two 12½" x 3" (31.8 cm x 7.6 cm) strips. Referring to the
    diagram (see below), cut scallops along one edge of each strip.

2.  Coat the backs of the floral strips with spray adhesive. With ¼" (5 mm) of the
    tan tissue exposed, place the floral strips on the tan strips and press to adhere.
    Coat the backs of the layered strips with spray adhesive. With ½" (1.3 cm) over-
    hanging the top edge of the pages, pinch the tissue together slightly at the
    scallops and press in place. Wrap the overhanging edge to the back of the pages
    and press to adhere.

3.  From the pink twine, cut eight 5" (12.7 cm) lengths. Using the sharp point of the
    craft knife, pierce the paper at each scallop. Carefully thread the twine through
    each hole and knot. Trim the twine ends.

### Instructions for Completing the Pages

1.  Trim the photos.

2.  Arrange the announcements, postcard, and photos on the pages. Use double-sided
    adhesive to attach the components to the pages. Attach the stickers to the pages.
    With the marker, write a messages on the stickers.

_____ 12½" (31.8 cm) _____

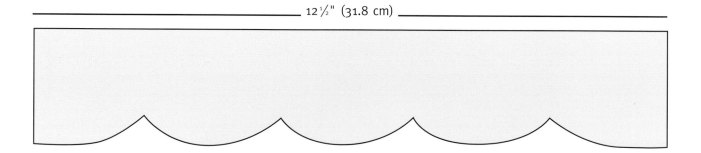

WITH LOVE.

PLEASE JOIN US
FOR A WEDDING BRUNCH HONORING
DANIEL AND JENNIFER
LITTLE AMERICA HOTEL
500 S. MAIN STREET, SALT LAKE CITY
MARCH 13, 2004 AT 10:30 A.M.

MR. AND MRS. CHADRICK DALE PERKINS
REQUEST THE PLEASURE OF YOUR COMPANY
AT THE WEDDING RECEPTION OF THEIR DAUGHTER
*Jennifer Lynn*
AND
*Daniel Joseph*
SON OF MR. AND MRS. BRUCE FRED GLADWELL
ON SATURDAY, THE THIRTEENTH DAY OF MARCH
TWO THOUSAND AND FOUR

XoXo

*Forever*

# Best Friends

## Paper pinwheel border

A border of cut and folded spinning pinwheels underlines the playful bond between a boy and his dog.

### Instructions for the Pinwheels

1. From the blue print paper, cut five 2½" (6.4 cm) squares. Refer to Diagram A (see below) and, from each corner, make a 1⅛" (2.8 cm) diagonal cut. Place the squares on the work surface with the solid side facing up. Referring to Diagram B (see below), fold the bottom left corner to the center of the square. Working counterclockwise, fold the remaining corners to the center, overlapping the points.

2. Stitch a button in the center of each pinwheel, securing all layers. Tape the thread ends to the back of the pinwheels. Trim the thread ends.

3. From the dark blue paper, cut five ⅜" x 2¼" (1 cm x 5.7 cm) strips. Align the strips to the pinwheels at right angles, and tape one end of each strip to the center back of each pinwheel.

### Instructions for Completing the Pages

1. From the vellum, cut one 2¾" x 8" (7 cm x 20.3 cm) rectangle. From the lavender paper, cut one 2¾" x 8" (7 cm x 20.3 cm) rectangle. With the computer printer, print the title on the white paper. Cut irregular shapes around each letter.

2. Trim the photos.

3. Arrange the rectangles, photos, and title on the pages. With the strips overhanging the bottom edges, place the pinwheels on the pages. Use adhesive to attach the components to the pages. Trim the overhanging ends of the strips. Use the marker to write captions.

**MATERIALS**

12" x 12" (30.5 cm x 30.5 cm) ivory paper

pink striped vellum

paper in the following colors: white, lavender, dark blue, blue print with a solid color on the reverse side

five miniature buttons

blue sewing thread

spray adhesive

double-sided adhesive sheet, such as Peel-N-Stick

**TOOLS**

metal-edged ruler

craft knife

sewing needle

scissors

computer printer

paper tape

black fine-tip marker

*Diagram A*

*Diagram B*

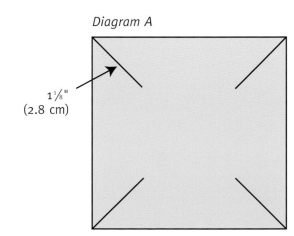

1⅛" (2.8 cm)

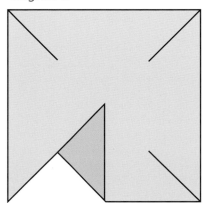

# At the Park

## Accented silver mesh border

This shiny mesh paper suggests the chain-link fences at a neighborhood playground. Add a little fun to the backdrop with brads and bright paper accents.

### Instructions for the Playground Border

1. Cut one 13" (33 cm) length of paper mesh. Remove the protective paper from the back of the mesh and, angling it up slightly, press it in place along the top of the left-hand page. Wrap the overhanging edges to the back of the page.

2. Cut one 4½" (11.4 cm) length and one 9½" (24.1 cm) length of silver paper mesh. Attach the paper mesh strips to the top of the right-hand page, with the short strip angling up and the long strip angling down. Overlap the strip ends slightly. Wrap the overhanging edges to the back of the page.

3. From the lavender paper, cut five ¾" (1.9 cm) squares. From the brown paper, cut two ½" (1.3 cm) squares. Place the squares at random points on the paper mesh. With the sharp point of the craft knife, pierce through the centers of the squares and through the rust paper. Insert the silver brads in the holes and secure through all layers.

### Instructions for Completing the Pages

1. Copy the selected photos on a copy machine. You can experiment with the copy machine settings to enhance the contrast.

2. Trim the photos and the black-and-white copies.

3. Arrange the photos and the black-and-white copies on the pages. Coat the backs with spray adhesive. Place on the pages and press to adhere.

4. From the red print paper, cut irregular shapes slightly larger than the letters. Arrange the pewter letters on the pages. Following the manufacturer's directions, attach the letters to the pages.

## MATERIALS

12" x 12" (30.5 cm x 30.5 cm) rust colored paper

silver paper mesh with self adhesive backing

small silver brads

paper in the following colors: lavender, brown, red print

pewter tack-on letters

spray adhesive

## TOOLS

metal-edged ruler

craft knife

scissors

copy machine

# *Paper Dolls*

## Accordion-style paper cut borders

Children everywhere love to make paper dolls. Weave these paper borders into your compositions to accent pages and to honor this timeless craft.

**Instructions for the Paper Doll Borders**

1. Use the tracing paper to make the templates (see below). From the pink print paper, cut two 2" x 4¾" (5.1 cm x 12.1 cm) strips. With the print side facing out, fold the strips accordion style with each fold measuring ¾" (1.9 cm) wide. Trace the heart template on the outside folds. Cut through the folded layers to make three connecting hearts per strip.

2. From the lavender paper, cut one 2½" x 6" (6.4 cm x 15.2 cm) strip. Fold the strip accordion style with each fold measuring 1" (2.5 cm) wide. Trace the doll template on the outside fold. Cut through the folded layers to make three connecting dolls. From the lavender paper, cut one 2½" x 4" (6.4 cm x 10.2 cm) strip. Fold and cut to make two connecting dolls.

**Instructions for Completing the Pages**

1. Trim the photos.

2. From the cream print paper, cut one 1" x 11" (2.5 cm x 27.9 cm) strip. Arrange the strip, photos, heart border, doll borders, and butterflies on the pages. Use adhesive to attach the components to the pages.

3. With the acrylic paint, paint the titles. Let dry. With the colored pencil, write captions.

*Heart Template*   *Doll Template*

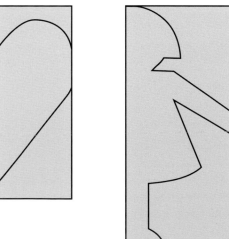

Cousins

Mary and Ivy

Sisters

Jane and

Cara and Megan

Friends

Calle and Melissa at the
wedding

Melissa Morgan
weds
Todd Anderson
June 8, 2004

# Angels

## Celestial ribbon borders

A heavenly mix of surfaces, textures, and techniques. Fashion these borders to commemorate special occasions and special relationships.

### Instructions for the Angel Borders

1. Spacing evenly, stamp three angels along the left edge of the left-hand page. Let dry.

2. Punch a hole in the top left corner, 1" (2.5 cm) from the top and the left side of the page. Repeat in the bottom left corner. Thread the ribbon from the back to the front through the top hole, and from the front to the back through the bottom hole. Referring to the photo for placement, stitch four cross-stitches to secure the ribbon to the paper. Tape the thread ends to the back of the page and trim. Bring the ribbon ends from the back and thread them through the holes again. Tape the ribbon ends to the back of the page and trim.

3. Stamp a band of leaf fronds along the right edge of the right-hand page, approximately 1½" (3.8 cm) wide. Alter the direction of the stamp to create an irregular pattern. Let dry.

4. From the mauve paper, cut three 2¼" (5.7 cm) squares. Stamp an angel in the center of each square. Let dry. Laminate the stamped squares. With the ruler and knife, trim the laminated squares to 2½" (6.4 cm).

5. Referring to the diagram (see below), punch holes in the top and bottom of each square. Loosely thread the ribbon through the holes. Use double-sided adhesive to attach the laminated squares to the right side of the right-hand page. Trim the ribbon ends.

### Instructions for Completing the Pages

1. Trim the pink print paper to 8½" x 11" (21.6 cm x 27.9 cm). Coat the back of the paper with spray adhesive. Place the paper on the left-hand page. Press to adhere.

2. Trim the photos.

3. Use adhesive to mount the selected photo on the gray paper. Trim the gray paper to make a narrow border.

4. Arrange the photos on the pages. Use adhesive to attach the photos to the pages. Write a caption with the brown colored pencil.

## MATERIALS

12" x 12" (30.5 cm x 30.5 cm) wheat paper

paper in the following colors: pink print, gray, mauve

laminating sheets

1 yard (0.9 m) of ⅝" (1.6 cm)-wide organza ribbon

cream thread

spray adhesive

double-sided adhesive sheet, such as Peel-N-Stick

tape

## TOOLS

metal-edged ruler

craft knife

scissors

needle

leaf frond rubber stamp

angel rubber stamp

brown ink pad

¼" (5 mm) hole punch

brown colored pencil

*Punch Diagram*

1" (2.5 cm)

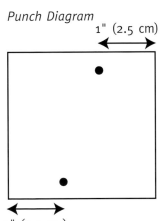

1" (2.5 cm)

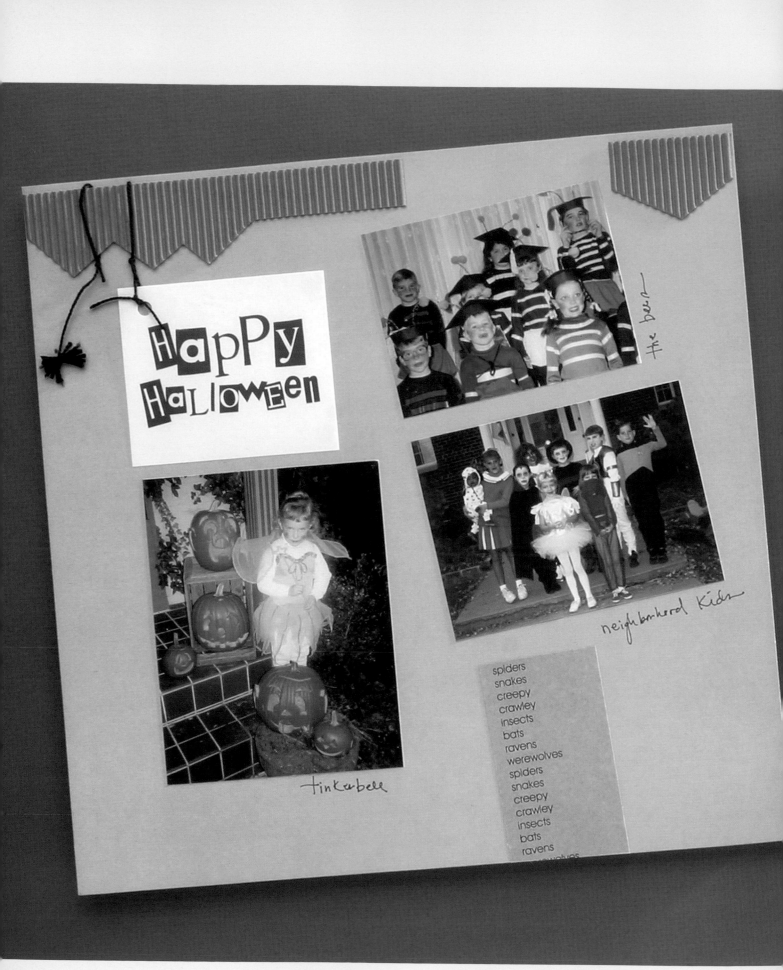

HaPPy HaLLOWeen

the bear

neighborhood kids

tinkerbell

spiders
snakes
creepy
crawley
insects
bats
ravens
werewolves
spiders
snakes
creepy
crawley
insects
bats
ravens

# Happy Halloween

## Strung spiders Halloween border

Funny, furry spiders dangle from this whimsical Halloween border. Use it to showcase your darling kids in their scary costumes. (Or is it scary kids in darling costumes?)

### Instructions for the Spider Border

1. Cut 1½" (3.8 cm)-wide strips from the corrugated paper. Cut notches along one side of the strips. Piecing as necessary, arrange the corrugated strips along the top edges of the pages. Break the strips for a diagonal photo if desired.

2. Cut five 9" (22.9 cm) lengths of pearl cotton. Wrap the lengths around the notches of the corrugated strips and knot to secure. Referring to the diagram (see below right), make small tassels for spiders. Tie the tassels to the pearl cotton at various lengths. Trim the thread ends of the spiders to shape.

### Instructions for Completing the Pages

1. Trim the photos and title box. Punch a hole in the top left corner of the title box. Use the computer printer to print a message box on the purple paper. Trim the message box.

2. Arrange the photos, title box, and message box on the pages. Tie the title box to the border. Trim the thread ends.

3. Use double-sided adhesive to attach the photos, title box, message box, and border to the pages. Use the marker to write captions.

**MATERIALS**

12" x 12"
(30.5 cm x 30.5 cm)
lavender colored
paper

rust colored
corrugated paper

purple paper

black pearl cotton

preprinted title box

double-sided
adhesive sheet,
such as Peel-N-Stick

**TOOLS**

metal-edged ruler

craft knife

scissors

¼" (5 mm) hole
punch

computer printer

black fine-tip marker

*Spider Diagram*

## MATERIALS

12" x 12" (30.5 cm x 30.5 cm) green printed paper

paper in the following colors: light green, dark green, orange, tan, purple, gray, blue, blue print

paper tape

spray adhesive

double-sided adhesive sheet, such as Peel-N-Stick

## TOOLS

metal-edged ruler

craft knife

tracing paper

pencil

scissors

¼" (5 mm) hole punch

black fine-tip marker

# Summer at the Lake

## Rippling seaside border

The bad news—the mosquitoes are biting; the good news—so are the fish. Delight young nature lovers and old fishermen alike with this animated border.

### Instructions for the Fish Border

1. Use the tracing paper to make the templates (see below). Referring to the photo for colors, cut the fish and the shadows from the assorted papers. Coat the backs of the fish with spray adhesive. Place the fish on the shadows and press in place.

2. From the gray paper, cut three ¼" x 3" (5 mm x 7.6 cm) strips. Tape the strips to the backs of the fish.

3. From the blue and blue print papers, tear several wavy strips of various lengths and widths. Overlapping where desired, arrange the waves on the bottom edges of the pages. Tuck the ends of the fish supports between the waves. Coat the backs of the waves and the fish with spray adhesive and press in place to adhere. Trim the overhanging edges of the waves.

### Instructions for Completing the Pages

1. Trim the photos. From the gray paper, cut one 1" x 8" (2.5 cm x 20.3 cm) strip for the title. Punch a hole in each end of the strip.

2. Arrange the photos and title box on the pages. Use adhesive to attach the components to the pages. Use the marker to write the title and captions.

*Fish Template*

*Shadow Template*

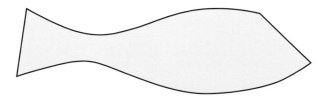

Summer @ the Lake

We met up at the Lake. We went fishing, hiking, and swimming.

Later we had lunch and posed for pictures by the water.

Miss Jennifer's
dance class
Spring 2004

# Sepia Dancers

## Magic wand and streamer borders

Grant your favorite dancer's wish with these dreamy borders. The magic will be preserved long after the pink slippers are put away.

### Instructions for the Magic Wand and Stars Border

1. Paint the dowel. Let dry. With the craft knife, cut a ½" (1.3 cm) long slit in one end of the dowel.

2. Use the tracing paper to make the star templates (see page 292). From the white paper, cut one large star. From the white vellum, cut three medium stars and two small stars. From the gold vellum, cut one medium star. From the yellow paper, cut one small star.

3. Coat the front of the large white star with spray adhesive. Sprinkle the front of the star with glitter. Slide the star into the slit at the end of the dowel to make a magic wand. Coat the fronts of three white vellum stars with spray adhesive. Sprinkle the stars with glitter.

4. From the gold vellum, cut one 1" x 12" (2.5 cm x 30.5 cm) strip. Referring to the diagram (see below), cut contours in the sides of the strip. With the craft knife, cut eleven small holes in the strip. Thread the wand through the holes. Place the wand on the work surface and crease to flatten slightly. Apply narrow strips of double-sided adhesive to the back of the creased vellum at the areas that will make contact with the page.

5. From the gold vellum, cut five narrow streamers. Curl the streamers with scissors. Place the streamers on the work surface and crease to flatten. Trim the streamers to various lengths.

6. Attach the wand to the top of the left-hand page. Arrange the streamers and the stars on the pages. Coat the backs of the stars and the streamers with spray adhesive, and press in place to adhere. Trim the overhanging stars. Use the foam spacers to attach the yellow star to the page.

### Instructions for Completing the Pages

1. Trim the photos.

2. Use adhesive to mount the photos on the burgundy and olive papers. Trim the colored papers to make narrow borders.

3. Arrange the photos on the pages. Use spray adhesive for the top photos and the foam spacers for the bottom photos. Attach them to the pages. Use the marker to write a caption.

*Diagram*

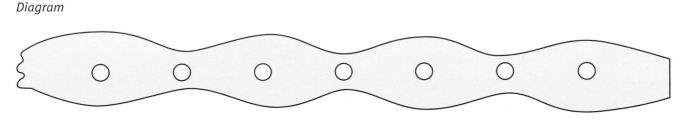

Come on OVER for a POOL PARTY!!!!!!!!!!!

the first day of summer 2004

# Pool Party

## Summer shapes paper and fiber border

Surf's up! Though the surfing takes place in a rubber wading pool, it's still a terrific way to cool off. Have fun making this splashy summer border.

### Instructions for the Pool Party Borders

1. From the white vellum, cut two 1¼" x 12" (3.1 cm x 30.5 cm) strips. Coat the backs of the vellum strips with spray adhesive. Place the strips along the top edges of the pages and press to adhere.

2. Use the tracing paper to make the templates for the beach ball, stripes, bucket, and shovel (see page 292). Referring to the photo for colors, cut the shapes from the assorted papers. Coat the backs of the beach ball stripes with spray adhesive. Place the stripes on the balls and press to adhere.

3. With the craft knife, cut small holes in three of the beach balls. Thread three of the beach balls, two buckets, and two shovels on the light blue yarn.

4. Coat the backs of the remaining beach balls with spray adhesive. Referring to the photo for placement, press in place on the top of the left-hand page. Coat the backs of the connected shapes with spray adhesive. Press in place on the top of the right-hand page.

### Instructions for Completing the Pages

1. With the computer printer, print the title on white paper. Trim the title box and photos.

2. Use adhesive to mount selected photos and the title box on the pink print paper. Trim the pink print paper to make narrow borders.

3. Punch a hole in the title box and thread a short length of dark blue yarn through the hole. Trim the yarn ends. Arrange the photos and title box on the pages. Use adhesive to attach the components to the page. Use the marker to write a caption.

12" x 12" (30.5 cm x 30.5 cm) green print paper

white vellum

paper in the following colors: white, gray, light green, dark green, light blue, turquoise, mauve, pink print

light blue decorative yarn

dark blue decorative yarn

spray adhesive

double sided adhesive sheet, such as Peel-N-Stick

## TOOLS

metal-edged ruler

craft knife

tracing paper

pencil

scissors

computer printer

green fine-tip marker

¼" (5 mm) hole punch

winding through-
# SAN FRANCISCO

Allison riding a trolley
in San Francisco
May 28, 2004

View of the Bay

Pacific Bell Park
San Francisco Giants
verses the Atlanta Braves
May 30, 2004

# Winding through San Francisco

## Asian accent borders

A city teaming with activity is represented by graphic Japanese icons. Use these borders to also decorate menus or invitations.

### Instructions for the Kimonos and the Chopstick Border

1. From the cream paper, cut one 1½" x 12" (3.8 cm x 30.5 cm) strip. With the craft knife, cut ¾" (1.9 cm) squares at each end of the strip. Note that the space between the squares should be less than the length of the chopstick.

2. From the medium gray paper, cut two ⅜" x 3½" (1 cm x 8.9 cm) strips. Place the cream strip along the top edge of the left-hand page. Slide the gray strips behind the cream strip and center them vertically behind the windows. With the double-sided adhesive, attach the bottom ends of the strips to the page. Place the chopstick on top of the cream strip and beneath the gray strips. Fold the top ends of the gray strips to the back of the page, pulling tightly enough to secure the chopstick. With the double-sided adhesive, attach the top ends of the strips to the back of the page. Remove the chopstick.

3. Use the tracing paper to make the kimono template (see page 292). From the blue print paper, make two kimonos. From the cream paper, cut two ¼" x 4" (5 mm x 10.2 cm) strips. Fold the kimonos over the strips and center. Use the double-sided adhesive to secure the kimono layers together.

4. Cut a 1" (2.5 cm) circle in a piece of scrap paper. Center the circle on the kimonos and apply a coat of rubber cement in the exposed circle. Let dry. Place the gold leaf paper right side down on the circles and burnish. Remove any excess gold leaf.

### Instructions for Completing the Pages

1. With the computer printer, print the title and captions on the white paper.

2. Trim the photos, title, and captions. Arrange the photos, kimonos, title box, and captions on the pages. Use adhesive to secure the components to the pages.

3. From the light gray paper, cut three narrow strips of varying lengths. Leaving loops large enough to insert the chopstick, thread the strips through the medallions, and secure the ends to the back of the strips with rubber cement. Thread the medallions on the chopstick and slide it under the gray strips.

## MATERIALS

12" x 12" (30.5 cm x 30.5 cm) light gray paper

paper in the following colors: white, light gray, medium gray, cream, blue print

chopstick

metal medallions

gold leaf paper

rubber cement

spray adhesive

double-sided adhesive sheet, such as Peel-N-Stick

## TOOLS

metal-edged ruler

craft knife

tracing paper

scissors

12" x 12"
(30.5 cm x 30.5 cm)
ivory paper

12" x 12"
(30.5 cm x 30.5 cm)
blue print paper

paper in the
following colors:
turquoise, medium
blue, orange, dark
gray, periwinkle
with white on the
reverse side

chipboard

one large
latex balloon

turquoise curling
ribbon

spray adhesive

double-sided
adhesive sheet,
such as Peel-N-Stick

TOOLS

metal-edged ruler

craft knife

tracing paper

pencil

scissors

tape

brown colored
pencil

# Birthday Balloons

## Layered shapes party borders

A high-flying parade of balloons for a birthday commemoration. The bright colors of these balloons and ribbons are the perfect contrast to the charming sepia-toned photos.

### Instructions for the Packages and Balloon Border

1. From the blue paper, cut two 2" (5.1 cm) squares. From the curling ribbon, cut four 3" (7.6 cm) lengths. Center and wrap the ribbon around the squares, both vertically and horizontally. Tape the ribbon ends to the backs of the squares with tape. From the curling ribbon, cut two 2½" (6.4 cm) lengths. Fold in half at the centers. With the ends exposed, tape the ribbon to the backs of the squares.

2. Use the tracing paper to make the template (see opposite, below). From the orange paper, cut two balloons with necks. From the periwinkle/white paper, cut two ¼" x 4" (5 mm x 10.2 cm) strips. Fold in half lengthwise and place on the bottoms of the balloons. Cut two ¼" x 2" (5 mm x 5.1 cm) strips. Wrap the strips around the necks of the balloons, overlapping the folded strips. Use double-sided adhesive to secure the ends. Trim the ends at an angle. From the turquoise, periwinkle, and orange paper, cut a total of six balloons with no necks.

3. From the chipboard, cut one balloon. Cut a slit in the back of the latex balloon and insert the chipboard balloon inside. Stretch the latex around the chipboard and trim away the excess. Secure the wrapped edges of the latex to the chipboard with several short strips of double-sided adhesive. Trim the rolled neck from the latex balloon. From the curling ribbon, cut one 13" (33 cm) length. Curl slightly and tie around the neck of the wrapped balloon.

### Instructions for Completing the Pages

1. Trim the photos. Trim the blue print paper to an 11" (27.9 cm) square.

2. Arrange the blue print paper, photos, packages, and balloons on the pages. Use adhesive to attach the components to the pages. Note, attach the latex balloon with double-sided adhesive. Trim the overhanging edges of the balloons.

3. Write the title on the gray paper. Cut out the title and coat the back of the trimmed title with the spray adhesive. Press in place on the left-hand page. Use the colored pencil to complete the title.

*Balloon*

# Gentler Times

## Gathered paper borders

Delicate paper ruffles can float above your favorite family photos. The gathered cream paper poses as aged lace without adding bulk.

### Instructions for the Gathered Paper Borders

1. From the tissue paper, cut four 2" x 20" (5.1 cm x 50.8 cm) strips. Layer two strips and machine stitch a gathering stitch along the center. Pull the bottom thread and gather evenly. Knot and trim the thread ends. Arrange the gathered strip on the page and press to flatten. Trim to the desired length. After trimming the strip, limit handling to avoid removing the gathers. Repeat with the second strip.

2. Attach the stickers to the left-hand page. Arrange one strip on the stickered page and carefully trim the tissue to frame any selected stickers.

3. Coat the back of the gathered strip with spray adhesive. Place the strip on the page and press to adhere. Arrange and attach the second strip on the right-hand page.

4. Place the beads on the right-hand page, repeating the curve of the tissue strip. With the needle, pierce the paper for bead placement. Stitch the beads to the paper and secure the thread ends to the back of the page with the tape.

### Instructions for Completing the Pages

1. Trim the photos.

2. Arrange the photos and announcement on the pages. Use adhesive to attach the components to the pages. Use foam spacers to attach the selected photo to the page.

3. To make the diagonal corner stays, cut four ¼" x 4" (5 mm x 10.2 cm) strips from the gray paper. Measure and cut parallel slits along the four sides of the photo with the craft knife. Thread the strips through the slits and secure the ends to the back of the page with tape.

## MATERIALS

12" x 12" (30.5 cm x 30.5 cm) blue print paper

light gray paper

birth announcement

cream tissue paper

pink sewing thread

glass flower beads

silver bugle beads

small stickers

spray adhesive

double-sided adhesive sheet, such as Peel-N-Stick

## TOOLS

metal-edged ruler

craft knife

scissors

sewing machine

needle

tape

foam adhesive spacers

black fine-tip marker

Switzerland

July 12, 2004

# Happy Wanderers

## Shingled paper and feathered grass frames

Two distinctive textures are represented with these frames: scarred and weathered wooden shingles and shining emerald meadows.

### Instructions for the Shingle Frame

1. The frame is made for a 7½" x 5" (19.1 cm x 12.7 cm) photo. Make adjustments if your photo is a different size. From the burgundy paper, cut an 8½" x 6" (21.6 cm x 15.2 cm) rectangle. Cut a 7" x 4½" (17.8 cm x 11.4 cm) window in the center.

2. From the black paper, cut several ¾" x 8½" (1.9 cm x 21.6 cm) strips. From the gray paper, cut one ¾" x 8½" (1.9 cm x 21.6 cm) strip. Cut shallow, irregular curves on one side of each strip. Cut each strip into shingles that measure from ½" to 3" (1.3 cm to 7.6 cm) long. Apply the chalk to the edges of several of the black shingles.

3. Starting at the bottom and overlapping rows, arrange the shingles on the burgundy frame. Note that random areas of the frame are left exposed and some sections overhang the outside and inside edges of the frame. Coat the backs of the shingles with spray adhesive. Press the shingles in place on the frame. Center and tape the photo to the back of the frame.

### Instructions for the Grass Frame

1. The frame is made for a 5½" x 4½" (13.4 cm x 11.4 cm) photo. Make adjustments if your photo is a different size. From the sage paper, cut a 7½" x 6½" (19.1 cm x 16.5 cm) rectangle. Cut a 5" x 4" (12.7 cm x 10.2 cm) window in the center.

2. From the fabric, cut a frame with the outside edge slightly larger and the window slightly smaller than the paper frame. Remove a few loose threads along the cut edges so it frays slightly. Place the feathers on the bottom left corner of the frame. Trim to the desired lengths. With small, even stitches, secure most of the feathers to the fabric. Weave the remaining feathers over and under through the fabric. Coat the back of the fabric with spray adhesive. Center and press the fabric on the paper frame. Tape the photo to the back of the frame in the center.

### Instructions for Completing the Pages

1. Trim the remaining photo. Trim the sage paper to 8" x 10" (20.3 cm x 25.4 cm). Arrange the colored papers, framed photos, unframed photo, and butterflies on the pages. Use adhesive to secure the components to the pages. Use the marker to write a caption.

## MATERIALS

12" x 12" (30.5 cm x 30.5 cm) wheat colored paper

paper in the following colors: gold, sage, burgundy, black, gray

sage textured fabric

fine peacock pin feathers

painted feather butterflies

gray decorative chalk

purple decorative chalk

spray adhesive

double-sided adhesive sheet, such as Peel-N-Stick

## TOOLS

metal-edged ruler

craft knife

sage sewing thread

needle

tape

green fine-tip marker

12" x 12"
(30.5 cm x 30.5 cm)
oatmeal colored
paper

paper in the follow-
ing colors: light
gray, dark gray,
cream print

one 6" x 11 ¾"
(15.2 cm x 29.8 cm)
sheet birch veneer,
¹⁄₆₄" (0.8 mm) thick

walnut wood stain

faux metal letter
disks

printed
announcement

spray adhesive

double-sided
adhesive sheet,
such as Peel-N-Stick

**TOOLS**

metal-edged ruler

craft knife

sewing thread

scissors

paintbrush

paper towel

tape

# Winter Love Scene

## Elegant wood veneer frames

Large, flat areas of rich wood grain give this frame an architectural
look. Small brackets provide an effective complement while keeping
with the style of clean corners and spare lines.

### Instructions for the Frame

1. The frame is made for a 4¼" x 6¼" (10.8 cm x 15.8 cm) photo. Make adjustments
   if your photo is a different size. From the dark gray paper, cut a 5" x 7" (12.7 cm x
   17.8 cm) rectangle. Cut a 3¾" x 5¾" (9.5 cm x 14.6 cm) window in the center.

2. Referring to the photo for placement, and with the ruler and knife, cut a 4¼" x 6¼"
   (10.8 cm x 15.8 cm) window in the veneer. It will take several passes of the knife
   to cut completely through the wood. Coat the veneer frame with the stain. Blot the
   stain from the veneer to expose the grain of the wood. Let dry. Center and tape
   the photo to the back of the paper frame. Center and tape the framed photo to
   the back of the veneer frame.

### Instructions for Completing the Pages

1. Trim the photos and announcement. Use spray adhesive to mount the announcement on the light gray paper. Trim the gray paper to create a narrow border. Attach
   the mounted announcement to the cream print paper. Trim the print paper to create
   a 1" (2.5 cm)-wide border.

2. From the dark gray paper, cut a 1" x 5½" (2.5 cm x 13.4 cm) strip. Referring to the
   photo for placement, stitch the disks to the paper. Tape the thread ends to the
   back of the strip.

3. From the remaining veneer, cut four ¾" (1.9 cm) strips. Stain the strips. Let dry.
   Arrange the framed photo, unframed photos, brackets, announcement, and message strip on the pages. Use double-sided adhesive to attach the components to
   the pages.

Dewey Jay & Jeanette Gill
are pleased to announce
the marriage of their daughter
Jealin Joyce
to
Jeremy Scott Dickamore
Son of Gene & Karleen Dickamore
On Saturday, March 6, 2004

Pinnochio

outside of Geppetti's Toy Shoppe

## Wish List

- puppy
- candy necklace
- paper
- stickers
- trip to the zoo
- snow cone maker
- sidewalk chalk

Mary and Santa- Christmas 2003

David and Melissa: Holiday Party

# Christmas Wish List

## Cut and fold-out paper frames

The folding sections of these easy-to-make frames open to reveal treasured photos and bring to mind the paper windows and doors of a holiday advent calendar.

### Instructions for the Square Frame

1. The frame is made for a 5" (12.7 cm) square photo. Make adjustments if your photo is a different size. From the wheat paper, cut a 7½" (19.1 cm) square. Draw a 4½" (11.4 cm) square in the center.

2. Referring to Diagram A (see below), cut a diamond in the square. Cut diagonal lines from corner to corner of the marked square. Score the paper along the dotted lines. Fold the points out at the scored lines. Remove any visible pencil marks with the eraser. Use the foam spacers to attach the points to the frame sides. Center and tape the photo to the back of the frame.

### Instructions for the Rectangle Frame

1. The frame is made for a 2½" x 3½" (6.4 cm x 8.9 cm) photo. Make adjustments if your photo is a different size. From the tan paper, cut a 3½" x 4½" (8.9 cm x 11.4 cm) rectangle. Draw a 2" x 3" (5.1 cm x 7.6 cm) rectangle in the center.

2. Referring to Diagram B (see below), cut diagonal lines from corner to corner of the marked rectangle. Score the paper along the dotted lines. Fold the points out at the scored lines. Remove any visible pencil marks. Trim the top and bottom points.

3. From the pink paper, cut a 2¾" x 3¾" (7 cm x 9.5 cm) rectangle. Cut a 2⅛" x 3⅛" (5.4 cm x 7.9 cm) window in the center. Fold the points of the tan frame to the center. Coat the back of the pink frame with spray adhesive. Center and press in place on the tan frame. Fold the points out and use the foam spacers to attach them to the frame sides. Center and tape the photo to the back of the frame.

### Instructions for Completing the Pages

1. With the computer printer, print the title on the white paper. Trim the title box to 3½" x 6½" (8.9 cm x 16.5 cm). Cut 3½" x 6½" (8.9 cm x 16.5 cm) rectangles from the red and tan papers.

2. Arrange the framed photos, rectangles, and title box on the pages. Use double-sided adhesive to attach the components to the pages. Use craft glue to attach the snowflakes to the pages. Use colored pencil to write captions.

**MATERIALS**

12" x 12" (30.5 cm x 30.5 cm) cream print paper

12" x 12" (30.5 cm x 30.5 cm) tan print paper

paper in the following colors: wheat, tan, pink, white, red

five tin snowflakes

spray adhesive

double-sided adhesive sheet, such as Peel-N-Stick

foam adhesive spacers

craft glue

**TOOLS**

metal-edged ruler

craft knife

pencil

computer printer

brown colored pencil

kneaded rubber eraser

tape

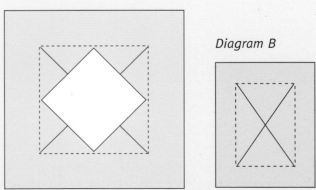

*Diagram A*

*Diagram B*

12" x 12"
(30.5 cm x 30.5 cm)
turquoise polka dot
paper

paper in the follow-
ing colors: white,
ivory, tan, blue,
pale green, dark
green

preprinted clock

preprinted letters

precut paper frame

foam adhesive
spacers

spray adhesive

double-sided
adhesive sheet,
such as Peel-N-Stick

TOOLS

metal-edged ruler

craft knife

tracing paper

pencil

alphabet rubber
stamps

turquoise ink pad

turquoise colored
pencil

black fine-tip
marker

tape

copy machine

# Graduation Celebration

## Classical column frames

After the ceremony, commence with the party. Go to the head of the class with frames that feature classic columns as playful props.

### Instructions for the Doorway Frame

1. The frame is made for a 4½" x 6¾" (11.4 cm x 17.1 cm) photo. Make adjustments if your photo is a different size. To achieve a gray cast, adjust the copy machine to the darkest setting. Make two copies of the column. Cut out the columns.

2. Use the tracing paper to make the pediment templates (see page 293). From the tan paper, make one large pediment. From the ivory paper, make one small pediment and two 2½" (6.4 cm) squares. From the pale green paper, cut one ¾" x 3⅛" (1.9 cm x 7.9 cm) strip.

3. Coat the backs of the small pediment, clock, and letters with spray adhesive. Center and press the small pediment on the large pediment, and then press the clock onto the small pediment. Press the letters on the squares. Use the colored pencil to shade the columns and clock.

4. Arrange the photo, columns, and green strip on the left-hand page. Use adhesive to attach the components to the page. Use the foam spacers to attach the pediment and the squares to the page.

### Instructions for the Window Frame

1. The frame is made for a 5" x 4" (12.7 cm x 10.2 cm) photo. Make adjustments if your photo is a different size. Coat the back of the photo with spray adhesive and press on the right-hand page. Trim around the paper to make a ½" (1.3 cm) border.

2. Make four copies of the columns. Cut out the columns and shade them with the colored pencil. With the top ends out and overlapping at the corners, arrange the columns around the photo. Trim the exposed ends. Trim the ends of the bottom right corner at a right angle.

3. From the tan paper, cut a 1½" (3.8 cm) square. Use the tracing paper to make the four-leaf clover template (see page 293). From the dark green paper, cut one clover. Place the square at the bottom right corner. Place the clover on the square. Use adhesive to attach the components to the page.

### Instructions for Completing the Page

1. Center and tape the small photo to the paper frame. Attach the framed photo to the page with double-sided adhesive. Stamp the message. Let dry. Use the marker to write a caption.

## MATERIALS

12" x 12"
(30.5 cm x 30.5 cm)
blue polka dot
paper

12" x 12"
(30.5 cm x 30.5 cm)
gray polka dot
paper

12" x 12"
(30.5 cm x 30.5 cm)
black paper

paper in the
following colors:
light pink, light
lavender, light blue,
blue print, silver,
lavender print, pink
print with white on
the reverse side

gold embossing
powder

spray adhesive

double-sided
adhesive sheet,
such as Peel-N-Stick

## TOOLS

metal-edged ruler

craft knife

scissors

rose rubber stamp

butterfly rubber
stamp

tan ink pad

black ink pad

angel clip art

tape

black fine-tip
marker

# Laughing Out Loud

## Glittering embossed and collaged frames

A spring day shared with an old friend and punctuated by a good laugh. Preserve a personal memory behind a sparkling, embossed, or collaged frame.

### Instructions for the Embossed Frame

1. The frame is made for a 7" x 5" (17.8 cm x 12.7 cm) photo. Make adjustments if your photo is a different size. From the black paper, cut an 8¾" x 6¾" (22.2 cm x 17.1 cm) rectangle. Cut a 6¼" x 4¼" (15.8 cm x 10.8 cm) window in the center.

2. From the lavender paper, cut an 8½" x 6½" (21.6 cm x 16.5 cm) rectangle. Cut a 6½" x 4½" (16.5 cm x 11.4 cm) window in the center.

3. With the tan ink and the rose stamp, stamp a random floral pattern on the frame. Sprinkle the wet ink with embossing powder. Remove the excess powder. Apply heat with a heat gun until the powder melds to the paper. Coat the back of the frame with spray adhesive. Center and press in place on the black frame. Center and tape the photo to the back of the frame.

### Instructions for the Collage Frame

1. From the blue print paper, cut a 7" x 5" (17.8 cm x 12.7 cm) rectangle. Referring to the diagram for placement, cut a 4½" x 3" (11.4 cm x 7.6 cm) window with rounded corners.

2. From the silver paper, cut a 1¼" x 6" (3.1 cm x 15.2 cm) strip. Refer to step 2 of the Embossed Frame and emboss the floral pattern on the strip. Coat the back of the strip with spray adhesive. Press in place along the wide side of the frame.

3. From the pink print/white paper, cut two ⅛" x 8½" (3 mm x 21.6 cm) strips. Coil the strips tightly. Place the strips on the work surface and crease to flatten. Coat the backs of the strips with spray adhesive, and press in place around the edge of the frame window. Trim around the clip art. Tape the clip art to the back of the frame. From the lavender paper, cut a 5½" x 4" (13.4 cm x 10.2 cm) rectangle. Center and tape the lavender paper to the back of the frame.

### Instructions for Completing the Pages

1. From the black paper, cut a 1¾" x 12" (4.4 cm x 30.5 cm) strip, and a 2½" x 12" (6.4 cm x 30.5 cm) strip. Coat the backs of the strips with adhesive spray. Press the narrow strip in place along the left edge of the blue page. Press the wide strip in place along the right edge of the gray page.

2. From the silver paper, cut one 2" x 1½" (5.1 cm x 3.8 cm) rectangle. Refer to step 2 of the Embossed Frame and emboss the butterfly on the rectangle.

3. From the blue paper, cut one 6¾" x 2½" (17.1 cm x 6.4 cm) rectangle. From the pink paper, cut one 9" x 6" (22.9 cm x 15.2 cm) rectangle. From the pink print paper, cut three 2¾" x 3½" (7 cm x 8.9 cm) rectangles. And from the lavender print paper, cut one 2¾" x 3½" (7 cm x 8.9 cm) rectangle.

4. Noting overlaps, arrange the trimmed papers, framed photo, and framed clip art on the pages. Use adhesive to attach the components to the pages. With the black ink, stamp the butterflies on the right-hand page. Use the marker to write a title and message.

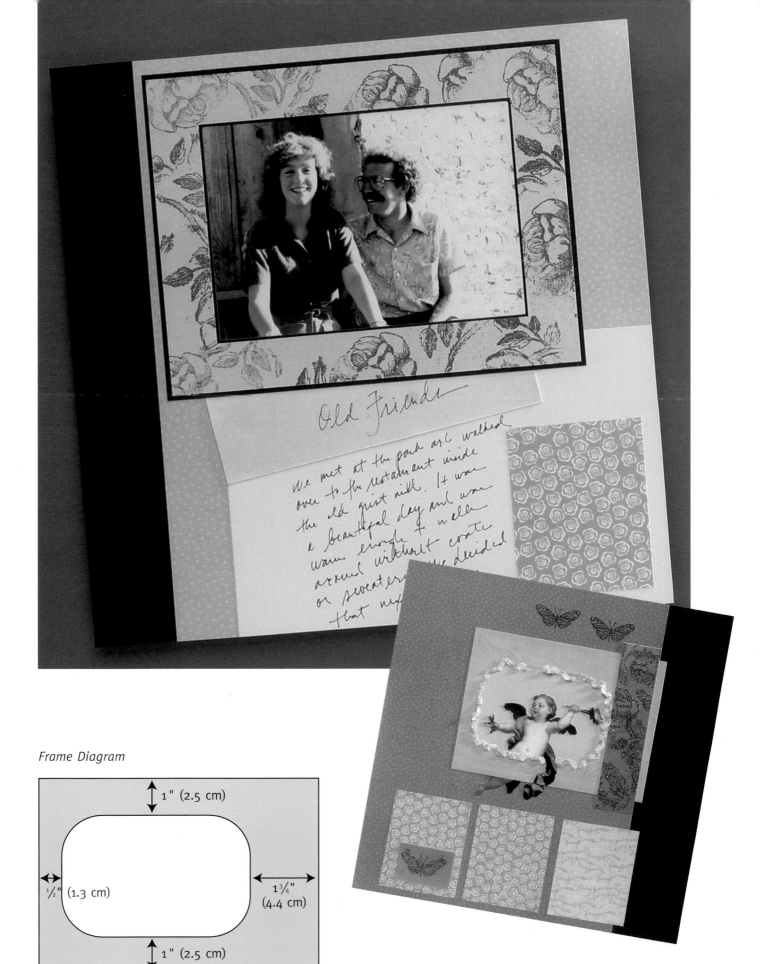

*Frame Diagram*

1 " (2.5 cm)

½" (1.3 cm)

1³/₄" (4.4 cm)

1 " (2.5 cm)

# When We Were Young

## Clever found-object frames

Flashback to the time of first crushes and lunch lines. Use the unique found-object decorations as your own personal time capsule.

### Instructions for the Necklace Frame

1. This arrangement is made for a 4" x 6" (10.2 cm x 15.2 cm) photo. Make adjustments if your photo is a different size. From the alphabet paper, cut a 5½" x 8½" (13.4 cm x 21.6 cm) rectangle. Coat the back of the paper with spray adhesive. Referring to the photo for placement, press in place on the top of the left-hand page. Cut a 3" (7.6 cm) length of paper ribbon. Align the ribbon with the bottom right edge of the alphabet paper, and use double-sided adhesive to attach it to the page.

2. Coat the back of the photo with spray adhesive, and press in place on the page.

3. Place the necklace on the photo and smooth out the chain. Carefully lift the chain from the paper at several different points and apply a small drop of the glue at the contact point. Press the chain in place to adhere.

### Instructions for the Shoelace Frame

1. This arrangement is made for a 4" x 6" (10.2 cm x 15.2 cm) photo. Make adjustments if your photo is a different size. From the alphabet paper, cut a 5½" x 8½" (13.4 cm x 21.6 cm) rectangle. Coat the back of the paper with spray adhesive. Referring to the photo for placement, press in place on the top of the right-hand page.

2. Coat the back of the photo with spray adhesive, and press in place on the page. Cut a 3" (7.6 cm) length of paper ribbon. Align the ribbon with the bottom left edge of the photo, and use double-sided adhesive to attach it to the page.

3. From the pink paper, cut a ½" x 3" (1.9 cm x 7.6 cm) strip. Use double-sided adhesive to attach the strip at a diagonal on the bottom right corner of the photo. Place the shoelace on the photo with the ends intersecting on top of the pink strip. Use short, narrow strips of double-sided adhesive to attach the shoelace to the page at three chosen contact points. Coat the back of the bubble gum label with spray adhesive and place over the lace and the pink strip, and press in place to adhere.

### Instructions for Completing the Pages

1. Arrange the alphabet tiles on the ribbon.
   Attach them to the ribbon with double-sided adhesive. Arrange the remaining components on the pages. Use adhesive to attach the components to the pages.

## MATERIALS

12" x 12" (30.5 cm x 30.5 cm) ivory paper

alphabet print paper

pink paper

peach paper ribbon

plastic letter tiles

one necklace

one shoelace

bubble gum label sticker

assorted items such as plastic slide frames, die-cut shapes, shirt pocket, paper tickets

spray adhesive

double-sided adhesive sheet, such as Peel-N-Stick

## TOOLS

metal-edged ruler

craft knife

scissors

craft glue

## MATERIALS

12" x 12"
(30.5 cm x 30.5 cm)
tan paper

paper in the follow-
ing colors: white,
black, gray, peri-
winkle

pewter star brads

yellow brads

laminating sheets

½ yard (0.5 m)
gray rayon braid

spray adhesive

double-sided
adhesive sheet,
such as Peel-N-Stick

## TOOLS

metal-edged ruler

craft knife

scissors

tape

pencil

computer printer

black fine-tip
marker

# Featured Artist

## Protective gallery display frames

Shine the spotlight on great art and a great artist with this sophisticated presentation. The laminated surfaces protecting the artwork
and the photo resemble shiny gallery glass.

### Instructions for the Lattice Frame

1. The frame is made for a 3½" x 5½" (8.9 cm x 13.4 cm) photo. Make adjustments if
   your photo is a different size. From the periwinkle paper, cut four ¼" x 9" (5 mm x
   22.9 cm) strips. With the ruler and knife, cut a 5" x 7½" (12.7 cm x 19.1 cm) rectangle
   from the laminating sheet.

2. Separate the layers of the trimmed laminating sheet. Place the dull layer on the
   work surface. Center and place the photo on top. Overhanging the corners of the
   photo slightly, arrange the strips to form a diamond. Align the clear layer of the
   laminating sheet on the dull layer and burnish.

### Instructions for the Picture Frames

1. The left frame is made for 4½" x 6¼" (11.4 cm x 15.8 cm) artwork. Make adjustments if your artwork is a different size. Cut around the outside edge of the artwork.
   Laminate the artwork. With the ruler and knife, trim the laminated artwork to a
   5½" x 7¼" (13.4 cm x 18.4 cm) rectangle.

2. From the black paper, cut one 5½" x 7¼" (13.4 cm x 18.4 cm) rectangle. Cut a
   4½" x 6¼" (11.4 cm x 15.8 cm) window in the center. Using double-sided adhesive,
   attach the frame to the front of the laminated rectangle.

3. The right frame is made for 4¼" x 5¼" (10.8 cm x 13.3 cm) artwork. Making
   adjustments for the smaller size, repeat steps 1 and 2 to laminate the artwork and
   complete the frame.

### Instructions for Completing the Pages

1. Referring to the photo for placement, attach the framed photo to the left-hand
   page with double-sided adhesive. From the gray paper, cut two 2¼" (6 cm)
   squares. Coat the backs of the squares with spray adhesive. Press in place beneath the strips at the top and bottom of the frame. With the sharp point of the
   craft knife, pierce through the intersecting strips and through the gray and tan
   paper. Insert the star brads in the holes and secure through all layers.

2. Cut an 8" (20.3 cm) length of rayon braid and tape the ends to the back of the
   large frame. Cut a 7" (17.8 cm) length and tape the ends to the back of the small
   frame. Place the framed pieces on the right-hand page and, with the pencil, mark
   the point at which they will "hang" from the rayon braid. Pierce the paper at the
   marked points with the craft knife. Insert the yellow brads and secure.

3. Attach small squares of double-sided adhesive to the corners on the backs of the
   frames. Loop the braid over the brads and attach them to the page. Use the computer printer to print a title and captions on the white paper. Trim the title and
   caption boxes. Use spray adhesive to attach them to the pages.

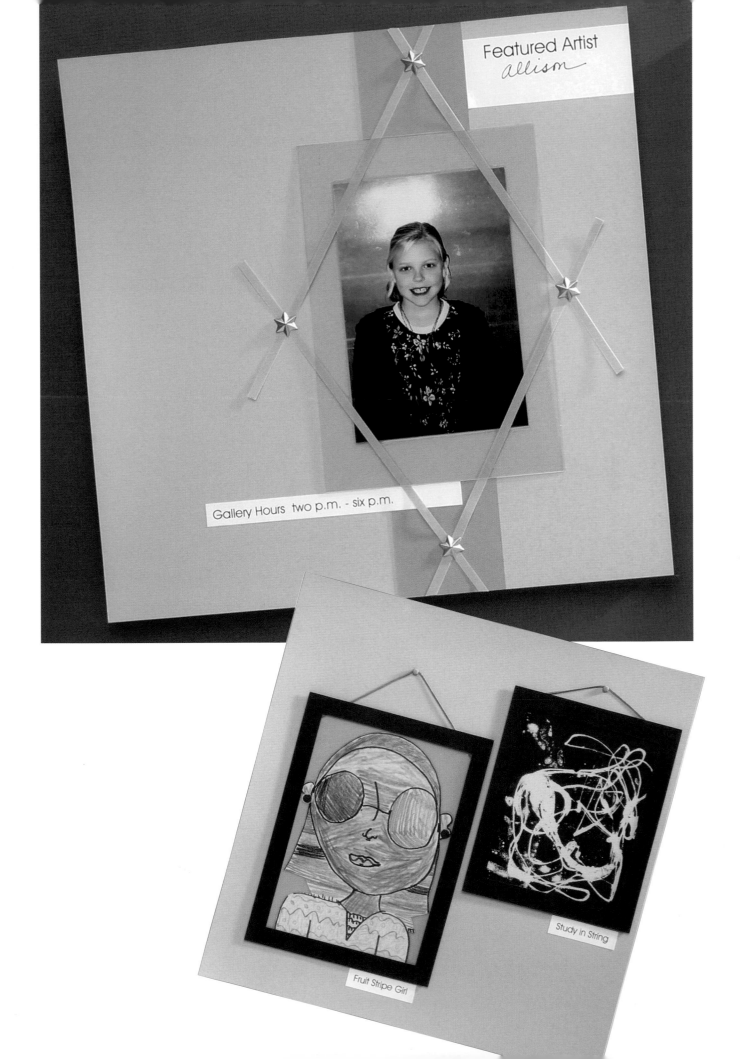

Featured Artist
allison

Gallery Hours  two p.m. - six p.m.

Fruit Stripe Girl

Study in String

## Heritage-style multimedia frames

A mélange of somber colors and rich textures honors the fabric of pioneer life.

### Instructions for the Herringbone Frame

1. The frame is made for a 5" x 7" (12.7 cm x 17.8 cm) photo. Make adjustments if your photo is a different size. From the brown paper, cut a 6¼" x 8¼" (15.8 cm x 20.9 cm) rectangle. Cut a 4½" x 6½" (11.4 cm x 16.5 cm) window in the center.

2. Referring to Diagram A (see below), mark the dots on the left side of the frame. With the sharp point of the craft knife, cut small holes at the marked points. Cut a 24" (61 cm) length of the ribbon. Place the frame right side down on the work surface. Tape the ribbon to the back of the frame ¾" (1.9 cm) above the top hole.

3. Thread one end of the ribbon through the needle. Bring the ribbon from the back to the front and insert the needle through the top hole. Wrap the ribbon around the edge of the paper, and on the front of the frame, reinsert the ribbon in the next hole. Continue stitching to complete one edge. Remove the needle and thread it on the remaining end. Repeat the stitching working in the opposite direction. When complete, the rows form seven V shapes. Tape the ends to the back of the frame. Trim the exposed ends. Center and tape the photo to the back of the frame.

### Instructions for the Edged Frame

1. The frame is made for a 3½" (8.9 cm) square photo. Make adjustments if your photo is a different size. From the brown paper, cut a 3¾" x 4¾" (9.5 cm x 12.1 cm) rectangle. Referring to Diagram B (see below), mark the dots on the bottom of the frame. With the sharp point of the craft knife, cut small holes at the marked points.

2. Cut two 7" (17.8 cm) lengths of ribbon. Thread the needle on one length. Working from the back to the front, bring the needle up through the first hole. Stitch over and under to the opposite hole. Keep the ribbon loose while stitching. Thread the needle on the second length. Working from the front to the back, insert the needle through the same holes. Trim the ends. Coat the back of the photo with spray adhesive. Center and press in place leaving ⅛" (3 mm) around the top and sides of the photo.

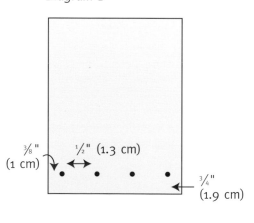

*Diagram A*

*Diagram B*

## Instructions for Completing the Pages

1. Trim the remaining photos, message box, and paper accent. Use spray adhesive to mount the photos and message box on the brown and black paper. Trim the papers to make narrow borders.

2. Trim the script paper to 8" x 12" (20.3 cm x 30.5 cm). Trim the patterned paper to 7" x 6" (17.8 cm x 15.2 cm). Trim the taupe print paper to 3" x 12" (7.6 cm x 30.5 cm). Tear one long side of the strip. Arrange the papers, framed photo, mounted photos, and message box on the pages. Use adhesive to attach the components to the pages. Loop the tag string around the bottom V of the Herringbone Frame and knot to secure.

## MATERIALS

12" x 12"
(30.5 cm x 30.5 cm)
brown paper

paper in the follow-
ing colors: gray,
black, yellow print

decorative papers

faux metal letter
disks

silver brads

fine purple wire,
24 mm

assorted beads

bronze eyelets

spray adhesive

double-sided
adhesive sheet,
such as Peel-N-Stick

## TOOLS

metal-edged ruler

craft knife

wire cutters

pencil

eyelet tool

tape

computer printer

yellow colored
pencil

# Families

## Beaded patchwork and license plate frames

In a play, on a park bench, or at a museum—it doesn't matter where you are as long as you are together. Patchwork frames highlight family memories.

### Instructions for the Beaded Frame

1. The frame is made for a $3\frac{1}{2}$" x 5" (8.9 cm x 12.7 cm) photo. Make adjustments if your photo is a different size. From the black paper, cut a $5\frac{1}{2}$" x 7" (13.4 cm x 17.8 cm) rectangle. Cut a 3" x $4\frac{1}{2}$" (7.6 cm x 11.4 cm) window in the center with the bottom of the frame slightly larger then the top and the sides.

2. From the gray paper, cut a 5" x $6\frac{1}{2}$" (12.7 cm x 16.5 cm) rectangle. Cut a $3\frac{1}{4}$" x $4\frac{3}{4}$" (8.2 cm x 12.1 cm) window in the center. Tear several strips from the decorative paper. Coat the backs of the strips with spray adhesive and place them on the gray frame in an irregular pattern. Trim the overhanging edges. Coat the back of the frame with spray adhesive. Center and press in place on the black frame.

3. Align the eyelets with the corners of the window and insert them in the black paper at the bottom of the frame. Cut an 8" (20.3 cm) length from the purple wire. Thread the beads on the wire and insert the wire ends in the eyelets. Twist the wire around itself to secure, and trim the wire ends. Center and tape the photo to the back of the frame.

### Instructions for the License Plate Frame

1. The frame is made for a $5\frac{1}{2}$" x $3\frac{1}{2}$" (13.4 cm x 8.9 cm) photo. Make adjustments if your photo is a different size. From the black paper, cut a $7\frac{1}{4}$" x $5\frac{3}{4}$" (18.4 cm x 14.6 cm) rectangle. Referring to the diagram (see opposite, below), trim away the top corners of the rectangle. Cut a 5" x 3" (12.7 cm x 7.6 cm) window, with the bottom of the frame slightly larger then the top and sides.

2. From the gray paper, cut a 7" x 5" (17.8 cm x 12.7 cm) rectangle. Cut a $5\frac{1}{4}$" x $3\frac{1}{4}$" (13.3 cm x 8.2 cm) window in the center. Refer to step 2 of the Beaded Frame to apply the decorative papers. Coat the back of the frame with spray adhesive. Center and press in place on the black frame.

3. Place the disks on the frame and mark at the holes. With the sharp point of the craft knife, pierce the paper at the marked points. Insert the brads through the disks and paper and secure.

### Instructions for Completing the Pages

1. Use the computer printer to print the title on the yellow paper. Trim the title box and remaining photos. Arrange the framed photos, unframed photos, and title box on the pages. Use adhesive to attach the components to the pages. Use the colored pencil to write captions.

**License Plate Frame**

2¼" (5.7 cm)   2¼" (5.7 cm)

½" (1.3 cm)   ½" (1.3 cm)

SNOW DAY

# Snow Day

## Tulle, frost, and painted lace frames

Bundling up has never been so much fun. This bundle of three frosty frames is a perfect wintery mix, with Scribble paint used to create lacy patterns of frost and ice.

### Instructions for the Tulle Frame

1. The frame is made for a 6" x 4" (15.2 cm x 10.2 cm) photo. Make adjustments if your photo is a different size. From the pink paper, cut a 7¾" x 5¾" (19.7 cm x 14.6 cm) rectangle. Cut a 5½" x 3½" (13.4 cm x 8.9 cm) window in the center. From the dark gray paper, cut a 7¾" x 5¾" (19.7 cm x 14.6 cm) rectangle. Cut a 5¾" x 3¾" (14.6 cm x 9.5 cm) window in the center. Coat the back of the gray frame with spray adhesive. Center and press in place on the pink frame.

2. Cut an 8" x 18" (20.3 cm x 45.7 cm) rectangle from the tulle and fold it lengthwise twice to 2" x 18" (5.1 cm x 45.7 cm). Tape it to the back bottom of the frame with the end extending diagonally 2" (5.1 cm) below the frame. Working from left to right, wrap the bottom of the frame several times. Tape to the back of the frame at the opposite end. From the floss, cut two 4" (10.2 cm) lengths. Wrap each around the ends of the tulle and knot to secure.

### Instructions for the Painted Frost Frame

1. The frame is made for a 4" x 3¾" (10.2 cm x 9.5 cm) photo. Make adjustments if your photo is a different size. From the periwinkle paper, cut a 4½" x 4" (11.4 cm x 10.2 cm) rectangle. Cut a 3½" x 3½" (8.9 cm x 8.9 cm) window to make a frame with only three sides.

2. Squirt two or three 1" (2.5 cm) lines of paint on the frame. Blot with wax paper to cover the paper and to create a crackle pattern. Let dry. Tape the photo to the back of the frame.

### Instructions for the Painted Lace Frame

1. The frame is made for a 4" x 6" (10.2 cm x 15.2 cm) photo. Make adjustments if your photo is a different size. From the polka dot paper, cut a 5½" x 7½" (13.4 cm x 19.1 cm) rectangle. Cut a 3½" x 5½" (8.9 cm x 13.4 cm) window in the center. From the light gray paper, cut a 6¼" x 8¼" (15.8 cm x 20.9 cm) rectangle. Cut a 4¼" x 6¼" (10.8 cm x 15.8 cm) window in the center. Trim to make diagonal corners 1¾" (4.4 cm) in from each corner.

2. Apply the paint in irregular swirls on the gray frame. Let dry. Coat the back of the gray frame with spray adhesive. Center and press in place on the polka dot frame. Center and tape the photo to the back of the frame.

### Instructions for Completing the Pages

1. Use the computer printer to print the title on the lavender paper. Trim the title box.

2. From the gray paper, cut two ½" x 12" (1.3 cm x 30.5 cm) strips. Arrange the framed photos, strips, and title box on the pages. Use adhesive to attach the components to the pages. Cut small sections from the paper doily. Place on the pages and press clear tiles over the top to secure.

## MATERIALS

12" x 12" (30.5 cm x 30.5 cm) blue print paper

12" x 12" (30.5 cm x 30.5 cm) gray paper

paper in the following colors: dark gray, light gray, lavender, pink, blue polka dot

white tulle

clear plastic tiles

paper doily

blue embroidery floss

spray adhesive

double-sided adhesive sheet, such as Peel-N-Stick

## TOOLS

metal-edged ruler

craft knife

scissors

tape

light blue paint with fine-tip applicator, such as Scribble Paint

wax paper

computer printer

# Traveling

## Punched paper and stamped fabric frames

Small accents can sometimes have a big pay-off. Add get-up-and-go to your travel photos with punched paper and stamped fabric corners.

### Instructions for Assembling the Pages

1. With the ruler and knife, trim the unframed photos. Arrange and, with double-sided adhesive, attach them to the left-hand page. With the black ink, stamp the sun in the top right quadrant of the page. Let dry.

2. The frame is made for a 3½" x 4¾" (8.9 cm x 12.1 cm) photo. Make adjustments if your photo is a different size. From the gray paper, cut a 4" x 5¼" (10.2 cm x 13.3 cm) rectangle. Cut a 3" x 4¼" (7.6 cm x 10.8 cm) window in the center. Center and tape the photo to the back of the frame. Place the framed photo on the right-hand page and attach with double-sided adhesive. With scraps of paper, mask around the framed photo 1½" (3.8 cm) from the sides and 1¼" (3.1 cm) from the top and bottom. With the green ink, stamp the fern fronds in a random pattern. Let dry. Use the colored pencil to write a title and captions.

### Instructions for the Punched Corners

1. Referring to the photo for colors, cut six 1½" (3.8 cm) squares. Punch a leaf in the center of three of the squares. Coat the backs of the punched squares with adhesive spray. Align the edges and press in place on the remaining squares. Use double-sided adhesive to attach to the corners of the photos.

### Instructions for the Pillow Corners

1. Corners are made for 1½" x 1" (3.8 cm x 2.5 cm) rubber stamps. Make adjustments for stamps of different sizes. Cut 1½" x 1¼" (3.8 cm x 3.1 cm) rectangles at each corner. Cut four 2" (5.1 cm) squares from the fabric. With the brown ink, stamp the images in the centers of the fabric squares. Let dry.

2. Align the backing paper behind the page and draw a light line around the inside edge of each window. Attach a 2" (5.1 cm) square of double-sided adhesive sheet over each marked window. Remove the remaining protective paper to expose the adhesive. From the batting, cut four 1¼" x 1" (3.1 cm x 2.5 cm) rectangles. Center each inside the marked rectangles and attach to the adhesive. Center and place the stamped cloth rectangles on the batting and press the edges on the adhesive to secure.

3. Coat the back of the polka dot paper with spray adhesive. Press in place on the backing paper.

---

## MATERIALS

12" x 12" (30.5 cm x 30.5 cm) gray paper

12" x 12" (30.5 cm x 30.5 cm) blue polka dot paper

12" x 12" (30.5 cm x 30.5 cm) backing paper

paper in the following colors: light green, sage green, yellow, dark gray

cream fabric

cotton quilt batting

spray adhesive

double-sided adhesive sheet, such as Peel-N-Stick

## TOOLS

metal-edged ruler

craft knife

pencil

scissors

rubber stamps with the following images: air mail medallion, suitcase, fern frond, sun

ink pads in the following colors: green, brown, black

oak leaf hole punch

maple leaf hole punch

brown colored pencil

MATERIALS

12" x 12"
(30.5 cm x 30.5 cm)
light gray paper

12" x 12"
(30.5 cm x 30.5 cm)
blue polka dot
paper

red paper

green paper

pink striped vellum

vintage postcard

vintage Valentine

die-cut wagon

button

cream pearl cotton

plastic letter tile

pewter star brad

spray adhesive

double-sided
adhesive sheet,
such as Peel-N-Stick

TOOLS

metal-edged ruler

craft knife

scissors

black fine-tip
marker

# Monochrome Kids

## Fun folded paper corners

Nostalgic tokens of childhood, and snippets of folded paper, act as subtle but clever photo additions.

### Instructions for Assembling the Pages

1. Trim the photos. Arrange the photos, postcard, Valentine, and wagon on the pages. Use adhesive to attach the components to the pages. Use the marker to write a title and caption.

### Instructions for the Button Corner

1. Thread a short length of pearl cotton through the button holes. Knot and trim the thread ends. From the green paper, cut a ¾" (1.9 cm) square. Use double-sided adhesive to attach the button to the paper and to attach the paper to the photo corner.

### Instructions for the Star Corner

1. From the vellum, cut a ½" x 4" (1.3 cm x 10.2 cm) strip. Referring to Diagram A (see below), fold at a right angle. Referring to Diagram B (see below), fold the ends to the center. Referring to Diagram C (see below), trim the ends. Place on the photo corner. Use the sharp point of the craft knife to pierce through the layered vellum and the page. Insert the star brad and secure through all layers.

### Instructions for the Triangle Corners

1. From the red paper, cut a 1¼" (2 cm) square. Cut in half diagonally. From the vellum, cut two ½" x 3" (1.3 cm x 7.6 cm) strips. Referring to Diagram D (see below), fold the strips over the triangles. Referring to Diagram E (see below), trim the ends. Use adhesive to attach the triangles to the photo.

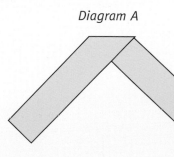

*Diagram A*

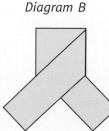

*Diagram B*

*Diagram C*

*Diagram D*

*Diagram E*

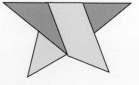

sight seeing

IMAGINE

- the aquatic Park
- the assui at Central Park
- up a down through the tree trunk
- exploring
- climbing
- discovering

# Imagine

## Micro bead starburst corners

Capture the moment in time when it actually seems that time has stood still. Afternoons of exploration and discovery are defined with iridescent paper and bursts of micro beads.

### Instructions for Assembling the Pages

1. From the silver film, cut four 5¾" (14.6 cm) squares. Coat the backs of the film with spray adhesive. Referring to the photo for placement, press in place on the right-hand page.

2. Trim the photos. Arrange the photos and the label on the pages. Use adhesive to attach them to the pages.

3. From the white paper, cut a 2" x 4½" (5.1 cm x 11.4 cm) rectangle. Coat the back of the rectangle with spray adhesive. Referring to the photo for placement, attach the rectangle to the right-hand page. From the white vellum, cut a 3¼" x 5" (8.2 cm x 12.7 cm) rectangle. Overhanging the bottom edge of the page, place the vellum rectangle over the white rectangle. Secure the vellum at the top corners with double-sided adhesive. Wrap the bottom edge to the back of the page and tape to secure. Use the marker to write captions.

### Instructions for the Cosmic Corners

1. From the gold vellum, cut three 1¼" x 1½" (3.1 cm x 3.8 cm) rectangles. Coat the backs of the rectangles with spray adhesive. Press in place at the photo corners. Use the tracing paper to make the swirl templates (see below). Make two small swirls and one large swirl from double-sided adhesive. Peel the backing from the swirls, and overlapping the gold rectangles, attach them to the pages. Remove the remaining protective paper and sprinkle the beads on the exposed adhesive. Remove excess beads.

**MATERIALS**

12" x 12"
(30.5 cm x 30.5 cm)
gray paper

white paper

gold vellum

white vellum

faux metal label

silver micro beads

silver film

**TOOLS**

metal-edged ruler

craft knife

tracing paper

pencil

scissors

tape

black fine-tip marker

*Small Swirl*

*Large Swirl*

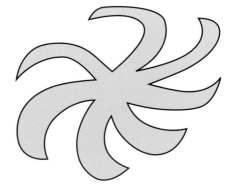

# Our Garden

## Torn paper foliage corners

You don't need a green thumb to tear paper into vines and leaves. (Only opposing thumbs.) This foolproof treatment is great for beginners since you can't make a mistake when tearing.

**MATERIALS**

12" x 12" (30.5 cm x 30.5 cm) green paper

paper in the following colors: red gray/green, tan

spray adhesive

brown acrylic paint

**TOOLS**

metal-edged ruler

craft knife

tracing paper

pencil

scissors

paintbrush

### Instructions for Assembling the Pages

1. Trim the photos and arrange them on the pages. Use adhesive to attach them to the pages. Paint the title on the page. Let dry.

*Rose*

### Instructions for the Vine Corners

1. Tear strips from green paper. Fold to create contours. Tear leaves from green paper. Coat the backs of the leaves with spray adhesive. Press in place on the photo corners.

### Instructions for the Rose Corners

1. Use the tracing paper to make the rose template (see above). From the red paper, cut two roses. From the tan paper, tear two 1½" (3.8 cm) wide ovals. From the green paper, tear six leaves. Coat the backs of the ovals, leaves, and roses with spray adhesive. Layer the elements in the same order and press in place at the corners.

### Instructions for the Vine Corners

1. Tear strips from green paper. Fold to create contours. Tear leaves from green paper. Coat the backs of the vines and the leaves with spray adhesive. Press in place on the photo corners.

12" x 12"
(30.5 cm x 30.5 cm)
ivory paper

paper in the follow-
ing colors: pink
print, pink stripe,
white, blue polka
dot, turquoise,
lavender

pink striped vellum

pink chenille sticks

copper wire, 18 mm

blue decorative cord

spray adhesive

double-sided
adhesive sheet,
such as Peel-N-Stick


TOOLS

metal-edged ruler

craft knife

scissors

tracing paper

pencil

wire cutters

needle-nose pliers

hot glue gun

computer printer

black fine-tip
marker

# *Babies*

## Diaper pin, teddy, and triangle corners

Nothing is cuter than a baby posing for a camera, but these corner accents come in a close second. You can coil, knot, and piece adorable corners for photos of diva babies.

### Instructions for Assembling the Pages

1. Coat the backs of the pink print and pink stripe papers with spray adhesive. Referring to the photo, press in place on the pages. Trim the photos. Use the computer printer to print the title on the white paper. Coat the back of the tracing paper with spray adhesive. Press the tracing paper on the printed paper. Trim the title box through both layers.

2. Arrange the photos and title box on the pages. Use adhesive to attach the components to the pages. Use the marker to write captions.

### Instructions for the Diaper Pin Corners

1. Use the tracing paper to make the diaper template (see page 294). From the white paper, cut four diaper corners. From the copper wire, cut two $4\frac{1}{2}$" (11.4 cm) lengths. With the pliers, shape the wire to match Diagram A (see page 294). Trim the wire ends. With the pliers, coil the chenille stems to match Diagram B (see page 294).

2. Attach narrow strips of the double-sided adhesive to the long sides of the diaper triangles. Overlapping at the centers, attach the triangles to the page corners. With the sharp point of the craft knife, pierce the top triangles at the marked points. Referring to the photo, insert the wire ends through the holes. Glue the coiled chenille over the wire ends with the hot glue gun.

### Instructions for the Teddy Bear Corner

1. From the white paper, cut one $3\frac{1}{2}$" (8.9 cm) square. Use the tracing paper to make the templates (see page 294). Referring to the photo for colors, cut the shapes. Coat the backs of the shapes with spray adhesive. Referring to Assembled Bear Diagram (see page 294), place the shapes on the white paper in the following order: arms, body, head, snout, and foot pads. Press in place to adhere.

2. Trim the white paper to $2\frac{1}{2}$" x $2\frac{3}{4}$" (6.4 cm x 7 cm). Use the marker to draw the eyes, nose, and mouth where indicated. Use adhesive to attach the corner to the page.

### Instructions for the Triangle Corners

1. From the polka dot paper, cut one $1\frac{1}{4}$" (3.1 cm) square. Cut in half diagonally. From the cord, cut two 3" (7.6 cm) lengths. Knot in the centers. Glue the knots to the triangles with the hot glue gun. Trim the cord ends. Attach the triangles at the photo corners with double-sided adhesive.

babies

babies

babies

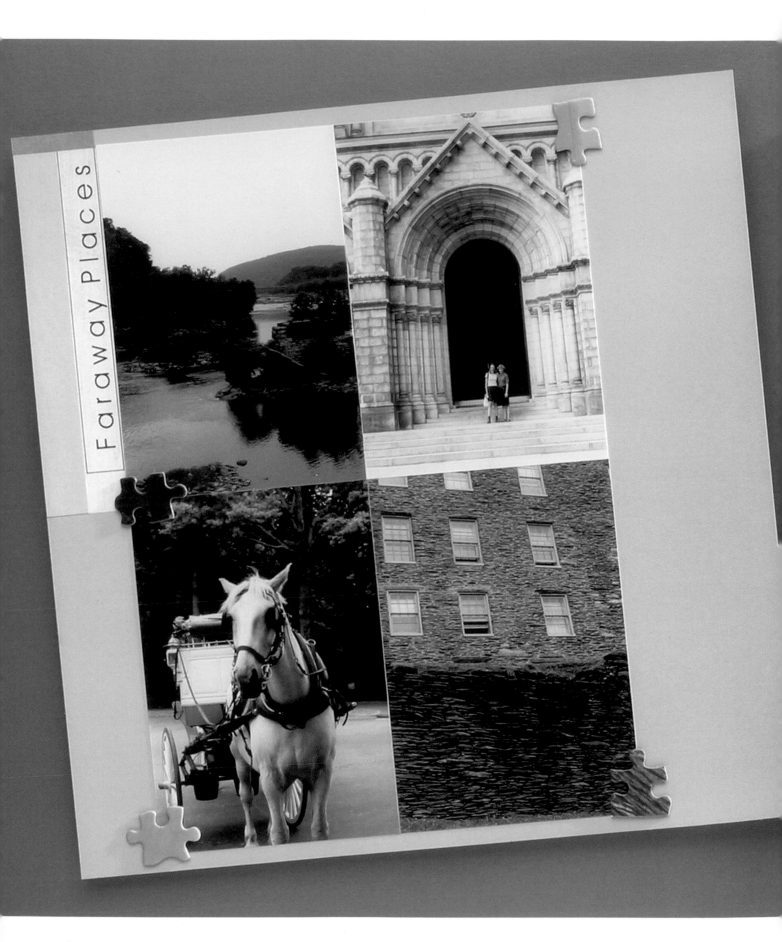

Faraway Places

# Faraway Places

## Puzzle piece corners

The original pixels: jigsaw puzzles pieces. Combine the pieces to create a graphic landscape and then break off the edges to accent your photos.

### Instructions for Assembling the Pages

1. Use the computer printer to print the title on the white paper. (Make the type size ¾" [1.9 cm] tall.) Trim the title. From the lavender paper, cut one ¾" x 5¾" (1.9 cm x 14.6 cm) strip. From the purple paper, cut one ¼" x ½" (5 mm x 1.3 cm) strip. Coat the backs of the title box and paper strips with adhesive. Referring to the photo for placement, press in place at the corner of the left-hand page.

2. Trim the photos. Align the edge of the top photo with the title box and place the photos on the page. Use adhesive to attach the photos to the page.

3. Assemble the selected section of the jigsaw puzzle on a sheet of paper. Place a second sheet of paper over the top and turn the puzzle upside-down. Use the tracing paper to make a template that roughly matches the assembled pieces. Piecing if necessary, cut the shape from double-sided adhesive and attach it to the back of the puzzle. Attach the puzzle to the right-hand page. Attach selected loose puzzle pieces to the page.

### Instructions for the Puzzle Corners

1. Attach selected loose puzzle pieces to the photo corners with double-sided adhesive.

**MATERIALS**

**12" x 12"** (30.5 cm x 30.5 cm) tan paper

paper in the following colors: white, lavender, purple

jigsaw puzzle

spray adhesive

double-sided adhesive sheet, such as Peel-N-Stick

**TOOLS**

metal-edged ruler

craft knife

computer printer

scissors

black fine-tip marker

*Diagram A*

TRIM

*Diagram B*

# Having Fun

## Pleated border and rainbow frames

What's black and white and hot all over? Black-and-white photos combined with glowing rainbow frames, of course. These eclectic outlines aren't confined to the edges of the photos. They zero in on the best parts of the images—the happy faces.

### Instructions for the Pleated Border

1. From the cream print paper, cut two 1½" x 12" (3.8 cm x 30.5 cm) strips. Referring to Diagram A (see opposite, below), fold the strips at ½" (1.3 cm) and at 1½" (3.8 cm) repeats. Cut triangles on both sides of the strips as indicated. Fold and trim the ½" (1.3 cm)-wide sections to match the trimmed 1½" (3.8 cm) sections. Place the folded strips, wrong-side-up, on the work surface. Cut short strips from double-sided adhesive. Referring to Diagram B (see opposite, below), attach them to the backs of the folded strips at the narrowest sections.

2. Starting in the top center of the page, overlap the narrow ends and attach the strips to the left-hand page. With the sharp point of the craft knife, pierce through the overlapping ends of the strips and through the page. Insert the silver brad and secure through all layers.

3. Use the tracing paper to make the Stem, Blossom, and Flower Center templates (see page 295). Referring to the photo for colors, cut four stems, blossoms, and centers. Slide the stems under the pleats. Coat the backs of the centers with spray adhesive and press in place on the blossoms. Coat the backs of the blossoms with spray adhesive and press in place on the tops of the stems. Attach the bottoms of the stems to the page with narrow strips of double-sided adhesive.

### Instructions for the Rainbow Frames

1. Use the tracing paper to make the templates for the frames (see page 295). Enlarge or reduce if necessary to fit the selected photos. Referring to the photo for colors, cut one of each frame.

### Instructions for Completing the Pages

1. Trim the background from the selected photo. Coat the back of the photo with spray adhesive. Mount the photo on the lavender paper. Trim the paper to a 7" x 5½" (17.8 cm x 13.4 cm) rectangle. Coat the back of the rectangle with spray adhesive and mount on the blue paper. Trim the blue paper to make a ¼" (5 mm) border. Stamp the title on the lavender paper. Let dry.

2. Trim the photos.

3. Arrange the mounted and unmounted photos on the pages. Use adhesive to attach the photos to the pages. Arrange the small frames on the photos. Coat the backs of the photos with spray adhesive and press in place to adhere.

## MATERIALS

12" x 12" (30.5 cm x 30.5 cm) tangerine paper

12" x 12" (30.5 cm x 30.5 cm) orange paper

12" x 12" (30.5 cm x 30.5 cm) cream print paper

paper in the following colors: lavender, blue, light turquoise, dark turquoise, mint, periwinkle, pink, light green

silver brad

spray adhesive

double-sided adhesive sheet, such as Peel-N-Stick

## TOOLS

metal-edged ruler

craft knife

tracing paper

scissors

pencil

alphabet rubber stamps

black ink pad

# Cherries Jubilee

## Cherries border with paper clip and double frames

What do an ice cream sundae and a polka-dot page have in common? They are both topped with cherries. (In this case, rows and rows of cherries.) You could also use this border to color picnic or reunion pages.

### Instructions for the Cherries Border

1. Use the tracing paper to make the templates (see opposite, below). From the red paper, cut two 12" (30.5 cm) long cherry strips. Referring to the diagram (see opposite, below), attach the wide bands of the strips to the pages with double-sided adhesive. From the light green paper, cut two ³⁄₈" x 11" (1 cm x 27.9 cm) strips. Coat the backs of the strips with spray adhesive. Press in place on the red bands. Attach a small square of double-sided adhesive to the center of each cherry. Fold each cherry over the red/green band and attach each to the pages.

2. From the Kelly green paper, cut eighteen leaves. Coat the backs of the leaves with spray adhesive. Referring to the photo for placement, press in place on the red/green band. Attach round stickers to selected cherries.

### Instructions for the Double Frames

1. The frame is made for a 5" x 6" (12.7 cm x 15.2 cm) photo. Make adjustments if your photo is a different size. From the blue paper, cut a 6¼" x 7¼" (15.8 cm x 18.4 cm) rectangle. Cut a 4½" x 5½" (11.4 cm x 13.4 cm) window in the center. From the tan paper, cut a 6¼" x 7¼" (15.8 cm x 18.4 cm) rectangle. Cut a 5" x 6" (12.7 cm x 15.2 cm) window in the center. Coat the back of the tan frame with spray adhesive. Center and press in place on the blue frame. Center and tape the photo to the back of the frame.

2. Repeat step 1 with blue and green papers. Center and tape the artwork to the back of the frame.

### Instructions for the Paper Clip Frame

1. Trim the artwork to the desired size. Coat the back with spray adhesive. Mount the artwork on the pink paper. Trim the pink paper to make a narrow border. Slide the paper clips on the top edge.

### Instructions for Completing the Pages

1. Attach the stickers to the light green paper for the title box. Use the marker to write a subtitle on the cream paper. Trim the green paper, cream paper, and decorative paper. Arrange the framed photo, framed artwork, mounted artwork, and title strips on the pages. Use adhesive to attach the components to the pages.

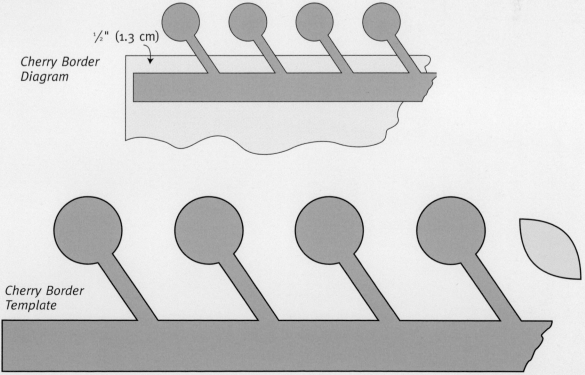

½" (1.3 cm)

*Cherry Border Diagram*

*Cherry Border Template*

Cami and Marissa at the airport

summer 2004

saying
good-bye
to GERMANY

after traveling from Munich to
Frankfurt, we left Germany for
New York City. It was hard
saying good-bye to everyone,
but we looked forward to going
home to begin fall semester.

FROHSINN

# Saying Good-Bye

## Rustic wooden frame and corners

Handcrafted wooden corners and a carved timber frame add elegance to picturesque travel photos. After being charmed by the old-world details, it's hard saying good-bye.

### Instructions for the Wooden Corners

1. Use the ruler and knife to cut two 1½" (3.8 cm) squares from the balsa wood. It will take several passes of the knife to cut completely through the wood. Cut both in half diagonally to make four triangles. Dilute the brown paint and paint the triangles. Let dry. Sand the edges and the tops to reveal the wood. Coat the backs of the tin corners with the craft glue and press in place on the wooden corners. Let dry.

2. Trim the photo. Use adhesive to mount the photo on the tan paper. Trim the paper to make narrow borders. Use double-sided adhesive to secure the corners to the photo.

### Instructions for the Wooden Frame

1. The frame is made for a 5" x 3" (12.7 cm x 7.6 cm) photo. Make adjustments if your photo is a different size. With the ruler and knife, cut a 6" x 4" (15.2 cm x 10.2 cm) rectangle from the balsa wood. It will take several passes of the knife to cut completely through the wood. Cut a 4½" x 2½" (11.4 cm x 6.4 cm) window in the center.

2. Carefully cut small notches around the outside edges of the frame. Note that the wood breaks easily when working in the same direction as the wood grain. Use the sandpaper and the emery board to smooth the notched edges. Dilute the rust paint and paint the frame. Let dry. Center and tape the photo to the back of the frame.

3. From the dark gray paper, cut a 6¼" x 4¼" (15.8 cm x 10.8 cm) rectangle. With the sharp point of the craft knife, cut a small hole in the corners of the wooden frame and the paper. Insert the brads and secure through all layers.

### Instructions for Completing the Pages

1. Coat the backs of the vellum sheet with spray adhesive. Align the outside edges and press in place on the tan paper. Trim the remaining photos.

2. Use the computer printer to print the title and a caption on the taupe print paper. Trim or tear the title and caption boxes. Arrange the unframed photos, framed photo, mounted photo, hinges, title box, and caption box. Use adhesive to attach the components to the pages.

3. Attach the sticker. Use the sharp point of the craft knife to pierce the caption box and the page. Pierce the sticker and the page. Insert brads and secure through all layers. Use the marker to write messages.

## MATERIALS

12" x 12" (30.5 cm x 30.5 cm) tan paper

12" x 12" (30.5 cm x 30.5 cm) printed vellum

paper in the following colors: tan, gray, taupe print

balsa wood

silver brads

sticker

tin filigree corners

silver hinges

brown acrylic paint

rust acrylic paint

spray adhesive

double-sided adhesive sheet, such as Peel-N-Stick

## TOOLS

metal-edged ruler

craft knife

emery board

fine sandpaper

craft glue

tape

computer printer

black fine-tip marker

# Doorways

## Bower borders and photo toppers

The symbol of the doorway is one of the most intriguing and
endearing in all of art, literature, and mythology. Who can resist
wondering what waits on the other side? Especially behind such
welcoming doorways as these.

### Instructions for Assembling the Pages

1. With the ruler and knife, trim the photos.

2. Use adhesive to mount the selected photos on the gray and pink papers. Trim the
   colored papers to make narrow borders. Note that the large photo has a border on
   only the top and sides.

3. From the lavender paper, cut a 1¼" x 12" (3.1 cm x 30.5 cm) strip. Use the computer printer to print captions on the white paper. Trim the captions. Apply a light
   coat of chalk to the caption boxes and rub with a tissue to distribute the color.

4. Arrange the mounted photos, unmounted photo, lavender strip, and caption boxes
   on the pages. Use adhesive to attach the components to the pages.

### Instructions for Bower Border

1. Use the tracing paper to make the sleeve template (see opposite, below). From the
   gold paper, cut one sleeve. Fold where indicated. Attach one small strip of double-
   sided adhesive to the back of the sleeve. Center and press in place on the top of
   the page.

2. With the wire cutters, cut four 7" (17.8 cm) lengths of stems. Overlapping the ends at
   the center, arrange on the open sleeve. With small stitches spaced approximately ½"
   (1.3 cm) apart, stitch the stems to the page to secure. Tape the thread ends to the
   back of the page.

3. Fold the sleeve ends in and use a small square of double-sided adhesive to secure
   the ends together. Apply a small drop of craft glue to the back of the angel charm
   and attach it to the sleeve. Let dry.

### Instructions for Bower Toppers

1. Cut one 5½" (13.4 cm) stem and two 7" (17.8 cm)
   stems. Place the short stem horizontally on the work
   surface. Referring to Diagram A (right), place the long
   stems perpendicular on the short stem, 1¼" (3.1 cm)
   from the left end. Use the embroidery floss to lash the
   stems together at the intersection. Knot the floss and
   trim the floss ends.

2. Referring to Diagram B (opposite, left), bend the long
   stems together and lash the ends together at the opposite end of the short stem. Knot the floss and trim
   the floss ends. Attach double-sided adhesive to the
   back of the green paper scraps. Cut into narrow strips.
   Remove remaining protective paper and place the
   strips over stems at selected points to secure to the
   page.

3. Repeat steps 1 and 2 to make second Bower Topper.

*Diagram A*

1"
(2.5 cm)

Church of the Good Shepherd
Monterey

The Cannery
San Francisco

Inn by the Lake
Chelsea

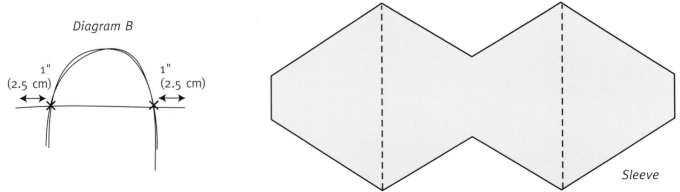

*Diagram B*

1"
(2.5 cm)

1"
(2.5 cm)

*Sleeve*

For photography we were assigned to take pictures of various nature scenes

(Old Barn by Far West)

(Junk yard by Grandmas house)

*Wrapping the Corner Diagram*

*Corner Template*

# Rust and Splinters

## Newsprint corners and railroad track border

A lazy afternoon that included a new roll of film and a full tank of gas produced a synthesis of aging textures and surfaces. Decorate studies of ordinary objects with ordinary accents that include old newspapers and silver wire.

### Instructions for the Print-Covered Corners

1. Use the tracing paper to make the templates (see opposite, below right). Use the ruler and knife to cut four corners from the balsa wood. It will take several passes of the knife to cut completely through the wood. Note that the wood breaks easily when working in the same direction as the wood grain.

2. Referring to the diagram (see opposite, below left), cut a piece from the newspaper. Coat the back of the newspaper with spray adhesive. Wrap the newspaper around the corner piece. Repeat with the remaining corners.

3. Trim the photo. Use adhesive to mount the photo on the gray paper. Trim the top and sides of the gray paper to make ¾" (1.9 cm) borders. Tear the bottom edge of the gray paper. Use double-sided adhesive to secure the corners to the photo.

### Instructions for the Railroad Tracks Border

1. From the black paper, cut two 6" (15.2 cm) lengths of railroad tracks (see below). Draw irregular outlines on the tracks with the white colored pencil. Coat the backs of the tracks with spray adhesive. Overlapping the ends slightly, place the tracks on the work surface. Cut a 45" (114.3 cm) length of silver wire and weave the wire around and through the tracks in a freeform pattern. Coil the wire ends in at the bottom of the tracks.

### Instructions for Completing the Pages

1. Trim the remaining photos and decorative paper. Arrange the mounted photo, unmounted photos, and decorative paper on the pages. Use adhesive to secure the components to the pages. Press the tracks along the edge of the paper. Use the black colored pencil to write the title and the tan pencil to write the captions.

*Railroad Tracks*

## MATERIALS

12" 12" (30.5 cm x 30.5 cm) brown paper

gray paper

black paper

newspaper

decorative paper

silver 32 mm gauge wire

balsa wood

spray adhesive

double-sided adhesive sheet, such as Peel-N-Stick

## TOOLS

metal-edged ruler

craft knife

tracing paper

pencil

scissors

wire cutters

colored pencils in the following colors: black, white, tan

Reflections

Lisa

High School Grad

College
Graduation
1980

# *Reflections*

## Jeweled corner and serpentine border

Foggy images, tender feelings, beckoning sounds, and flowery smells are important memory snippets that describe who we are. Make a paper and photo collage to chronicle your past and to provoke personal ephemera.

### Instructions for Assembling the Pages

1. Cut a 6" x 8" (15.2 cm x 20.3 cm) rectangle from the dictionary and toile papers. From the olive polka dot paper, cut one 8½" x 12" (21.6 cm x 30.5 cm) rectangle. Trim the photos.

2. Stamp a rose on one large tag. Let dry. Shade the rose with the colored pencils. Cut small scraps from the decorative papers. Coat the backs of the scraps with spray adhesive and attach them to the medium tag and the remaining large tag. From the rayon trim, cut three 4" (10.2 cm) lengths. Thread the lengths through the tags and knot.

3. Trim the photos. Arrange the photos, polka dot paper, dictionary paper, toile paper, and tags on the pages. Use adhesive to attach the components to the pages.

4. Stamp the pears on the tops of the pages. Let dry. Shade the pears with the colored pencils. From the green vellum, tear a 2½" x 6½" (6.4 cm x 16.5 cm) rectangle. Coat the back of the rectangle with spray adhesive and press in place over the two stamped pears. Tear a 3" x 3" (7.6 cm x 7.6 cm) square. Coat with spray adhesive and press in place over the single stamped pear.

### Instructions for the Jeweled Corner

1. Cut a 1" (2.5 cm) square from the fabric. Remove a few loose threads along the cut edges to fray slightly. Press the prongs of the jewel stud through the fabric scrap. Place the jewel on the photo corner and mark the insertion points for the prongs. With the sharp point of the craft knife, pierce the fabric at the marked points. Insert the prongs through all layers and bend them flat with the spoon or knife.

### Instructions for the Serpentine Border

1. Cut one yard (0.9 m) of rayon trim. Overhang the top edge of the page with the looped end, and place the trim on the paper. Shape the trim into freeform lines of bends and curls. Place the jewels over the trim, and mark the insertion points for the prongs. With the sharp point of the craft knife, pierce the paper at the marked points. Insert the prongs through all layers and bend them flat with the spoon or knife. Tape the top loop of the trim to the back of the page. Trim the ends.

## MATERIALS

12" x 12" (30.5 cm x 30.5 cm) cream paper

12" x 12" (30.5 cm x 30.5 cm) olive polka dot paper

dictionary print paper

lavender toile paper

turquoise vellum

decorative papers

1¼ yards (1.1 m) tufted rayon trim

square jewel studs

two large paper tags

one medium paper tag

scrap pink moiré fabric

spray adhesive

double-sided adhesive sheet, such as Peel-N-Stick

## TOOLS

metal-edged ruler

craft knife

scissors

tape

rose rubber stamp

pear rubber stamp

brown ink pad

colored pencils

blunt tool (spoon or knife)

black fine-tip marker

12" x 12"
(30.5 cm x 30.5 cm)
lined composition
paper

12" x 12"
(30.5 cm x 30.5 cm)
gold print paper

preprinted title

paper in the follow-
ing colors: tan, gray,
mauve, red, green

paper clips

photo of stairs

small notebook
with spiral binding

air-drying
modeling clay,
such as PaperClay

acrylic paint in the
following colors:
gold, orange, white,
black

stickers

alphabet paper

spray adhesive

double-sided
adhesive sheet,
such as Peel-N-Stick

craft glue

TOOLS

metal-edged ruler

craft knife

tracing paper

pencil

tape

scissors

paintbrush

sandpaper

colored pencils

black fine-tip marker

# Back to School

## School-themed frames and apple corner

School photos—they go from the classroom to the refrigerator door to the junk drawer to the shoe box. Rescue your favorites and choose these elementary techniques to make display frames. Then, they can go straight to your album.

### Instructions for the Paper Clip Frame

1. The frame is made for a $3\frac{1}{4}$" x $4\frac{1}{2}$" (8.2 cm x 11.4 cm) photo. Make adjustments if your photo is a different size. From the tan paper, cut a 4" x 6" (10.2 x 15.2 cm) rectangle. Cut an off-kilter $2\frac{3}{4}$" x 4" (7 cm x 10.2 cm) window. Center and tape the photo to the back of the frame. Slide the paper clips on the side of the frame.

### Instructions for the Doorway Frame

1. The frame is made for a $2\frac{1}{2}$" x $3\frac{3}{4}$" (6.4 cm x 9.5 cm) photo. Make adjustments if your photo is a different size. From the gray paper, cut a $2\frac{3}{4}$" x $4\frac{3}{4}$" (7 cm x 12.1 cm) rectangle. Leaving $1\frac{1}{4}$" (3.1 cm) on the bottom of the frame, cut a 2" x $3\frac{1}{4}$" (5.1 cm x 8.2 cm) window. Use the colored pencils to draw a recessed panel and a doorknob on the frame. Center and tape the photo to the back of the frame.

### Instructions for the Notebook Frame

1. The frame is made for a $2\frac{1}{2}$" x $3\frac{1}{2}$" (6.4 cm x 8.9 cm) photo. Make adjustments if your photo is a different size. Cut a 2" x 3" (5.1 cm x 7.6 cm) window in the cover of the notebook. Center and tape the photo to the back of the cover. Place the notebook on the work surface and flatten the wire coils.

### Instructions for the Pencil Frame

1. The frame is made for a $3\frac{1}{4}$" x $4\frac{1}{4}$" (8.2 cm x 10.8 cm) photo. Make adjustments if your photo is a different size. From the clay, shape a $\frac{3}{8}$" x 3" (1 cm x 7.6 cm) tube. Let dry. Trim the ends. Shave one end to resemble a pencil point. Flatten a long flat side by sanding down with sandpaper. Paint with the acrylic paints: Use gold paint for the shaft, orange for the eraser, white for the point, and black for the tip. Let dry.

2. From the mauve paper, cut a 4" x 5" (10.2 cm x 12.7 cm) rectangle. Center and cut a $2\frac{3}{4}$" x $3\frac{3}{4}$" (7 cm x 9.5 cm) window. Center and tape the photo to the back of the frame. Use the craft glue to glue the pencil to the top of the frame. Let dry.

### Instructions for the Apple Corner

1. Use the tracing paper to make the templates (see opposite). From the red paper, cut an apple. From the green paper, cut a stem/leaf.

### Instructions for Completing Pages

1. Trim the title box. Cut out the selected paper letters. Cut the stairs from the stairs photo. From the gold print paper, cut a $2\frac{1}{2}$" x 12" (6.4 cm x 30.5 cm) strip. Tear one long side of the strip. Arrange the torn strip, framed photos, unframed photo, title box, and stairs on the pages. Use adhesive to attach the components to the pages. Attach the stickers to the pages. Use the marker to write captions.

Stem/Leaf

Apple

# The Adventures of Super Dog

## Book border and bed frame

It isn't just kids who dream of growing up to become superheroes. Immortalize your mild-mannered underdog with a special story and a visual tribute. You may not get applause, but you will get a nice, wet kiss.

### Instructions for the Book Border

1. From the white paper, cut two $3\frac{1}{4}$" x $1\frac{1}{2}$" (8.2 cm x 3.8 cm) rectangles. From the red paper, cut two $3\frac{1}{4}$" x $1\frac{3}{4}$" (8.2 cm x 4.4 cm) rectangles. Fold the white rectangles in half. Attach narrow strips of double-sided adhesive to the short sides. Apply a thin line of glue to the folded edges with the glue gun. Press in place in the centers of the red rectangles. Let dry. Remove the remaining protective paper from the adhesive strips and, with the paper slightly bowed, attach the sides to the red rectangles.

2. From the vellum, cut two $\frac{1}{4}$" x $3\frac{1}{4}$" (5 mm x 8.2 cm) strips. Tape the ends to the back of the books. Fold over the tops of the books and crease the strips. Attach small squares of double-sided adhesive to the ends of the strips.

3. From the vellum, cut two $3\frac{3}{4}$" x 12" (9.5 cm x 30.5 cm) strips. Coat the backs of the strips with spray adhesive. Press in place along the tops of the pages. Coat the backs of the books with spray adhesive. Press in place at the top corners of the pages. Remove the remaining protective paper from the adhesive squares and, with the bookmarks slightly bowed, attach them to the pages.

### Instructions for the Bed Frame

1. Use the tracing paper to make the templates (see page 296). Referring to the photo for colors, cut one of each shape.

2. Arrange the shapes on the right-hand page. Coat the backs of the shapes with spray adhesive. Noting overlaps, press in place on the page.

### Instructions for Completing the Pages

1. With the ruler and knife, trim the photos. Cut the artwork into a cloud shape. Cut two small cloud shapes from the white paper. Assemble the photos, artwork, and small clouds on the pages. Use adhesive to attach the components to the pages. Use the pink colored pencil to write a story. Use the black colored pencil to write a caption.

happy birthday !

Party Guests:
Brianne
Liza
Beck
Spencer
Mackay
Angela
Tracee
Blair
Annabelle
Lake

# Birthday Cake

## Candle frames and cake slice border

Question: Who has more fun—the birthday kid, the party guests, or the photographer? Answer: None of the above. You will have the most fun of all making these paper pieced party pages.

### Instructions for the Candle Frames

1. The large frame is made for a 5" x 3¼" (12.7 cm x 8.2 cm) photo. Make adjustments if your photo is a different size. From the polka-dot paper, cut one 6¼" x 4½" (15.8 cm x 11.4 cm) rectangle. Center and cut a 4½" x 2¾" (11.4 cm x 7 cm) frame. Center and tape the photo to the back of the frame.

2. Cut three 1" (2.5 cm) lengths of pearl cotton. Place them on the frame. From the green paper, cut three ¼" (5 mm) strips of various lengths. Covering the bottoms of the wicks, attach the candles to the frame with double-sided adhesive.

3. The small frame is made for a 2½" x 3" (6.4 cm x 7.6 cm) photo. Making adjustments for the smaller size, repeat steps 1 and 2 to complete the frame.

### Instructions for the Cake Border

1. Use the tracing paper to make the templates (see page 297). Referring to the photo for colors, cut out four frosting shapes, four cake-top shapes, eight layer shapes, and three forks. From the purple paper, cut two ¾" x 12" (1.9 cm x 30.5 cm) strips. Cut shallow scallops along one side of the strips.

2. Trim the photos. Slide the photos between the fork tines. Noting overlaps, arrange the scallops, forks, and cake shapes on the pages. Note that the layers overlap the cake-top shapes. Coat the backs of the shapes with spray adhesive and press in place on the pages. Cut four 1" (2.5 cm) lengths of pearl cotton. Place them on the cake slices. From the green paper, cut four ¼" x 1" (5 mm x 2.5 cm) strips. Covering the bottoms of the wicks, attach the candles to the cake slices with the double-sided adhesive.

### Instructions for Completing the Pages

1. Use the computer printer to print a caption on the lavender paper. Trim the caption box to an irregular shape. Coat the back of the caption box with spray adhesive and press in place on the page. Use the yellow chalk to write a title.

## MATERIALS

12" x 12" (30.5 cm x 30.5 cm) brown paper

paper in the following colors: turquoise, gold, lavender, green, gray, purple, blue polka dot

cream pearl cotton

spray adhesive

double-sided adhesive sheet, such as Peel-N-Stick

## TOOLS

metal-edged ruler

craft knife

tracing paper

pencil

tape

scissors

computer printer

yellow chalk

**4B** Saturday, March 13, 2004

## SPORTS BRIEFS

homes will eventually fill a 6.5-acre parcel in an area originally intended for less dense housing, although the rezone approval by the Hooper City Council raised the question of when development will slow in the small rural community.

"Look at all the building that's going on out here right now. We have more than 900 homes on the books, our plate's pretty full. . . . We don't need any more building right now," said Councilman Richard Noyes.

Nonetheless, the small acreage owned by Ralph Miles at 4924 W. S500 South was rezoned by a vote of four to two.

The development, which was originally zoned for one-acre lots, will be comprised of properties that can accommodate smaller homes on lots of a minimum of 13,000 square feet.

According to City Engineer Tracy Allen, the property in question suits the city's master plan for smaller lots. He also said collateral factors such as its proximity to the Legacy Highway and adjacent higher-density developments make it a good fit for a rezoning action.

Resident Shawn Beus agreed. "I hope you will consider the effectiveness of the land. The useage as a residential setting is in the property owners' best interest and fits the overall community plan. Please consider (the proposal to rezone) independently of other large developments," he said.

Mayor Glenn Barrow said he was intrigued by developer Miles' ideas of building some housing for seniors that would have handicapped access and other features such as one-story construction.

"There's a huge question mark about how all this is going to play out. We do have 900 homes approved . . . We're on a train and we don't know when it will stop," added Councilman Theo Cox.

Lyle Taylor, newly elected to the council, made it clear that his constituents desire no further action on approving more dense developments and, along with Noyes, voted against the rezoning action.

continue to wring our chubby little hands over how to fix this obesity epidemic. The answer seems obvious, yet few of us have the will power to put down that drumstick and pick up that dumbbell.

But Dave Greiling has an idea.

Dave is an editor here at the Standard-Examiner. As any writer can tell you, editors rarely have ideas — let alone good ones — so when they do actually hit upon something like this, it's vitally important to reward that initiative by mocking it in print.

His suggestion? A fat tax.

No, not a "flat" tax, but an actual "fat" tax. Make Americans pay their taxes by the pound. For example, you take the combined total weight of a taxpayer and his or her dependents and divide that number by their combined height. Then, using a complicated IRS formula that, frankly, you just wouldn't understand (multiply by 10), we arrive at a tax-burden percentage.

For example, consider a family of four with an annual income of $80,000. If their combined height is 18 feet 4 inches, and together they weigh a slightly portly 783 pounds, they'll pay $28,473 in taxes. But if each family member lost just 10 pounds, the resulting tax break would save them nearly $1,500 annually. And imagine if they lost some serious weight, like one of them developed an eating disorder or got sick or something.

But the best part of all this would be that the weeks leading up to an April 15 weigh-in become a festive time of anticipation, with the entire country resembling a high school

### g earns praise

The findings were published in Thursday's New England Journal of Medicine. The research was partly funded by Pfizer Inc., the maker of Aromasin.

Dr. Jeff Abrams, the National Cancer Institute's associate chief of clinical research, said a recent study on exemestane "cousin" letrozole showed important advantages over tamoxifen for the class.

"I think with these two studies together, the strategy of switching from tamoxifen to these aromatase inhibitors will become a new standard," said Abrams, who was not involved in the study.

Several recent studies have shown that exemestane and other aromatase inhibitors also work longer, with less toxicity, than tamoxifen in women whose breast cancer had spread to other areas. Exemestane also has been shown to prolong the survival of women with advanced breast cancer after tamoxifen and other drugs fail.

"This whole class of drugs looks very promising, very active," said Dr. Julia Smith, clinical associate professor of oncology at the NYU medical school and cancer institute.

The study, which involved 4,742 postmenopausal women in 37 countries, focused on women with breast cancer in which the hormone estrogen fuels tumor growth — the type responsible for about 70 percent of breast cancer.

Tamoxifen, the celebrated drug credited with slashing breast cancer death rates worldwide, could be eclipsed by a newer medicine that is even more effective at preventing recurrence of the disease in women whose tumors were caught early and removed.

A large, international study of postmenopausal women with early-stage cancer found that those who took tamoxifen for 2½ years and then switched to exemestane for another 2½ years were one-third less likely to suffer a recurrence than those who took tamoxifen the whole time.

The women switching to exemestane also had less-serious side effects, were 56 percent less likely to get cancer in the other breast and were half as likely to develop unrelated cancer in other parts of the body.

Lead researcher Dr. R.C. Coombes, professor of cancer medicine at Imperial College School of Medicine in London, predicted doctors will give exemestane to many women at high risk for recurrence, such as those whose breast cancer has spread to multiple lymph nodes.

Exemestane, which went on the market in advanced breast cancer, is a hormone the brand Aromasin. It

## LOCAL GIRL MAKES GOOD

Coverings - Home Depot
Demonstration – Home Depot, Ogden
Home Interiors & Gifts - Lisa Anderson
Gerry Richards, Team One at Coldwell Banker Residential Brokerage
stand of eco-system maintenance & filtration, Jeff Booth, Tesch Landscaping

strand of eco-system maintenance & filtration, Jeff Booth, Tesch Landscaping
Demonstration – Home Depot, Ogden
Fallon, ASID, CKD, Instile & Rail
Gerry Richards, Team One at Coldwell Banker Residential Brokerage
Birds And Blooms – Bill Fenimore, Wild Bird Center
Coverings – Home Depot
Home Depot, Ogden
Home Interiors & Gifts - Lisa Anderson
– Gerry Richards, Team One at Coldwell Banker Residential Brokerage
lly Wahlstrom, director

ome Depot, Ogden
Birds And Blooms – Bill Fenimore, Wild Bird Center
chards, Team One at Coldwell Banker Residential Brokerage
Demonstration – Home Depot, Ogden
Coverings – Home Depot
Gerry Richards, Team One at Coldwell Banker Residential Brokerage

seconds on the shot clock," Drisdom said of Woodberry's critical foul. "He was pressuring me, and I had no choice but to try to drive on him. He didn't want me to get by him, so he had to reach out. I started to get by him and he lunged at me a little bit and lost his balance.

"It was so ridiculous. I would kick myself if I v him."

"The fact that we g a new clock (thanks t Woodberry's untimel foul), it really was b us," said Utah senio Nick Jacobson, wh a game-high 19 po "With the things t

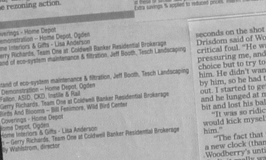

"That's why I do what I do."

First Place

# Local Girl Makes Good

## Newsprint frame and soccer ball border

Stop the presses! You can scoop your local sports writer with the release of these sensational pages. With this kind of encouragement, it won't be long before your budding athlete is featured in the real thing.

### Instructions for the Newspaper Frame

1. The frame is made for a 4" x 5½" (10.2 cm x 13.4 cm) photo. Make adjustments if your photo is a different size. Make a black-and-white copy of your photo with the copy machine. Lightly shade the photo with the colored pencils. In the top left quadrant of the left-hand page, cut a 3½" x 5" (8.9 cm x 12.7 cm) window. Center and tape the photo to the back of the page.

2. Use the computer printer to print the title on the white paper. Trim the title box. Cut sections from the newspaper and piece them together to cover the page. Coat the backs of the title box and newspaper sections with spray adhesive. Press in place to adhere.

### Instructions for the Soccer Border

1. From the olive polka dot paper, cut a 1¾" x 12" (4.4 cm x 30.5 cm) strip. Cut an irregular edge along one side. From the white paper, cut two 1¾" (4.4 cm)-wide circles, and two 1⅝" (4.1 cm)-wide circles. From the tan paper, cut one 1¾" (4.4 cm)-wide circle. From the black and the brown papers, cut confetti shapes, measuring between ¼" and ⅜" (5 mm and 1 cm) square. Noting overlaps, arrange the strip, circles, and confetti on the right-hand page. Coat the backs with spray adhesive and press in place along the edge of the page.

### Instructions for Completing the Pages

1. Trim the photos. From the taupe print paper, cut one 4" x 6" (10.2 cm x 15.2 cm) rectangle. From the blue paper, tear a blue ribbon. Trim the message box into an irregular shape.

2. Noting overlaps, arrange the photos, paper rectangle, blue ribbon, message box, and remaining confetti on the page. Use adhesive to attach the components to the page. Use the black colored pencil to decorate the ribbon.

**MATERIALS**

12" x 12" (30.5 cm x 30.5 cm) tan paper

12" x 12" (30.5 cm x 30.5 cm) olive polka-dot paper

newspapers

paper in the following colors: black, white, tan, brown, blue, taupe print

preprinted message

spray adhesive

double-sided adhesive sheet, such as Peel-N-Stick

**TOOLS**

metal-edged ruler

craft knife

scissors

tape

copy machine

computer printer

black colored pencil

**Basics**

## TOOLS AND SUPPLIES

If you are diving into 3-D scrapbooking, you have probably been introduced to the basics of this craft and have a few pages under your belt and a cache of supplies in your closet. When designing with 3-D embellishments, I find myself frequently using tweezers for picking up and placing small objects, mini craft scissors for snipping ribbon and cutting fine detail, a personal die-cutting system for creating die-cut shapes and titles, and wire cutters for snipping and bending wire. A hammer, eyelet punch, and eyelet setter are necessary for, of course, setting eyelets and fastening all the other metal embellishments that require the setter. And a ruler, craft knife, and self-healing mat are general essentials for precision cutting.

Adhesives will be an important consideration. There are many different kinds of acid-free adhesives on the market, but you need to decide which one will work best depending on the embellishment you are using. Some items that have a shiny metallic surface or a bumpy texture will require a more aggressive adhesive than others. Glue dots, foam adhesive, and scrappy tape are all aggressive adhesives. Less aggressive, but highly dependable, are adhesive machines, such as Xyron, and acid-free double-sided tape.

Perhaps the most important factor to consider when creating 3-D pages is safety. One of the reasons we scrapbook is to preserve photos for generations to come. As we start adding textural items to our pages, it becomes even more important to maintain a protective, acid-free environment. There are a number of ways to achieve this in the realm of dimensionality.

## Keep it acid-free

When adding 3-D paper-based items to your layouts that you aren't sure are acid-free, there are a few things you can do to insure protection for your albums and memorabilia. If you incorporate items such as road maps, menus, or newspaper clippings on your page, follow these three simple rules:

- **Test it.** Use a pH testing pen to test the level of acidity in the item.
- **Spray it.** There are now sprays on the market that neutralize the acid in paper-based materials. Simply spray the entire paper item, and it will be preserved and protected.
- **Copy it.** If you are really unsure about the item, one of the easiest solutions is to make a color photocopy of it onto acid-free paper.

There are a variety of 3-D embellishments and stickers available in scrapbook stores, many of which are produced for scrapbook pages and are acid-free.

## Safe design

When designing your layout, a little careful planning can make all the difference between album preservation and disintegration. Make sure that 3-D objects that aren't labeled "acid-free" don't come in contact with your photos—and that includes the photos on the facing page. When you close your album, you don't want 3-D objects pressing into the photos on the opposite page leaving scratches, tears, or imprints. Plastic page protectors will also prevent damage, though the glare will diminish the texture and dimensionality of a 3-D page.

Also, pay attention to the placement of 3-D objects throughout the album. If you like adding enhancements to your page titles, which are often at the top of the page, you will likely be left with a giant bulge along the top of your album when you close it. Over time, that will warp and disfigure your entire album. Vary the placement of your embellishments throughout the album—it's not only good for the health of the album, but it's good for your creative health, too.

## Safe storage

The best way to store your albums, even if you aren't using textured items, is to place them upright on a shelf. Laying them flat puts pressure on the pages, and, if you are using 3-D embellishments, it could lead to damaging impressions.

Refer to the tips and instructions for each project for additional insights on tools and creating safe pages. You'll be amazed at the wealth of ideas you'll find in these pages and will no doubt start looking at everyday objects with a newfound appreciation for their creative possibilities.

Paper

## LAYERING PAPERS, DIE-CUTS, POP-UPS, AND FOLDOUTS

The incredible variety and versatility of paper is enough to make your head spin. Walk into any scrapbook or craft store and you will be faced with racks of dazzling colors, designs, and textures. But while you might think of paper as flat, there are a number of techniques you can use to manipulate paper into dimensional designs.

In this chapter, you will learn how to add depth and texture to your pages with paper, card stock, and vellum. Paper engineering can be as simple as raising designs with pop-dots or as intricate as multiple layered pop-ups. Using paper die-cuts is a quick and inexpensive way to add character to your pages. Whether you have a personal die-cutting system at home, use the machine at your local scrapbook store, or buy pre-made die-cuts, look for shapes that include perforation marks that denote detail. Those perforation marks serve as guides to help you layer paper onto the die-cut to create beautiful, nuanced designs.

Pop-ups and sliders might sound like baseball terms, but in the scrapbook world they serve as interactive paper ele-

ments that add motion and surprise. Paper mosaics create a ceramic tile effect from cutting and reassembling small pieces of paper. Vellum windows offer a sneak peak of the photo or journaling underneath. Folding, creasing, embossing, cutting, punching, quilling, tearing, layering—whew! What a workout! But all those active terms will bring visual interest and liveliness to your pages.

As you shop for paper, the most important things to look for are the words "acid-free" and "lignin-free." The heart of scrapbooking lies in long-term preservation—capturing memories to share with your family and future generations. If your paper isn't labeled "acid-free," it's wise to check the pH-level of your paper in order to protect your photos and maintain the artistry of your books. Thick, handmade papers add warmth and texture, but make sure they are archivally safe. Shop for paper at scrapbook, craft, rubber stamp, stationery, and art stores, or on the Internet. And let the paper games begin!

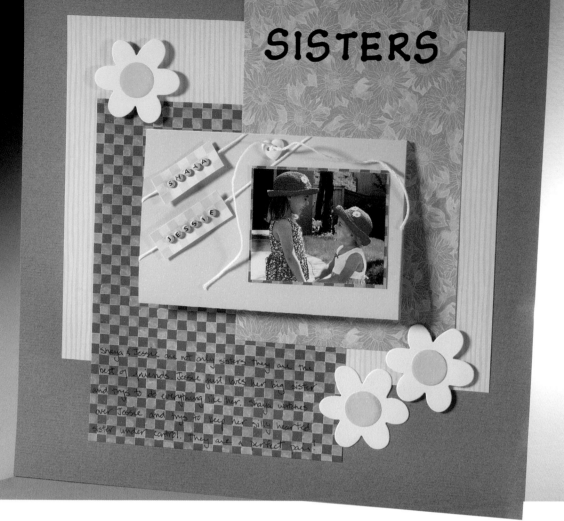

DESIGNER: CARA MARIANO

# Sisters

Brads and buttons are a fast and easy way to add embellishments. They come in a variety of colors, shapes, and sizes.

## MATERIALS

plain paper

patterned paper

embroidery floss

press-on letters

brads

buttons

adhesive

foam adhesive

scissors

die-cutting machine and dies

1. Start with a 12" x 12" (30.5 cm x 30.5 cm) blue background page. Arrange and layer three coordinating patterned papers onto the background page.

2. Accordion fold yellow paper into three separate panels and attach to the center of the page.

3. Mat photographs in a complementary patterned paper. Place a photo on each panel, making sure the photograph on the cover is slightly smaller.

4. Cut two small rectangles out of yellow patterned paper. Spell out each person's name using white brads and rub-on letters. Attach the finished brads to the yellow rectangles.

5. Place a white piece of embroidery floss behind each finished rectangle and attach the finished rectangles to the accordion card. Secure the excess thread with tape on the back of the card.

6. Attach a white heart button at the top of the card with embroidery floss. Leave the thread long to use as a pull to open the accordion card.

7. Die-cut the daisies out of white and yellow paper. On the yellow daisies, cut around the perforation marks in the center. Place the yellow circles onto the white daisies. Arrange the finished daisies onto the page using foam adhesive to create dimension.

8. Add press-on letters at the top to create a title and a journaling block at the bottom to tell the story.

# Hunting for chestnuts

Layering with paper is a simple yet effective way
to add dimension to scrapbook pages.

1. Cut a narrow rectangular frame out of paper that matches the background paper. The frame should be slightly smaller than the photo it will encase.

2. Run leaf-patterned paper through an adhesive machine to apply adhesive before cutting out the individual leaves.

3. Fasten the leaves to the frame, occasionally raising leaves with foam adhesive.

4. Crop and mat additional photos and a title bar.

5. Die-cut leaves from fall-colored papers and fasten them to the page where journaling will be placed.

6. Tear a piece of vellum, journal in a black pen, and attach over the die-cut leaves with a nail head in each corner.

## MATERIALS

plain paper

patterned paper

vellum

leaf die-cuts

nail heads

foam adhesive

scissors

black pen

adhesive machine, such as a Xyron

DESIGNER: SANDI GENOVESE

## MATERIALS

**card stock**

**grosgrain ribbon**

**embroidery floss**

**buttons**

**rubber stamps**

**ink pads, watermark**

**scissors**

# What a card!

Add additional dimension to stamped images by raising them off the page with foam adhesive.

1. Stamp stars and hearts onto card stock in contrasting colors and cut out the images.

2. Stamp vertical stripes along the bottom quarter of the background page using a watermark ink pad. Visually separate the bottom quarter of the page from the top three quarters by placing a horizontal strip of grosgrain ribbon along the top edge of the vertical stripes.

3. Add additional embellishments, such as buttons and embroidery floss, to the stamped images.

4. Place the hearts and stars on the page in a repeating pattern.

5. Stamp the title. Repeat the star and heart on the header.

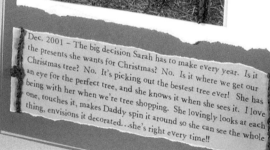

DESIGNER: KELLY JONES

# The tree

String fiber across a photograph to recreate the look of a
wrapped package as well as add some dimension to the page.

**MATERIALS**

1. Place a strip of corrugated paper across the top of the layout. Cut the title out
   of card stock and glue to the corrugated strip.

2. Tear a strip of contrasting colored card stock and adhere it to the center third
   of the background page.

3. String fiber across one of the photos. Place both photos onto the background
   paper.

4. Type journaling on vellum, tear the top and bottom, adhere to the page, and
   place fiber along the left and right edges of the vellum.

5. Using a paper punch, cut three pinecones from card stock, double-mat them
   onto three rectangles, and place them side-by-side to tie the theme together.

card stock

corrugated
paper

fiber

scissors

paper punch

personal
computer

# Peace

Layer vellum, sheer black ribbon, and matted, stamped squares of card stock in varying shades of black and silver. The simplicity of light and dark colors creates visual interest that is stunning.

DESIGNER: KELLY JONES

## MATERIALS

card stock

vellum

ribbon

foam adhesive

rubber stamp

ink pad

scissors

gel pen

1. Double-mat the photograph with a small black border and a larger white one, and then place the photograph onto black card stock to make the picture stand out.

2. Across the bottom, layer a piece of vellum on the card stock, sheer ribbon over the vellum, and then adhere three evenly-spaced squares onto the ribbon, raising them with foam adhesive.

3. Cut black card stock into 2" (5 cm) squares and stamp a pattern that relates to the photograph. Adhere 2" (5 cm) squares to larger squares, using foam adhesive to raise them.

4. Write the page title with a gel pen.

# Rosemary Ann Wilson

Paper can be pleated in the same way as fabric for a terrific three-dimensional effect.

1. Cut approximately eight strips of patterned paper 12" long x 1" wide (30.5 cm x 2.5 cm).

2. Using an embossing or scoring tool, score lines along the green paper, measuring ¼" (6 mm), then ¾" (1.9 cm), then ¼" (6 mm), then ¾" (1.9 cm), continuing until the end of the paper is reached. This will create lines for folding the pleats. Using this pleat, a 12" (30.5 cm) strip of paper will be 6" (15.2 cm) long when pleated.

3. Mount the pleats along the sides of a sheet of ivory card stock and miter the corners.

4. Trim a second sheet of patterned paper in a coordinating print to 11" (27.9 cm).

## MATERIALS

patterned paper

card stock

vellum

journaling block

wire-stemmed paper flowers

foam adhesive

glue dots

scissors

embossing or scoring tool

paper trimmer

Mat with another coordinating patterned paper, leaving approximately ⅛"
(3 mm) around the floral.

5. Mat the photo with ivory card stock and pink patterned paper.

6. Adhere a larger vellum mat to the floral page, then mount the photo onto that
using foam adhesive.

7. Roughly lay out the position of the flowers around the photo and connect them
by twisting the bottom of the wire stem around the next flower's stem. This will
lock them together. Doing this with the flowers in place will help to achieve
perfect placement. Adjust the leaves and flowers as desired and glue the
flowers into place with mini glue dots.

8. Handwrite the child's name and date in a pre-cut journaling block to complete
the page.

# Patchwork garden quilt

Use card stock and stickers to fashion a purse that is three-dimensional
and can be used to hold a removeable journaling card.

**MATERIALS**

plain paper

patterned paper

vellum

ribbon

stickers

gift card

foam adhesive

baby powder

scissors

glue or tape

1. Cut photographs and accent paper into nine equal-sized squares.
Trim the accent paper with sliver stickers and place grass stickers
along the bottom edge of four of the accent paper squares.

2. Place the various puppy stickers onto the squares. Use foam
adhesive to pop a second puppy on top of the first one in the
top two squares. Cut segments of grass and pop them over
the top of the existing grass for greater dimension. The same
technique can be done with the daffodils in the right square
by placing daffodils (with their stems cut off) over the top
of the existing flowers.

3. Pop the baby carriage in the lower left square so that the puppy appears to be
inside the carriage. To create the square with the gate, carefully place a second
gate on the back of the first one. Place the bottles at the top and bottom of the
gate to create hinges. Use baby powder to neutralize the glue on the segment
of bottles that hang over the edge of the gate. Fold the bottles around the edge
of the gate, trimming them slightly.

4. Cut small squares of foam adhesive and attach them to the fold under the
baby bottles.

5. After attaching the gate to the square with the foam adhesive, place the shrubs
and trees, popping them so that the right side of the gate can rest on them
when it is closed.

6. Each 3-D butterfly requires three stickers. Begin with either a blue or yellow
butterfly, and alternate the colors. Attach the right wing of the first butterfly to
the left wing of the second butterfly, and then attach the right wing of the second

butterfly to the left wing of the third butterfly. Attach the 3-D butterfly to the page with the remaining two "unstuck" wings. This will become easier with practice!

7. Attach the squares to the page, alternating them with four photographs of the same size. Place the blank accent paper square in the center after attaching a 4" x 2¼" (10.2 cm x 5.7 cm) vellum pocket to it. Create the pocket by folding in the sides of the vellum ½" (1.3 cm) each and the bottom ¼" (.6 cm) and sliding the gingham square into the pocket.

8. Complete the page by creating the journaling purse. Using a small yellow gift card (or yellow card stock), cut the edges so that they taper in at the top of the card, where the fold is. Attach the ribbon handle with tape or glue, and trim the edges of the purse with stickers. Top it off with a popped dog bone.

9. Trim the inside of the purse with sliver stickers, a butterfly, and a brush and comb to complete the page.

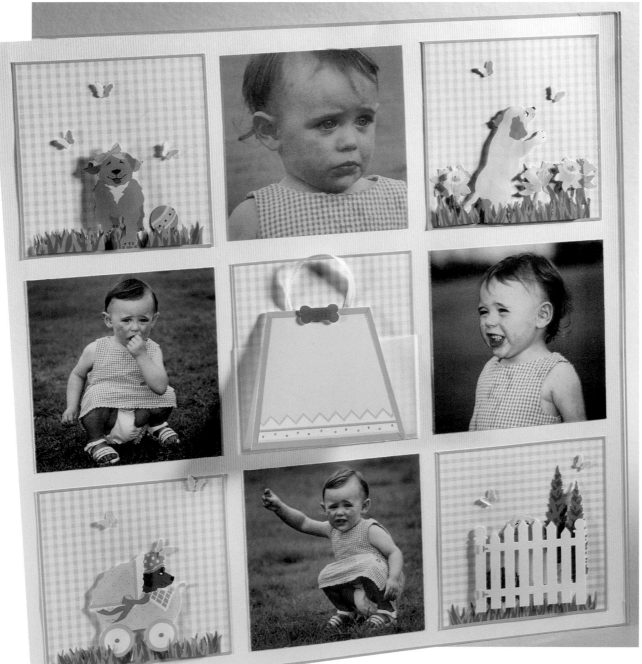

# How long is a girl a child?

Paper quilling is a simple technique that adds dimension and elegance to a scrapbook page.

MATERIALS

patterned paper

card stock

printed frame

adhesive

quilling tool

scalloped
scissors

craft knife

1. Cut along one edge of cream card stock with scalloped scissors. From each scallop, make downward slits in the card stock almost to the bottom edge. Roll these pieces with the quilling tool to make the flowers, spreading petals when finished.

2. From cream card stock strips, create eleven marquise-shaped leaves and sixteen tight circles. (Refer to the Basic Quilling Shapes diagram at left.) Attach a strip of cream card stock to the black card stock as a stem, curving up the page. Attach flowers, leaves, and dots.

3. Mount a strip of black card stock to the left side of the patterned paper background. Cut strips from second patterned paper and apply them to the background.

4. Mount a photo in the frame and mount on the page. Mount a journaling block onto the other piece of black card stock, adding quilled details as desired.

## BASIC QUILLING SHAPES

Tight circle/peg

Loose circle/closed coil

Teardrop

Marquise/eye

Shaped marquise/leaf

Square

Heart/rolled heart/shield

Loose coil scroll

Scroll heart

V scroll

C scroll

S scroll

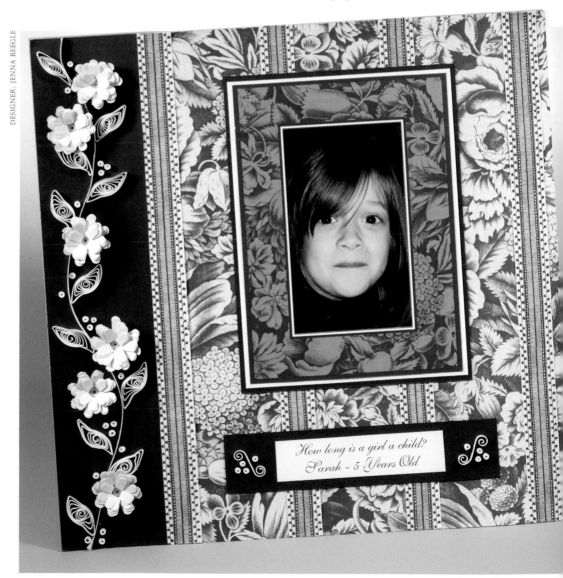

DESIGNER: JENNA BEEGLE

How long is a girl a child?
Sarah - 5 Years Old

DESIGNER: JENNA BEEGLE

# Jenna Carol Johnston

**patterned paper**

**card stock**

**journaling block**

**ribbon photo corners**

**adhesive**

**scissors**

Create a unique border with paper quilled flowers, leaves, and vines.

1. Begin with a 12" x 12" (30.5 cm x 30.5 cm) page of blue gingham paper.

2. Cut a smaller square of patterned paper to sit in the middle of the blue gingham page. Mat that with ivory card stock and attach it to the page.

3. Use blue card stock strips to create thirty-two leaf-shaped pieces for flower petals and thirty-six smaller leaf-shaped pieces for leaves. (Refer to the Basic Quilling Shapes diagram on page 196.) Use cream card stock to create ivory flower centers and mount them on each corner of the page. Add petals to the flowers. Add strips of cream card stock as stems between the flowers; add leaves.

4. Mount a photo using ribbon corners and a small journaling block.

DESIGNER: ANDREA GROSSMAN

# *Antarctica page*

Incorporate multiple photos onto one page with a unique accordion folding technique.

MATERIALS

plain paper

vellum

stickers

black tape

scissors

craft knife

journaling pen

pencil

1. Border one sheet of black cover paper with silver sliver stickers and miter the corners.

2. Using a sheet of lined paper underneath, handwrite journaling onto vellum and, using transparent photo squares, affix a journaling panel to the background paper with an even border all around.

3. To make the foldout, cut four rectangles 4 $\frac{1}{4}$" x 6 $\frac{1}{4}$" (10.8 cm x 15.9 cm) from the additional black papers and tape them together from the back, leaving a sliver of space between so they will fold up. Attach photos.

4. For the cover panel, cut another rectangle of black paper 6 $\frac{1}{4}$" x 4 $\frac{3}{4}$" (15.9 cm x 12.1 cm). Score it $\frac{1}{2}$" (1.3 cm) from the top.

5. From the back, tape the top of the first photo panel and foldout to the bottom edge of the cover panel.

6. Position your foldout on the page, then mark with a pencil at each top corner of the foldout. With a craft knife, cut a line from dot to dot. Slip the top of the foldout through the slit and tape it to the back of the page.

7. Using identical snowflake stickers, stick one on the front bottom edge photo panel in the foldout and one back-to-back on the back of that panel.

8. Mount the journaling panel under the foldout.

# Domo Arigato

Add a touch of ancient times to your page by creating a scroll with paper that has been distressed with water.

1. Stamp the left half of the background paper. Mat onto a slightly larger piece of complementary colored paper.

2. Stamp the title onto a contrasting colored paper. Mat the title onto the background paper and adhere to the page.

3. Journal onto white card stock. Tear the long edges and stamp the fan border with mustard ink over the journaling, stamping off once first to lighten the image.

4. Spray the journaling piece with water and distress the paper. Roll the top and bottom to form a scroll and allow to dry.

5. Trim black pieces to fit behind the fans and the journaling.

6. Crimp the pieces and mount the fans and journaling as shown.

7. Mount the photos onto card stock and adhere to the background page as shown.

DESIGNER: SHELLI GARDNER

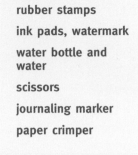

## MATERIALS

plain paper

patterned paper

card stock

foam adhesive

scissors

stylus

plastic spoon

pigment marker

die-cutting machine

alphabet and
wave dies

# 1st dive

Layering die-cuts with foam adhesive adds dimension. Take it one step further and give some shape to the die-cut with paper tolling.

1. Cut various-sized waves from complementary blue papers.

2. To paper tole: Turn a wave to the back side. Using the back of a plastic spoon, rub from the center out across the entire surface. The paper will begin to curl. Then trace the outline of the paper shape with a stylus. Repeat this for each wave.

3. Layer and arrange the waves with foam adhesive.

4. For the title, die-cut letters and numbers. Use foam adhesive to lift alternate letters. Outline some letters with a pigment marker to make letters stand out against the background.

5. Silhouette and mat photos, and then adhere. Journal as desired.

The kids were naturals. We swam with fish, stingrays and dolphins!

DISCOVERY COVE · AUG 2001

# Analisa

Create multidimensional scrapbook pages with foam adhesive that help images or elements pop out from the background.

1. Cut a strip of turquoise paper and place it across the top of a red 12" x 12" (30.5 cm x 30.5 cm) scrapbook page.

2. Using a paper trimmer, cut ½" (1.3 cm) strips of gold and yellow paper. Arrange the strips on the page, alternating each color. Vary the height of each strip by adding foam adhesive.

3. Cut a photograph into ½" (1.3 cm) strips like the gold and yellow paper. Place a strip of picture onto each yellow piece of paper.

4. Hang an eyelet letter from the strips of yellow paper to spell out a name. Attach the letters with thread and heart stickers.

5. Die-cut the teeth out of white and cream paper. Cut away detail and layer to create shading.

6. Double-mat a journaling rectangle and place it on the page at a diagonal. Attach the finished teeth to the corner of the rectangle.

## MATERIALS

plain paper

embroidery floss

stickers

adhesive

foam adhesive

eyelet setting tool and eyelet letters

pre-cut die-cuts or die-cutting machine and dies

paper trimmer

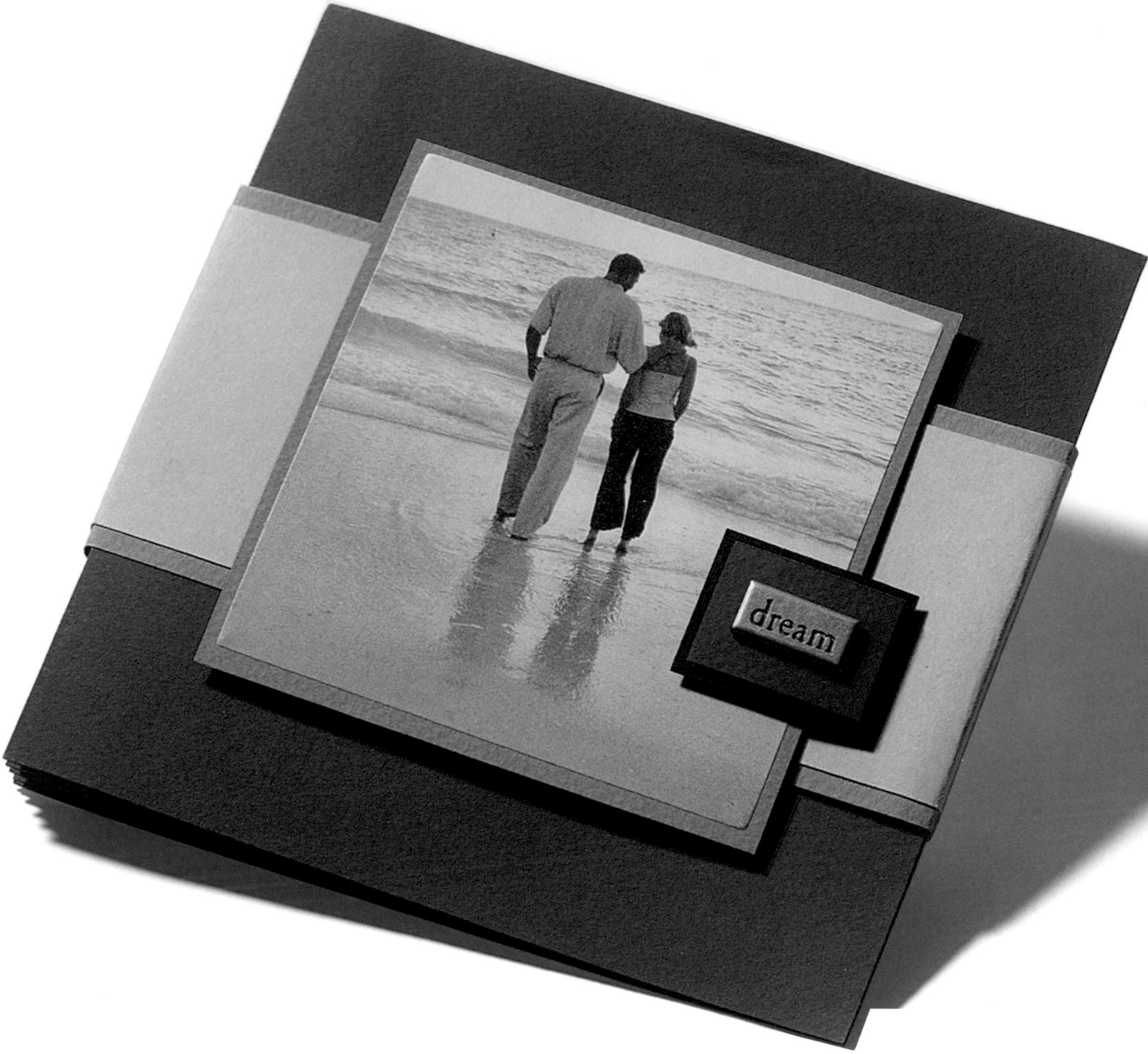

## MATERIALS

plain paper

zebra paper

ribbon

stickers

silver charm

adhesive

foam adhesive

silver pen

eyelet word

eyelet setting tool

pre-cut die-cuts
or die-cutting
machine and dies

# Tag along mini memory book

The accordion pleats in this mini book create a wonderful dimensionality even before the addition of ribbon and metal charms. When the album is closed, all the tags sit up; but as the album is opened, the tags form a crisscrossing pattern.

1. Cut a red strip of paper 6" x 17" (15.2 cm x 43.2 cm).

2. Accordion fold the middle section into four evenly spaced pleats, allowing 6" (15.2 cm) on each end for the front and back covers.

3. Line the inside front and back cover with zebra paper (allow a slight edge of red to show all around). Mat a photo and a journaling panel and center them inside each front and back inside cover.

4. Die-cut twelve black tags and thread a red ribbon through each tag hole.

5. Attach the first four tags onto the front side of each pleat. Attach the middle row of tags onto the back side of each pleat. Attach the final four tags onto the front side of each pleat. There should be a slight gap between each row of tags allowing the tags to form a crisscrossing pattern when the album is opened.

6. Decorate each tag with photos, die-cuts, stickers, and journaling (with a silver pen). Three-dimensional embellishments, such as a silver heart charm, can be added where desired.

7. Mat the title of the album and attach it to the front cover.

8. Create a long strip of matted paper to wrap around the album using a double fold on the sides to accommodate the width of the mini book. Overlap the strip in back and glue together to form a band that slides over the album to hold it closed.

9. Decorate the slider with a matted photo and matted eyelet word that is raised with foam adhesive to complete the mini book.

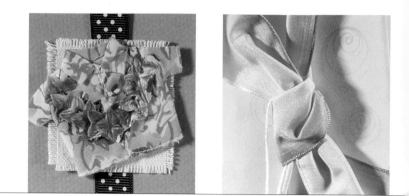

# Fabric

## DECORATING WITH RIBBONS, FIBER, BUTTONS, TRIMS, AND NOTIONS

More and more, the crafting lines are becoming blurred. Quilters are adding photographs to their heirloom-quality creations, and scrapbookers who flunked home economics in high school are now roaming the aisles at the local fabric store. As our page embellishments become more diverse, we are learning surprising new skills—such as threading a needle! Fabrics and notions are softer, gentler embellishments, and often give pages a homey, comfortable quality.

Working with notions can be as simple as gluing buttons onto a page, or as intricate as stitching a pocket or border directly onto the page. Small, portable sewing machines or hand-held machines are inexpensive and ideal for creating simple, basic stitches onto small page embellishments. I love working with beautiful ribbons—an elegant ribbon that matches the background paper makes a lovely addition to a wedding or baby page. Other notions, such

as lace, yarn, rickrack, twisted paper yarn, and raffia, make wonderful embellishments. Use fiber to create laces on die-cut shoes or to hang decorative elements, such as tags or charms.

Fabric can be used in place of patterned paper—it provides nice dimension without a lot of bulk. It's also fun to match fabric to an item of clothing that someone is wearing in a photograph. Most die-cutting machines will cut fabric and felt nicely so you can stitch titles and shapes onto your pages or cut out paper doll clothes for a realistic touch. Spray adhesive works well when adhering fabric to a page, and you can also run fabric through an adhesive machine to make it self-adhesive. Whether you stitch or glue it on, fabric and notions will liven up your pages and provide soft, subtle dimension.

# Favorite things

Combine lots of photos that feature several different events with a theme, such as favorite things. All photos don't need to be scrapbooked chronologically. Page titles like "Favorite Things" can encompass photos that cover several years. If you are overwhelmed with tons of photos, this is a great way to start.

## MATERIALS

patterned paper

card stock

ribbon

tag

adhesive

eyelet

eyelet
setting tool

paper punch

personal
computer

1. Punch photos into equal-sized squares and roughly lay out the photos, but do not attach them to the page.

2. Print journaling onto the background page.

3. Adhere photos onto the background page and mat onto a slightly larger contrasting colored paper.

4. Place the matted photos layout onto a larger piece of background paper in a coordinating color and pattern.

5. Tie a ribbon vertically along the left edge of the background paper to create a border and to support the title tag.

6. Place an eyelet through the hole in the tag and tie into the ribbon.

# Elena and Nick's wedding day

Don't forget to check the upholstery section of your favorite fabric store when hunting for scrapbook embellishments. Decorative cording provides a distinctive and textural way to frame a picture.

1. Cut foam core into a 10" (25.4 cm) square block. Cut another square from the center, leaving 2" (5 cm) on all sides. The opening will be 8" (20.3 cm) square. Cut a scrap of foam core to the size of the photo and mount the photo onto it.

2. Add patterned paper to the foam core, cutting it to fit.

3. On the back of the foam core, add double-sided tape. Apply cording to the inside and outside edges of the foam core. Be sure to apply cording with the flange on the underside of the cording. On the outside edge, the flange will want to double onto itself at the corners; trim the overlap. On the inside edges, add a slit in the flange at the corner to allow the cording to bend smoothly around the corner. Be sure to keep the cording smooth and even by checking how it looks from the front.

4. Mount a 9" (22.9 cm) square of patterned paper onto the center of the coordinating patterned paper. Mount the foam core square over that, centering it on the page.

5. Cut Vs in the ends of the ribbon. Fold the edges to pleat as shown. (This is much easier with wire-edged ribbon.)

6. Mount the ribbon onto the page. Mount the journaling block onto the ribbon, and then mount the photo to the center of the page.

DESIGNER: JENNA BEEGLE

## MATERIALS

patterned paper

ribbon

decorative cording

journaling block

foam core

double-sided tape

craft knife

## MATERIALS

- embroidery floss
- plain paper
- die-cut tags
- rubber stamps
- ink pads
- eyelets
- eyelet setting tool
- embroidery needle
- paper punches
- journaling marker
- pencil

# Home for the holidays

Hand embroidering a title on a scrapbook page adds a homey feeling to a holiday page.

1. Use a pencil to write the word "home" in cursive. Use an embroidery needle to punch holes in the pattern over the word and embroider the greeting.

2. Stamp the words "for the" and "holidays" using red ink.

3. Create the tags for the page by stamping a small Christmas tree on each of the tags.

4. Layer the tags onto card stock and secure them with eyelets.

5. Add additional embellishments to the tags using paper-punched stars, buttons, and embroidery floss.

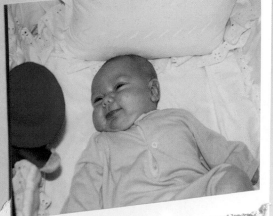

Who would Sarah give her first smile to? Would it be her beloved brother? Would it be her adoring mother? Would it be the father she had wrapped around her little finger?

FIRST SMILE

One day when Sarah was about four weeks old, I heard her cooing for the first time. I snuck into her room, camera in tow, just in time to catch her smiling and talking to Paddington Bear! It was her first real smile!

# First smile

Multicolored letter beads strung from fiber make charming titles for scrapbook pages.

1. Print journaling on the upper left of the background paper and the lower right of the foreground paper.

2. Tear the foreground paper on the diagonal and place it over a portion of the background paper, making sure the journaling on both the background and foreground pages is visible.

3. Unravel a piece of acid-free twisted paper yarn, flatten it, and glue it down. Thread a coordinating color of fiber through various-sized buttons, knot the fiber, and glue the buttons down.

4. String multi-colored letter beads from coordinating fiber across the center of the page to draw the eye to both pictures.

5. Place three squares on the bottom to balance the layout and attach them to the page with tiny eyelets to keep the square from appearing ordinary.

## MATERIALS

plain paper

acid-free twisted paper yarn

fiber

buttons

letter beads

glue

eyelets

eyelet setting tool

personal computer

## MATERIALS

- plain paper
- canvas fabric
- ribbon
- 3-D stickers
- adhesive
- foam adhesive
- scissors
- pen
- eyelet letters
- eyelet setting tool
- die-cutting machine

# Cancun

Enhance a scrapbook page with 3-D stickers that offer intricate detail featuring fabric, beads, foil, and more.

1. Start with turquoise and green 12" x 12" (30.5 cm x 30.5 cm) sheets of paper. Cut down the green paper and attach it to the turquoise along the right side of the page, leaving a small strip of turquoise exposed.

2. Run a piece of black-and-white dotted ribbon down the left side of the page. Attach the loose ends of the ribbon to the back of the page using tape.

3. Die-cut three squares out of canvas fabric. Fray the edges of each square and attach them, evenly spaced out, over the black-and-white ribbon. Add 3-D stickers to each fabric square.

4. Triple-mat each photograph using two shades of turquoise and black paper.

5. Arrange the photos on the green paper and add a journaling panel raised with foam adhesive for dimension.

6. Attach eyelet letters over two shades of turquoise paper to create a title for the page.

# What Sarah is doing at seven months

Fasten a bow to a page with Velcro, allowing the viewer to lift the bow and reveal the handwritten journaling behind the photo.

1. Cut three of the patterned papers to make quadrants on the other patterned paper and mount them.

2. Mount ribbon on the page between the quadrants.

3. Adhere a photo onto the card stock with ribbon corners.

4. Cut another piece of card stock the same width as the photo, but twice as long. Score it, fold it in half, and journal.

5. With the long piece of card stock closed, and the fold at the bottom, mount the photo to the folded card stock, sandwiching the tail of the hanging ribbon between the papers in the center. About 1" (2.5 cm) of ribbon and the bow will hang out at the top.

6. Mount this to the page, carefully lining up the bow with the ribbon on the page. Add a piece of Velcro to the back of the bow and to the ribbon on the page. Now, the Velcro will keep the card closed, but it can be opened by lifting the ribbon.

7. Add buttons with mini glue dots.

## MATERIALS

patterned paper

ivory card stock

blue ribbon

blue bow

blue ribbon corners

ribbon

buttons, various sizes

adhesive

mini glue dots

Velcro

scissors

journaling pen

paper trimmer

## MATERIALS

card stock

corrugated paper

vellum

ribbon

metal charm

adhesive

rubber stamps

ink pad

scissors

eyelets and
eyelet setting tool

paper punch

personal computer

# Mimi & me

Corrugated paper combined with ribbon and
charms can help add dimension to a special photo.

1. Tear a strip of red paper vertically to create a border.

2. Punch photos using a square punch to create an accent border.

3. Cut corrugated paper lengthwise to create a visual stand on which the
   focus photo can rest. Wrap corrugated paper with coordinating ribbon,
   threading the charm through the ribbon before tying. Adhere the ribbon
   to the page.

4. Mat the photo onto card stock and then again onto the corrugated paper.

5. Punch a heart out of card stock.

6. Adhere a vellum subtitle over the heart using eyelets.

7. Stamp the title.

# Charles Augustus Melville

Distinctive elegance is achieved on this heritage page by weaving ribbon through the background paper. Varying the width of the ribbon enhances the beauty.

1. Trim a sheet of background paper to 11 ½" x 11 ½" (29.2 cm x 29.2 cm).

2. Working on the back sides, determine the ribbon placement and lightly draw in ribbon outlines. Using a ruler for accurate placement, determine slits for the ribbon to weave through the paper. The slits are made in the same places for all four sides and for both sides of the ribbon. Cut slits with a craft knife.

3. Cut ribbon slightly more than 12" (30.5 cm) in length. This will allow extra ribbon in case it frays as it is woven. Weave the ribbon through the slits.

4. Use glue to hold the ends, adding a tiny bit of glue to the edge of the ribbon to prevent fraying.

5. Allow the ends of the narrow ribbon to extend beyond the edge of the paper.

6. Mount the paper by weaving it onto a second sheet of patterned paper. Adhere ribbon ends to that page.

7. Add a square of patterned vellum to the center of the page with ribbon corners. Trim the ribbon corners so that the underside does not show through the vellum.

8. Mount the photo and a journaling block.

MATERIALS

plain paper

patterned paper

vellum

ribbon

ribbon corners

glue

scissors

craft knife

ruler

personal computer

DESIGNER: JENNA BEEGLE

# Pocket-full of treasure

Use denim on a scrapbook page and add new meaning to
"Jeanealogy!" Turn a pair of worn-out jeans into a page by filling
the pocket with photos, journaling, or treasured souvenirs.

1. Die-cut a button cover out of the corner of the pocket of a denim square.

2. Mount the denim squares onto a piece of card stock using star eyelets
   and snaps.

3. Accent the layout with narrow strip stickers in the corners.

4. Fold the denim paper into thirds and make a photo booklet by adhering
   the first two "pages" with snaps.

5. Insert the booklet into the pocket and adhere stickers.

6. Record a message on the audio recording device and cover with the denim
   die-cut button cover. Adhere the audio recording device with glue dots.

Lindsay Spero began babysitting McKenna and Payton in July of 2002 while Mommy would leave to teach her scrapbooking classes. I knew from the moment she interacted with the girls she would be terrific. So when I saw them sitting in McKenna's closet playing with the tub full of toys, I couldn't resist snapping this photo.

Miss Lindsay

DESIGNER: DONNA DOWNEY

# Miss Lindsay

Using light colors with black-and-white photos creates visual interest on a page. A strip of ribbon across the page can soften the seam where the two papers meet.

1. Layer a piece of contrasting colored card stock over the bottom half of the background paper after printing the journaling on the computer.
2. Obscure the seam by covering it with a strip of ribbon.
3. Tie a separate ribbon bow and slide onto the ribbon strip.
4. Thread a tag through the bow's knot with embroidery floss.
5. Mat a photo in black.
6. To create a perfect bow that sits straight, tie the bow onto the ribbon strip after creating the bow.

**MATERIALS**

card stock

ribbon

embroidery floss

tag

adhesive

personal computer

Miss Lindsay

DESIGNER: CARA MARIANO

## MATERIALS

plain paper

patterned paper

ribbon

gold press-on numbers

foam adhesive

glue dots

tape

scissors

die-cutting machine and dies

personal computer

# Megan's sugar plum wishes

Ribbon comes in a large variety of colors and patterns, and it is a simple way to add texture and dimension to a scrapbook page.

1. Out of two shades of green paper, cut two rectangles—one slightly smaller than the other but the same width as the background page. Layer the two rectangles and position them at the top of the page to create a border.

2. Layer two different red ribbons over the green border. Attach the loose ends on the back of the scrapbook page using tape. Finish the border by adding a bow in the center.

3. Crop and mat a photograph as well as a title bar printed on the computer.

4. Die-cut gifts out of plain and patterned paper. Complete the gifts by adding red and green ribbon to each gift.

5. Attach the gifts along the bottom of the page. Use foam adhesive to create dimension.

6. Finish the page by adding a date with press-on numbers at the bottom of the green border.

The letter in the image reads:

> dear santa,
> define good.

The journaling block reads:

> It's the same story every year: Ashley always hems and haws about going to see Santa, but once we get there, she's thrilled to sit on his lap and tell him what she wants. Sarah, on the other hand, is always eager to see him BEFORE we got there, but when she finally gets on his lap, she's a little intimidated. This year she was actually stunned into silence!
> Ashley, 9 and Sarah, 3

# Dear Santa, define good

Decorate the seam where two textured papers meet with a little glue and glitter. Popping up parts of your layout really makes it stand out!

1. Place a die-cut tree on the bottom corner of paper and adorn with sequins for ornaments.

2. Place glue dots and silver glitter at random intervals near the top of the page.

3. Single-mat the photograph and adhere to the background paper. Place "Dear Santa" letter on the background paper, barely overlapping onto the photograph.

4. Place a journaling block below the photograph and adhere to the page with eyelets.

5. Choose coordinating paper and embellishments to create gifts.

6. Adhere gifts to the page, raising with foam adhesive for added dimension.

## MATERIALS

patterned paper

journaling block

die-cuts

glitter

adhesive

foam adhesive

glue dots

eyelets

eyelet setting tool

personal computer

# Model extraordinaire

Sheer fabric accents are a perfect complement to translucent vellum.
Fabric flowers can be strategically placed to hide the vellum adhesive.

1. Select a background paper that coordinates with the colors in your photographs.

2. Evenly space photos on a solid band of coordinating colored card stock and place the band across the center of the layout.

3. Print the title on vellum, and then chalk and place at an angle to give a little dimension. Fasten fabric flowers on the ends of the title block to hide the glue spots under the vellum.

4. Select a few choice words that depict the moods of the child in the pictures and print the words on vellum.

5. Cut the words into circles and place them in round tags.

6. Punch a hole and string fiber through the holes to draw them together for a smooth flow.

## MATERIALS

**plain paper**

**card stock**

**vellum**

**fiber**

**tags**

**flowers**

**glue**

**scissors**

**chalk**

**hole punch**

**personal computer**

# A star is born

Color blocking is a wonderful way to highlight a special photograph. The simple use of two colors adds subtle style to the page. Connect the color blocked squares with ribbon.

MATERIALS

**plain paper**

**vellum**

**ribbon**

**journaling block**

**letter stickers**

**adhesive**

**scissors**

**eyelets and eyelet setting tool**

**personal computer**

1. Select two contrasting colors for the overall page layout.

2. Use the darker of the two colors for the background page, and then cut two squares, each equaling one-fourth the size of the background paper. On this page, the artist used 12" x 12" (30.5 cm x 30.5 cm) paper, so the contrasting squares are each 6" x 6" (15.2 cm x 15.2 cm).

3. Diagonally place the light squares onto the dark background page.

4. Hand-cut four stars—two dark and two light. Place one of the light stars near the top of the dark paper and fasten it to the page with a dark eyelet. Repeat this process for the right side of the page, using the opposite colors.

5. Place a dark star at the center of the page so that it lays half on the light side and half on the dark side. Cut the remaining light star in half (roughly) and set the light half on top of the dark half.

6. Anchor a ribbon on the center star and tuck the ribbon through each of the eyelets.

7. Place a photograph onto the background paper. Placing the photograph slightly off center adds more visual interest to the page.

8. Print journaling onto a sheet of vellum, tear the edges, and adhere the journaling block to the page.

9. Create the title from letter stickers and place above the stars.

DESIGNER: KELLY JONES

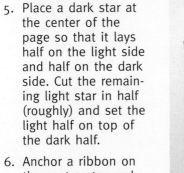

card stock

vellum

fiber

vellum bubble
stickers

liquid glaze

embossing powder

adhesive

rubber stamp

ink pad

watermark pen

chalk

eyelets and eyelet
setting tool

heat tool

hole punch

personal computer

# One fish, two fish, red fish, blue fish

Combine heat embossing with liquid glaze to create a dimensional title that is sure to make a big splash.

1. Print the page title on card stock and chalk inside the letters as desired. On top of the chalk, use a watermark pen and sprinkle embossing powder over the watermarked areas. Use a heat tool to emboss the letters.

2. Do a second layer of embossing by using liquid glaze over the paper to make the embossing powder bubble up and resemble water.

3. Tear three pieces of card stock horizontally in colors that are similar to the ones in the photograph.

4. Chalk the card stock as desired and place onto the background page. Stamp a few images along the bottom layer that coordinate with the images in the photograph.

5. Mount the photograph onto card stock, punch a hole in two corners, and thread the holes with several pieces of fiber that are knotted at the top to make it appear as if the picture is hanging.

6. Print the journaling on vellum and tack it down on the card stock at an angle. Then anchor the journaling into place with a vellum bubble sticker.

DESIGNER: KELLY JONES

Ashley got 'Fishy' for Valentines Day and absolutely loves her! Feeding her is funny because she swims around wildly in her tank snatching at the food. This is one of the best pets we have ever had (certainly one of the quietest and cleanest!) Feb. 2002

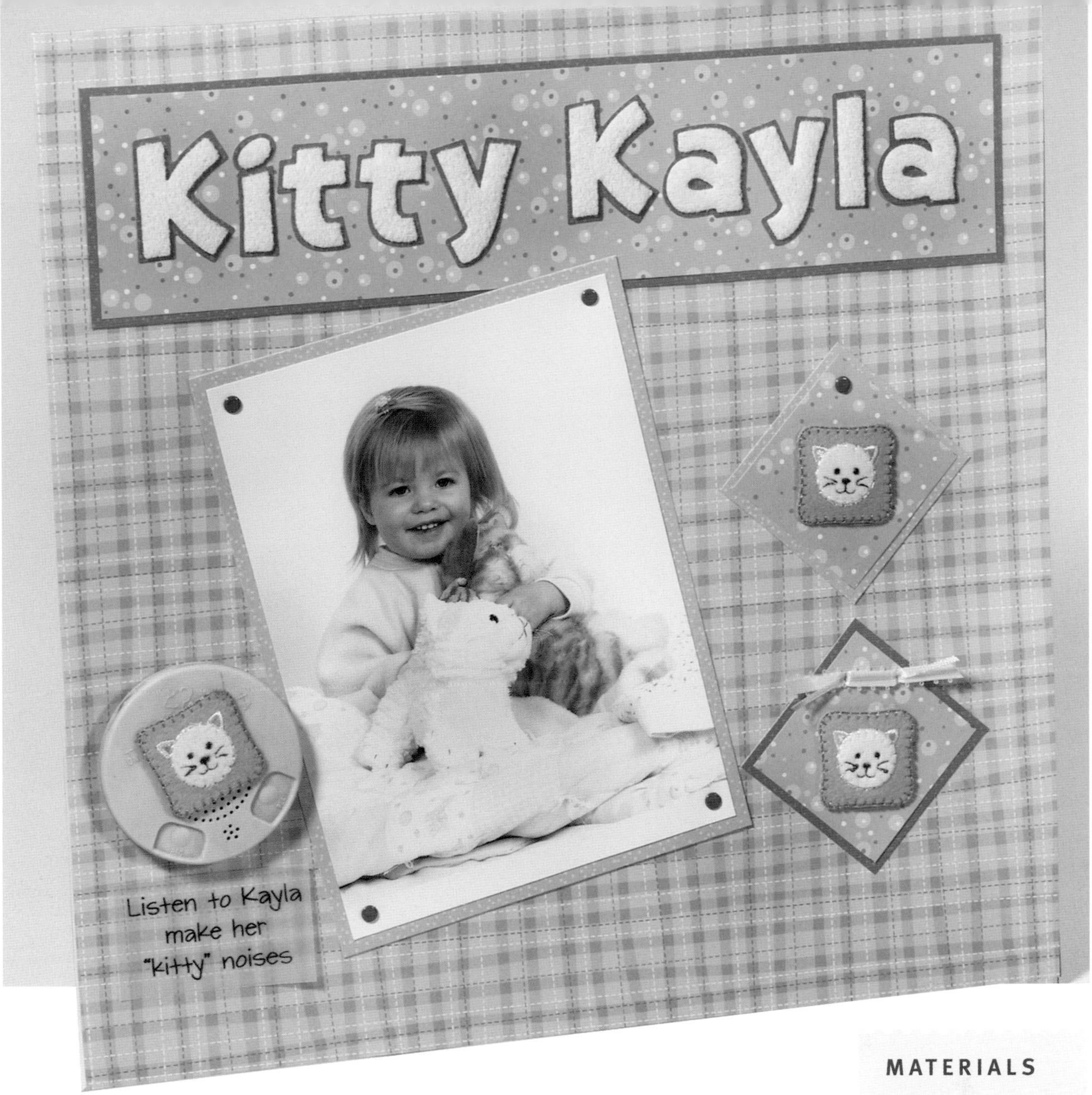

Kitty Kayla
Listen to Kayla make her "kitty" noises

DESIGNER: CAROL RICE

# Kitty Kayla

Record a child's voice on an audio recording device and make scrapbook pages come alive with sound.

1. Die-cut the title, mount it onto the background paper, and make a title box.
2. Adhere the box to the background page.
3. Mount and attach the photographs with snaps.
4. Make accent boxes using snaps or ribbon and apply patches in a coordinating theme.
5. Paint the audio recording device using a sponge applicator and an archival stamp pad.
6. Record a message on the audio recording device and decorate it with a kitty patch. Adhere the kitty patch to the audio recording device with glue dots.
7. Print text squares on vellum and adhere them to the page with spray adhesive.

**MATERIALS**

- plain paper
- patterned paper
- vellum
- small fabric patches
- ribbon
- snaps
- audio recording device, such as the Memory Button
- spray adhesive
- glue dots
- sponge applicator
- archival ink pad
- die-cutting machine and dies
- personal computer

Summer Fun

98

John Thomas (J.T.)

Karen & Noa

Maddie

Robert

# Summer fun keepsake box

A gift box is the perfect place to store photos from a particular event or occasion. Whether the box is die-cut or recycled from a previous birthday, it is decorated using the same tools and supplies as a scrapbook page. Connecting the lid and the photos with ribbon creates a 3-D display the moment the lid is lifted. Leave the box out for visitors to view and kiss your coffee-table books goodbye!

**MATERIALS**

plain paper or card stock

ribbon

sun die-cuts

foam adhesive

double-sided tape

eyelet numbers

eyelet punch

hammer

die-cutting machine and dies

1. Die-cut a box that will accommodate the size of your photos. The placement of the box decorations will be dictated by whether the photos are horizontal or vertical.

2. Poke a hole in the center of the box lid with an eyelet punch. Thread ribbon through the hole, taping one end to the top of the lid and leaving the remainder of the ribbon long enough to position all of your photos. (Half of the photos are on one side and half are on the back side.)

3. Decorate the box top with a colored band, the title, and eyelet numbers to designate the year. The sun die-cut is raised with foam adhesive. The colored band will effectively cover the hole and the ribbon.

4. Mat each photo on larger paper, leaving room to label each one. One paper can be left without a photo for journaling.

5. The matted photos are sandwiched together in pairs with a ribbon in the middle, leaving almost 1" (2.5 cm) of ribbon exposed in between to allow accordion folding of the photos.

6. Accordion fold the photos and place them inside the box so that when the lid is lifted the photos will begin to lift out of the box.

DESIGNER: SANDI GENOVESE

## Metal

### WORKING WITH WIRE, EYELETS, FOIL, SNAPS, MESH, CHARMS, AND CHAIN

It sounds unbelievable, doesn't it? Adhering metal objects onto paper that you intend to last for generations. Well, applied correctly, small metal objects won't cause any harm to your pages; but they will add sparkle to your layouts and functionality to your design elements. Best of all, many manufacturers have taken extra measures to make metal embellishments scrapbook-friendly.

Eyelets have become a new staple in scrapbook supplies. They not only add a decorative touch, but they also are used to attach items such as tags and labels to a page. I like to use them to dangle die-cuts and charms from ribbon, which adds movement to pages. Eyelets are available in all sorts of colors, shapes, and sizes. You need a hole punch, an eyelet setter, and a hammer to attach some brands, while others simply snap onto your page. Brads offer a similar functionality and flair.

Gold and silver beaded metal chain, which has been commonly used on key rings, is one of my favorite metal embellishments. I use it to outline die-cuts, photos, or mats, and it's amazing how much vibrancy and pop it adds to my pages. It is particularly striking when used against black background paper. Wire is another fun material to add to your pages, and it comes in a range of colors and gauges. Wrap it around letters or die-cuts or form it into curvaceous borders.

Foils, charms, metal tags, snaps, mesh, washers, paper clips—you name it. The most utilitarian household item can become a dazzling scrapbook embellishment. If you use the appropriate adhesive and keep an eye out for sharp edges, your heavy metal pages should offer long-lasting glimmer and enjoyment.

DESIGNER: JULIE LARSEN

# Girlfriends

## MATERIALS

card stock

vellum

satin ribbon

charm photo
corners

charm frames

metal words

adhesive

medium
glue dots

eyelet words
and eyelet
setting tool

Some metallic embellishments look like pewter and are perfect to enhance black-and-white photos. When adding ribbon to a layout, it's fun to attach it so that it looks loose and free.

1. Trim purple card stock $\frac{1}{8}$" (3 mm) on all sides and adhere to maize card stock.

2. Trim vellum $\frac{3}{4}$" (1.9 cm) larger than the large photo on the right side of the page.

3. Trim maize card stock $\frac{1}{8}$" (3 mm) larger than vellum and mat behind the vellum.

4. Adhere the large photo to the vellum.

5. Adhere photo corners to the corners of the vellum using glue dots.

6. Cut small pictures to fit three charm frames and place them inside the frames.

7. Using satin ribbon behind them, arrange the frames at the bottom of the page with glue dots to adhere the frames to the ribbon.

8. Trim three small pieces of vellum matting on maize card stock trimmed $\frac{1}{16}$" (1.5 mm) larger than vellum.

9. Set three eyelet words to each matted piece of vellum.

10. Adhere metal "girlfriends" word with small glue dots at an angle in the left corner of the page.

11. Place the eyelet words—one beneath another—below "girlfriends."

# Camp Arrowhead

Create hand-looped photo holders from wire to embrace vintage photographs.

1. Mount an 11" x 11" (27.9 cm x 27.9 cm) square of patterned paper onto black background paper.

2. Layer a 10" x 10" (25.4 cm x 25.4 cm) square of vellum and four strips of black stripe, wrapping the strips around to the back of the background page.

3. Make the bottom ribbon with a 2" (5 cm) strip of green patterned paper, two black ribbon strips, and two $\frac{1}{2}$" (1.3 cm) strips of floral patterned paper.

4. Form small loops at the ends of 8" (20.3 cm) of 20-gauge wire. Wrap around a 1" (2.5 cm) circular item to form the holder.

5. Mount the pictures in die-cut frames and mat them in green and black paper.

**MATERIALS**

plain paper

patterned paper

vellum

20-gauge wire

die-cut frames

adhesive

paper trimmer

DESIGNER: JENNIFER MASON

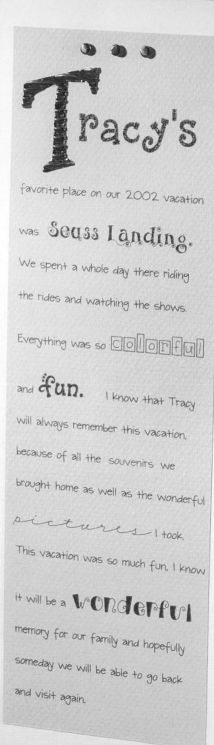

# Tracy's

favorite place on our 2002 vacation was **Seuss Landing.**

We spent a whole day there riding the rides and watching the shows.

Everything was so colorful and **fun.** I know that Tracy will always remember this vacation, because of all the souvenirs we brought home as well as the wonderful pictures I took. This vacation was so much fun, I know it will be a **wonderful** memory for our family and hopefully someday we will be able to go back and visit again.

## Seuss Landing

# Seuss Landing

Decorative foil is a lightweight, soft, pliable metal, which is easy to cut and use to add texture. Combine it with a photograph to add a special gleam to any scrapbook page.

1. Start with a yellow 12" x 12" (30.5 cm x 30.5 cm) background page.

2. Die-cut the first letter of the person's name out of red decorative foil. Run the letter through a crimper to get a wavy texture.

3. On the computer, print out a story for the page. The top of the story should be the person's name, but make sure to leave off the first letter—it will be replaced with the one made of foil.

4. Place the finished journaling panel on the far left side of the page. Add three red brads to the top of the panel. Punch holes out of red decorative foil the same size as the brads and attach the circles onto the brads.

5. Double-mat a photograph in two shades of red paper and attach to the page.

6. Die-cut three squares out of blue decorative foil. Turn the foil squares over and place them on a soft surface like a mouse pad. Take a stylus tool and create a decorative design in the foil. When the squares are turned over, they will look embossed.

7. Attach the three finished squares under the picture using foam adhesive to create dimension.

8. Hand-cut three wavy designs. Run the cut pieces through a crimper to create texture. Attach the waves at the bottom of the page. Place three brads underneath each wave. Add foil circles over each brad.

9. On the computer, print out a title and mat it using two shades of red paper.

DESIGNER: CARA MARIANO

## MATERIALS

plain paper

patterned paper

decorative foil

brads

adhesive

foam adhesive

scissors

stylus

paper crimper

paper punches

die-cutting machine and dies

personal computer

## MATERIALS

card stock

24-gauge wire, nontarnish silver

beads

nail heads

adhesive

paper crimper

paper trimmer

die-cutting machine and dies

# Kirstin at the park

Dimension is fundamental with the addition of wire to a scrapbook page. Bend it, twist it, and crimp it for various looks.

1. Add the beads to the wire. Bend and twist the wire to spell out the title.
2. Adhere the title card stock and add nail heads for dots on the letters.
3. Mat the photographs.
4. Die-cut three tags in contrasting colors of card stock.
5. Bend the wire to form flower petals and adhere to the card stock with nail heads.
6. Crimp the wire and thread it through the tags. Adhere the tags to the page.

# Our family Christmas

Combine upper and lower case letters to spell out page titles for a less symmetrical look. Colored eyelets are a nice touch when combined with silver-colored metal frames.

1. Trim striped paper ¼" (6 mm) on all sides.

2. Don't adhere to the hunter green card stock until the eyelet word "family" has been set.

3. Triple-mat a family photo on celery green, hunter, and off-white card stock.

4. Trim 1 ½" (3.8 cm) squares from celery card stock and mat on brick red card stock, tearing around all edges of the brick card stock.

5. Using a small glue dot, adhere holiday charms on each of the four squares.

6. Using two glue dots on each letter to spell "our," center the alphabet charms in the upper center of the page.

7. Set the eyelet word "family" under "our" through the back of the striped paper. Adhere the striped paper to the hunter paper, creating a mat.

8. Place a family photo in the center.

9. Back the tag with hunter card stock and set four eyelets in each corner of the tag (through the card stock).

10. Set the words "Merry Christmas" eyelet in the middle of the tag on hunter card stock.

11. Adhere the completed tag with glue dots.

DESIGNER: JULIE LARSEN

## MATERIALS

striped paper

card stock

alphabet charms

metal words

glue dots

eyelet words and eyelet setting tool

## MATERIALS

- plain paper
- decorative foil
- decorative wood frames
- wire
- die-cuts
- adhesive
- foam adhesive
- alphabet letter stamps
- ink pads
- craft knife
- silver pen
- hole punch
- die-cutting machine and dies
- personal computer

# Amanda and Dennis

Decorative wooden frames painted with gold metallic paint add an elegant touch to festive photographs for a memorable holiday page.

1. Start with a red 12" x 12" (30.5 cm x 30.5 cm) paper for the background.

2. Crop photos to fit inside decorative frames. Make small wire rings to connect the frames together. Punch holes in each picture and attach wire rings.

3. Die-cut ornaments out of decorative green and gold foil. With a craft knife, cut away detail.

4. Connect all the frames and the ornament together with gold wire rings and attach them to the left side of the scrapbook page.

5. Die-cut holly out of three shades of green paper. Add detail to each holly leaf with a silver pen.

6. Double mat a photograph with green and metallic gold paper. Arrange the picture on the page. Attach the holly leaves around the picture and the page. Use foam adhesive to add dimension.

7. On the computer, create a journaling block on metallic gold paper. Add completed holly leaves on the bottom corner.

8. Create a title with alphabet letter stamps and holly stickers.

DESIGNER: CARA MARIANO

One of Landon's Easter eggs from Grandma and Grandpa promised him a trip to the zoo, so Memorial Day weekend we decided to call them on it. We all made the 3 hour drive to the closest zoo in St. Louis. The kids really enjoyed seeing all of the animals and our family had a great time together.

# Zoo

Go a little wild when selecting dimensional elements for your scrapbook pages. The wire elephant on this page is actually a paper clip found at an import store.

1. Crop photographs into six equal squares and mount them onto solid-colored card stock.
2. Cut a hole in another piece of card stock and use foam adhesive to set mounted pictures behind it to create an inset window.
3. Use fiber to thread through a dated bookplate and foam adhesive to hold it in place.
4. Stitch an elephant paper clip to the page using embroidery floss and use the clip to hold the journaling block in place.

## MATERIALS

**card stock**

**fiber**

**embroidery floss**

**bookplate**

**journaling block**

**elephant paper clip**

**foam adhesive**

**glue dots**

**tape**

**scissors**

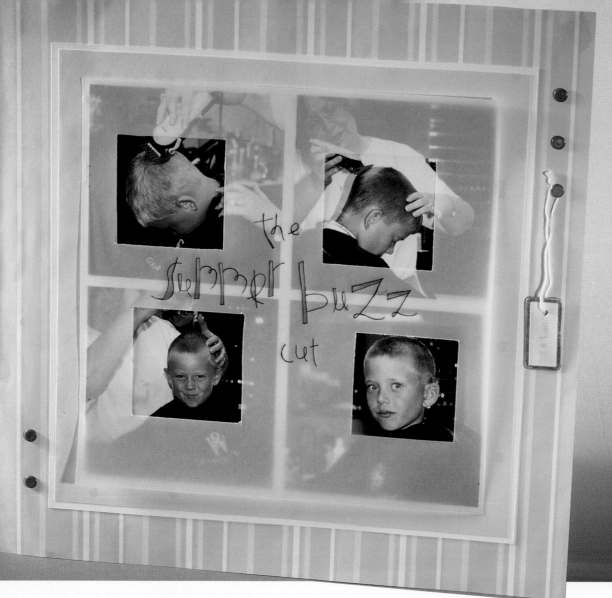

## MATERIALS

patterned paper

card stock

vellum

ribbon

tag

snaps

vellum adhesive

date stamp

ink pad

craft knife

pencil

colored pencils

paper punch

personal computer

# The summer buzz cut

Cut squares out of plain vellum paper and fasten over the top of photos creating "see-through" mats that focus your attention on the subject of the photos.

1. Crop photos and center them on polka-dotted background paper. Mount the polka-dotted page onto a contrasting colored solid page.

2. Place the single-matted layout onto a larger striped piece of paper.

3. Cut vellum slightly larger than the photos. Place the vellum over the pictures so that there is a small border extending beyond the photos.

4. Punch a square out of scrap vellum. Place the square over the desired window and trace it with a pencil. Cut out the windows using a craft knife.

5. Practice writing a freehand title on plain computer paper. When the desired look is achieved, trace it onto vellum and shade in using colored pencils.

6. Adhere the vellum over the photographs with vellum adhesive.

7. Stamp a small tag with a date that relates to the photographs.

8. Add snaps to the layout, using one of the snaps to hold the date-stamped tag in place.

# Siblings

Combine the straight edges of photographs and wire mesh with the torn edges of vellum for a unique layout.

1. Cut a strip of wire mesh to fit along the left side of the page.

2. Place a black-and-white picture somewhat centered on the page, barely overlapping the mesh.

3. Print the title and journaling on vellum and tear and chalk the edges in a coordinating color.

4. Place the title on the upper right side of the page and the journaling on the bottom left side.

5. Use eyelets to make the kids' names and attach them to the bottom right of the picture.

**MATERIALS**

card stock

vellum

wire mesh

chalk

eyelet letters and eyelet setting tool

personal computer

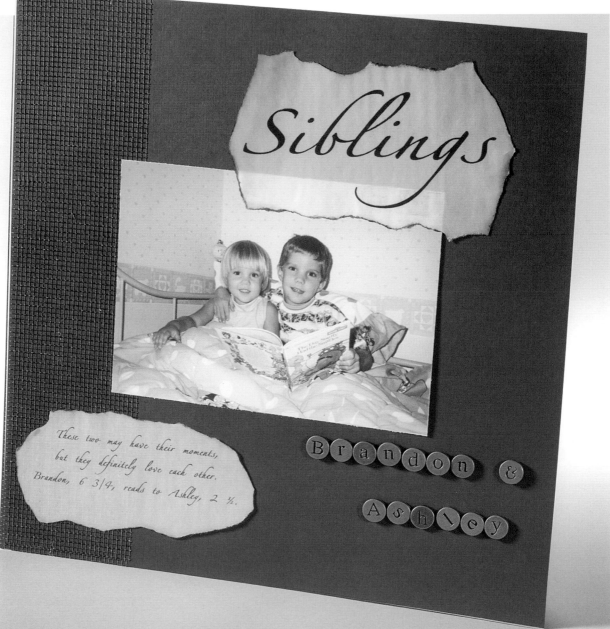

DESIGNER: KELLY JONES

My Wish

I often sit
and wish that I

Could be a kite
up in the sky.

Ride upon the wind
and go.

Whichever way
I chanced to blow.

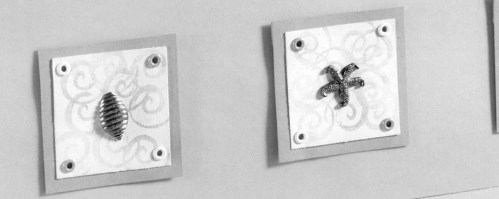

# My wish

Bronze charms fastened to rubber stamped paper squares add dimensionality to ocean-themed pages. Rubber stamped swirls mimic the feeling of water within each paper square.

1. Select two coordinating card stocks. Tear the foreground card stock in half horizontally and adhere it to the background card stock.

2. For the title, string fiber through two tags, and attach the fiber on either end of the layout through eyelets.

3. Put a letter sticker on the first tag and tack it down with mini glue dots. Finish the rest of the word with a watermark pen, simulating the letter sticker, and then chalk in shades that coordinate with the torn foreground paper. Repeat for the second word of the title.

4. Mat the photograph in a color that will make the subject stand out.

5. Print the journaling (in this case a poem) on vellum. Tear it, chalk the edges, and tack it down to the page.

6. To balance the layout, cut three squares of complementary colored card stock, and layer with a contrasting, trimmed piece of card stock.

7. Stamp a design on the smaller piece of card stock with a watermark pen and then chalk in the same colors as the title.

8. Add seashell charms to the stamped pieces of card stock, tying the squares in with the picture, and attach them with tiny white eyelets.

## MATERIALS

card stock

vellum

fiber

stickers

vellum tags

seashell charms

glue dots

watermark pen

chalk

eyelets and eyelet setting tool

personal computer

## MATERIALS

card stock

vellum

fiber

embroidery floss

poetry tags

buttons

scissors

craft knife

eyelets and eyelet setting tool

personal computer

# Sassy

Tags are a wonderful way to make a journaling block or title take center stage on a page.

1. Print a title on vellum and adhere to card stock of a contrasting color from the background page.

2. Cut the title into the shape of a tag, allowing portions of the letters to hang over the edges of the tag. Trim excess vellum with a craft knife in the space between the top and bottom of overhanging letters and the edge of the tag.

3. Attach an eyelet to the hole in the top of the tag and string contrasting colored fiber through the hole. Attach poetry tags to the ends of the fiber and place the tag on the page.

4. Mat the picture and place it at an angle for a different look.

5. Journal on vellum and cut it into strips, attaching strips with threaded buttons at intersecting corners.

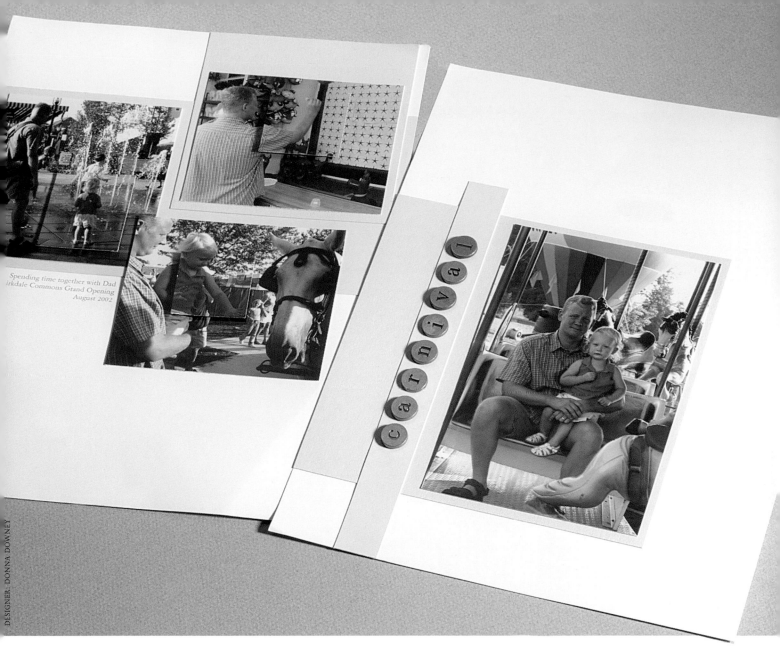

# Carnival

Create the look of a photo within a photo by printing an extra copy, cropping a small piece and raising it with foam adhesive before attaching it to the "parent" photo.

1. Create a graphic background by using perpendicular strips of contrasting card stock.

2. Place the focal point photo within the large strip of card stock.

3. Place photos on the second page within the other two strips.

4. Crop a double print of the photos to focus on action and mount on foam adhesive.

5. Use eyelet letters to create the title.

## MATERIALS

card stock

foam adhesive

eyelet letters and eyelet setting tool

paper punch

## MATERIALS

card stock

vellum

ribbon

fiber

charms

adhesive

glue dots

cotton balls

watermark pen

chalk

eyelets and eyelet setting tool

paper punch

personal computer

# That first day

Create a charming page combining ribbon and silver charms.

1. Print the titles on white card stock and frame them by threading ribbon into eyelets placed on the top and bottom of the title boxes.

2. Mat photographs, leaving an approximate 1" (2.5 cm) border on the top only. Punch two holes on the top section, approximately 1" (2.5 cm) apart, centering them. Thread ribbon through the holes, leaving enough ribbon to run the length of the mat.

3. Print journaling blocks and then trim. Place a watermark pen line around the boxes and go over with chalk on a cotton ball.

4. Highlight some of the charms by framing them with vellum tags, and "hanging" them from the pictures, using fine fiber. Attach charms to the tags with small glue dots.

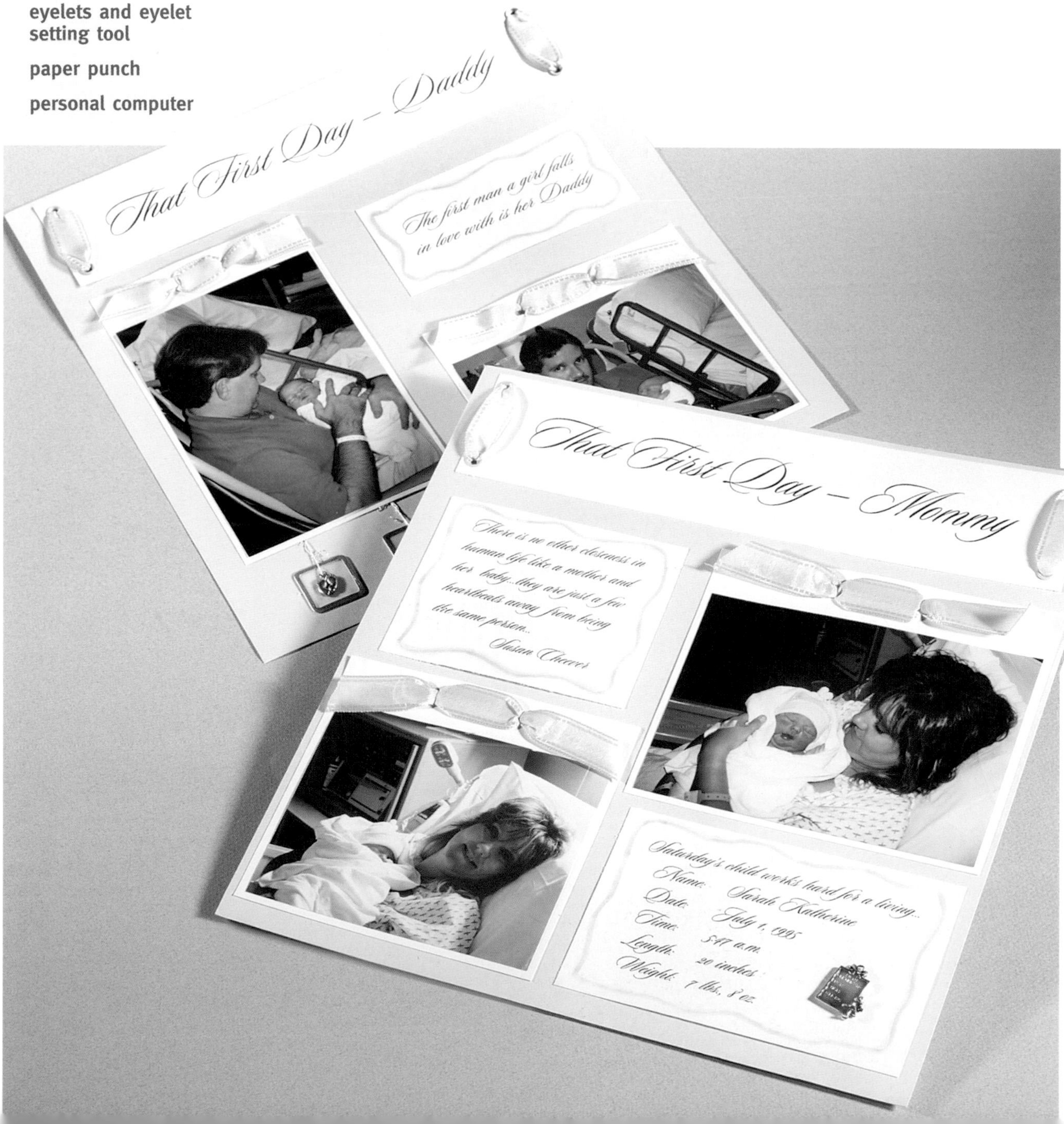

# Ski Utah

Create stunning three-dimensional snowflakes
using a rubber stamp, embossing powder, and a heat tool.

1. To create the 3-D snowflakes, pour a small pile of embossing powder directly onto the card stock. Carefully hold the card stock in the air without spilling the powder and hold the heat tool beneath the card stock so the powder will melt without blowing away.

2. As soon as the powder is melted, put the card stock down and press the stamp into the liquid powder. Allow it to set for 10 to 15 seconds, then remove the stamp.

3. Place the photos and layer vellum on top, leaving a space for part of the photograph to show through. Mount vellum to the page with mini deco fasteners.

4. Stamp title letters onto white tags and fasten them to the page with mini deco fasteners.

5. Die-cut a snowflake and embellish with snowflake-printed vellum. Add journaling to the vellum.

DESIGNER: SHELLI GARDNER

## MATERIALS

plain paper

card stock

patterned vellum

tags

die-cut snowflake

mini deco fasteners

rubber stamps

ink pad, watermark

embossing powder

journaling pen

paper punch

heat tool

DESIGNER: CAROL RICE

## MATERIALS

card stock

vellum

ribbon

flag (memorabilia)

letter tags

letter stickers

audio recording device, such as the Memory Button

die-cut audio recording device cover

snaps

spray adhesive

glue dots

eyelet setting tool

die-cutting machine

# All American boy

Metal letter tags are a great way to give a title added dimension.

1. Mount the fabric flag onto the card stock.

2. Color copy a photo onto vellum. Tear the edges and mount on top of the flag.

3. Adhere letter tags with snaps using an eyelet setting tool.

4. Apply stickers to complete the title.

5. Record a patriotic song, scout oath, and so forth, on the audio recording device.

6. Color copy a patriotic sticker onto vellum and die-cut the button cover.

7. Adhere the button cover over the audio recording device with spray adhesive, tie a ribbon, and adhere the audio recording device to the page with glue dots.

# Rebecca Carter Colefax

Create the illusion of a lacy border to separate patterned papers with colored eyelets. The eyelet holes allow the colored paper sitting behind them to peek through for a dramatic, two-toned effect.

1. Trim a sheet of patterned paper to 10" (25.4 cm) square. Trim a sheet of contrasting patterned paper to 11 ¾" (29.8 cm) square. Mount the smaller square of paper onto the larger square.

2. Using a ruler for guidance, add eyelets along the edge between these two papers, staggering the rows of eyelets.

3. Cut a piece of coordinating patterned paper as a mat for the photo and mount it using eyelets.

4. Cut a sheet of coordinating patterned paper twice as long as the top block. Cut the same size of plain vellum and card stock. Line all the pieces of vellum, patterned paper, and card stock together and fold in half. Punch two ³/₁₆" (4.8 mm) holes for eyelets near the fold line.

5. Punch matching holes where the booklet will be placed and above the booklet's fold line in the background paper. Add eyelets to all holes. Thread ribbon through the holes, going down through the booklet and up through the page above it. Tie off the ribbon and cut Vs into the ends.

6. Mount the whole page onto a sheet of coordinating patterned paper, leaving a thin edge of contrasting colored border.

MATERIALS

patterned paper

card stock

vellum

ribbon

adhesive

scissors

eyelets, ³/₁₆"
(4.8 mm) and ⅛"
(3 mm)

eyelet setting tool

ruler

hole punch

paper trimmer

DESIGNER: JENNA BEEGLE

# Hearty mini memory book

A handmade mini memory book makes a perfect gift for friends and family. While this one is themed with a heart trimmed with beaded metal chain, the theme can be adapted for any special event by simply changing the color scheme and cover decoration.

1. The book's spine is a black strip of paper 24" x 6" (61 cm x 15.2 cm). The first and last fold create the front and back cover at 3 ¼" (8.3 cm). The inside is accordion folded with each pleat measuring 1 ¾" (4.4 cm) (for a total of five pleats).

2. Cut two red covers each measuring 6" x 8" (15.2 cm x 20.3 cm) and attach them to the inside of the front and the back black covers.

3. Cut four additional red sheets to 6" x 8" (15.2 cm x 20.3 cm) and attach one to each of the inside pleats.

4. To hold the pages together, place red ribbon along the inside of the back cover, around the bottom of all the pleats, and up along the inside front cover. Tie a bow at the top.

5. To decorate the front cover, die-cut a red heart and fasten it to a square of sheet adhesive (with the exposed adhesive facing up).

6. Snake gold beaded metal chain along the perimeter of the heart in three rows, using wire snips to cut the chain in the cleavage and at the tip.

7. Use scissors to trim the adhesive flush with the ball chain.

8. Remove the protective backing from the heart back and attach the decorated heart to a black square matted in gold.

9. Raise the square with foam adhesive and attach to the album's front cover.

## MATERIALS

plain paper
or card stock

ribbon

heart die-cut

gold beaded
metal chain

sheet adhesive

foam adhesive

scissors

wire snips

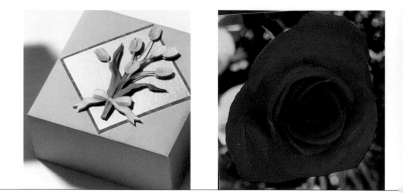

# Keepsakes

## USING SOUVENIRS, MEMENTOS, DRIED FLOWERS, SEASHELLS, AND AUDIO RECORDING DEVICES

A lock of hair from your baby's first hair cut. Dried flowers from your bridal bouquet. The key to your first sports car (in my dreams!). Keepsakes from big moments in your life can bring back a memory like no other 3-D embellishment. And, if they aren't too big and bulky, they can find a home on a scrapbook page.

Oftentimes, a keepsake is safest when placed in a clear, acid-free keepsake envelope or pocket. But items such as postcards, menus, invitations, cards, concert tickets, and stamps can be directly adhered to a page. If an item, like a road map or a college degree, is too large for your page, stick it in the color photocopier and reduce it down to a manageable size, or enlarge it to become a background element on the page. Keepsake items can also serve as decorative elements. Extra fabric or beading from a wedding gown can create an elegant border. A tassel from a graduation

cap can dangle from a page title. Birthday candles can be pieced together to form letters in a celebratory title.

Thanks to the wonders of technology, you can now incorporate sound into your pages. Small, flat audio recording devices, such as the Memory Button, enable you to record sound—like a child singing a favorite song—and attach it to your page for a lifetime of listening pleasure.

Hearing a person's voice can conjure up all sorts of emotions. I'll never forget one such instance when I was taping a segment of a scrapbooking television program that I host. My guest had incorporated the audio recording device in her layout of her father talking to his granddaughter. I didn't even know these people, and I started getting all choked up as I listened to the message. I asked the director to do another take, and I got all choked up the second time—even though I knew it was coming! It just goes to show that keepsakes—both real and virtual—can be powerful additions to your scrapbook pages.

McKenna & Payton
Myrtle Beach
May 2002

As they greet the beach they
hold out their hand
And I watch them scoop tiny
handfuls of sand
A look of pure wonder washes
over each face
On the edge of the blanket they
sit in one place
Wiggling their toes and having
such fun
As they enjoy the day and bask in
the sun.

the beach
explorers
Summer '02

# The beach explorers

This project uses seven layers of complementary patterned paper that are trimmed progressively smaller. Build the foam core section first and then adhere it to the background page to create a shadow box that will protect the seashells.

1. Cut a piece of foam core smaller than your background paper and wrap it with patterned paper, like a gift. The one we show is 10" x 10" (25.4 cm x 25.4 cm).

2. Adhere a second piece of slightly smaller patterned paper over the first layer on the foam core.

3. Cut a rectangle window on the left side of the foam core using a craft knife.

4. Cut a piece of patterned vellum to fit the open space on the foam core, large enough to show a mat around the photographs, and adhere to the foam core.

5. Mount the two larger photos on the vellum.

6. Attach smaller, framed photos, thread together with complementary colored ribbon, and add the title tag.

7. Raise small photos with foam adhesive.

8. Line the back of the rectangle with complementary patterned paper, drill holes in seashells, and thread ribbon through. Fasten the ribbon to the back of the foam core.

9. Cut another piece of complementary patterned paper slightly larger than the rectangle and attach it to the back of the foam core to anchor the ribbon in place.

10. Double mat the foam core onto two pieces of patterned paper in coordinating colors.

## MATERIALS

**patterned paper**

**patterned vellum**

**silk ribbon**

**die-cut frames**

**four seashells**

**foam core**

**foam adhesive**

**craft knife**

**drill**

DESIGNER: JENNIFER MASON

# Roses

Document a special anniversary by including
dried flowers from the special event.

DESIGNER: KELLY JONES

## MATERIALS

card stock

fabric roses

dried baby's breath

adhesive

paper punch

personal computer

1. Select the background card stock.

2. Place photographs and journaling block in a geometric fashion onto
   the card stock.

3. Anchor the journaling block to the page with fabric roses at each corner.

4. Fill in empty spaces with geometric shapes containing words that pertain
   to the pictures.

5. Select a prominent empty space to place dried flowers from the bouquet.

# Balboa Island

Incorporate found objects such as seashells and sand
on layouts with the use of embossing powder.

1. Make background paper for the square accents by using several scrap pieces
   of coordinating card stock. Run the paper through an adhesive machine to apply
   adhesive to the back. Randomly tear and cut the paper into strips. Press the
   strips onto a coordinating background sheet.

2. Randomly stamp on top of the paper.

3. Mix sand with transparent embossing powder. Use a paintbrush to randomly
   apply white glue to the paper. Sprinkle the sand and embossing powder mixture
   onto the glue and shake off the excess. Heat to emboss.

4. After the glue has dried, die-cut squares from random spots on the newly
   created paper.

5. Trim around the outside of the square hole to create a frame for the squares.

6. Add shells to the squares with glue.

7. Apply the squares to the inside of the frames using foam adhesive to raise them.

8. Apply sand and seashells to the tags using the sand and embossing powder mixture and the same technique.

9. Highlight a focus photo by mounting a 4" x 6" (10.2 cm x 15.2 cm) print to a
   duplicate 5" x 7" (12.7 cm x 17.8 cm) print with foam adhesive.

## MATERIALS

card stock

tags

sand

seashells

embossing powder

foam adhesive

white glue

rubber stamps

ink pad

scissors

paintbrush

adhesive machine,
such as a Xyron

die-cutting machine
and dies

heat tool

## MATERIALS

**card stock**

**vellum**

**ribbon**

**fabric hearts**

**drawstring bag**

**audio recording device, such as the Memory Button**

**adhesive**

**glue dots**

**hole punch**

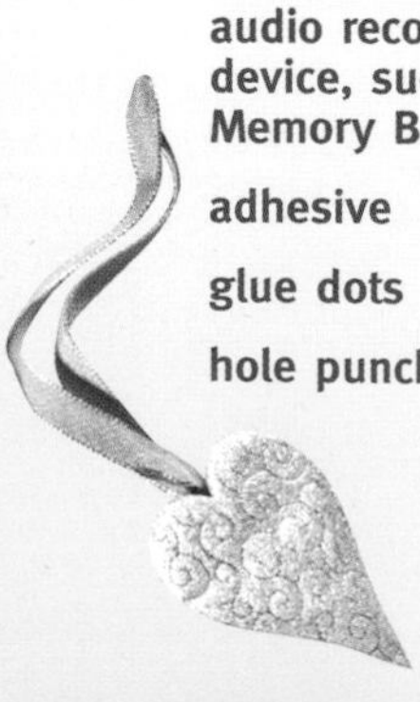

# Our love

Place a keepsake item, such as an audio recording device, in a sheer bag on a scrapbook page to cleverly conceal the audio element.

1. Trim the edges of the vellum and adhere to the card stock.

2. Mount a photo on card stock, punch a hole and thread ribbon through, and mount the silver heart in the center.

3. Record a love song, vows, and so forth, on an audio recording device and slip it into a silver drawstring bag.

4. Adhere the drawstring bag and ribbons to the page using glue dots.

5. Adhere the silver hearts over the knots of ribbon.

# Myrtle Beach

Souvenirs like seashells collected on vacation set the mood for a beach page. If your shell collecting was not successful, you can purchase beach embellishments like shells, starfish, and sand dollars.

1. Tear sand-colored card stock to create a sand border.

2. Mat the focus photo in coordinating blue paper.

3. Create the journal tag. On the page shown, the letters that spell "beach" were pulled out of the journaling.

4. Thread three shades of coordinating embroidery floss through the hole in the tag. Chalk and mat on coordinating blue card stock.

5. Chalk the title and "bury" in the sand.

6. Adhere shell, sand dollar, and starfish to create the beach feel.

**MATERIALS**

**plain paper**

**card stock**

**embroidery floss**

**handmade tag**

**seashells**

**adhesive**

**chalk**

# A day at the circus

Create dimensionality on scrapbook pages with souvenirs such as ticket stubs and programs. Additional dimension can be added by layering stickers with foam adhesive. Layering is made simple by neutralizing the adhesive on the back of stickers with baby powder.

1. Apply blue polka-dot stickers around the outside edge of the page. Apply red-checkered stickers around the whole page, just inside the border of blue dots.

2. Cut along the mouth of the giraffe sticker and insert one end of the gold thread underneath, leaving about 1" (2.5 cm) dangling. Add the giraffe to the bottom of the page, standing on the checkered line. Tape the other end of the gold thread to form a tightrope wire. Adhere the photo to cover the end of the wire. Add two yellow star stickers back-to-back on the end of the dangling "wire" to keep it from unraveling. Make a star necklace and add a hat sticker for the giraffe.

3. Add the cycling bear sticker to the tightrope wire. Add mounting tape to the back of the umbrella sticker leaving the protective layer in place. Powder the open umbrella only, to neutralize the adhesive. Remove the protective paper and place the umbrella in the bear's hand. Glue the tickets together, add some mounting tape to them to give them dimension, and slip them under the bear's other hand.

4. Cut one side of the blue striped square from a geometric sticker to match the curve in the elephant's back, and add it to create a blanket. Trim the square with a red and gold striped sticker, a silver star sticker, and a small purple star sticker. Add the elephant sticker to the parade, overlapping the giraffe slightly in order to create dimension. Add a party hat sticker and a monkey balancing a ball.

5. Add the circus elephant leaning against the rear of the lead elephant. Pop a large lollipop sticker with mounting tape and tuck it under the trunk. Add a crown sticker.

6. Pop the pink cotton candy sticker, put it in the hand of the dressed dog sticker, and add it to the parade.

7. End the parade with the juggling monkey sticker and some ball stickers.

8. Add red sliver stickers to mat the photo.

9. Trim the title from the circus program, attach above the photo, and trim with sliver stickers.

MATERIALS

plain paper
gold thread
stickers
baby powder
tape
glue
scissors

## MATERIALS

plain paper or
card stock

patterned paper

vellum

thread

beads

adhesive

foam adhesive

double-sided tape

scissors

pencil

ruler

creasing tool

pre-cut die-cuts
or die-cutting
machine and dies

# "I do" nesting keepsake boxes

Nesting boxes provide a unique way to enjoy your photos and
store souvenirs. This is a grouping of seven boxes, each one
slightly smaller than the next. Three-dimensional souvenirs—
like a champagne cork—that are too thick to include on a
scrapbook page can be placed inside the smallest box.

1. To make the largest box lid, begin with paper or card stock that measures
   12" x 12" (30.5 cm x 30.5 cm). With a ruler and a pencil, draw an X from corner
   to corner on the back side of the paper (Figure A).

2. Fold in each corner to the middle of the box, which is the intersection of the X
   (Figure B). Use a creasing tool to make crisp folds. (Figure C).

3. Fold in the corners again, this time so that they touch the first fold lines (Figure D).

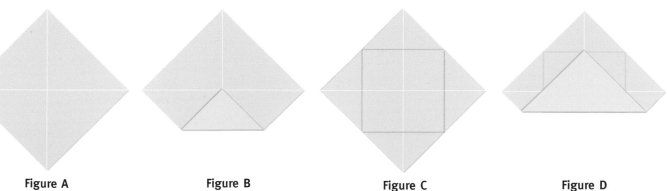

**Figure A**     **Figure B**     **Figure C**     **Figure D**

A

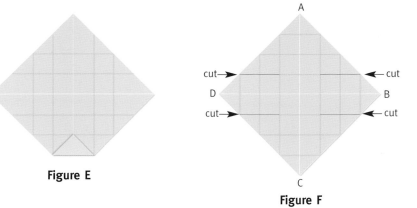

cut→          ←cut

D          B

cut→          ←cut

**Figure E**

C

**Figure F**

A

D          C          B

**Figure G**

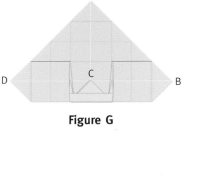

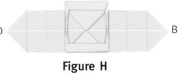

D          B

**Figure H**

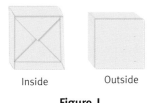

4. Fold the corners again, so that they touch the closest fold lines (Figure E).

5. Cut along two side folds, stopping at the fold that indicates the top of the box (Figure F).

6. Position corners B and D so they are on the sides with corners A and C as the top and bottom. Fold in corner C so that it touches the penciled X in the center and use double-sided tape to hold it in place (Figure G). Bring up the box side, reinforce the fold line, and swing in the arms that will become the other two sides (Figure G).

7. Repeat this step with the corner directly opposite (Figure H).

8. Bring in corner D, trapping the side arms underneath, and stick to the inside with double-sided tape.

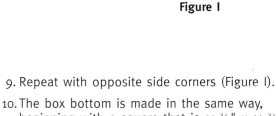

Inside          Outside

**Figure I**

9. Repeat with opposite side corners (Figure I).

10. The box bottom is made in the same way, beginning with a square that is 11 $^3/_4$" x 11 $^3/_4$" (29.8 cm x 29.8 cm). Each successive box (lids and bottoms) will be $^1/_4$" (6 mm) smaller than the preceding box. For a fit that is not quite as snug, use $^1/_2$" (1.3 cm) between each box (lids and bottoms) instead of $^1/_4$" (6 mm).

11. After building all fourteen boxes (seven lids and seven bottoms) add photos, journaling, and themed die-cuts to each of the box lids. Place souvenirs inside the final, smallest box. (Photos are matted and attached to box lids. Die-cuts and punches are raised with foam adhesive, sometimes in multiple layers. Beads are strung onto thread and wrapped around heart die-cuts.)

12. When all of the boxes are nested inside each other, cut a vellum strip to wrap around the outside box and decorate the strip with a matted eyelet word. If you can't locate vellum that is long enough, attach each end to a square of coordinating paper that will sit on the bottom of the nested boxes.

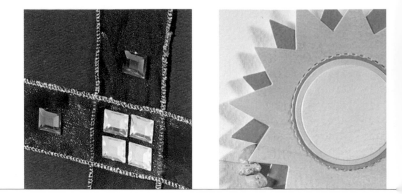

## Beads & Baubles

**DESIGNING WITH BEADS, MIRROR, SEA GLASS, GLASS PEBBLES, GLITTER, TURQUOISE, AND RHINESTONES**

As I'm designing my pages, I sometimes feel like I'm regressing into my childhood. Discovering an object that I can incorporate into a layout brings out an exhilarating excitement. As I look at the layouts in this chapter, I remember cherishing objects, such as pieces of smooth sea glass and beaded friendship bracelets, as a young girl, and I get just as excited seeing them used in scrapbook pages. Besides giving these pages dimension, shine, and color, they add a nice dose of sentimentality.

Scrapbook stores now carry beads, word pebbles, mosaic tiles, and glass do-dads in all sorts of shapes and colors—many of which are self-adhesive. Did you ever think you'd be making Shrinky Dinks after the age of ten? Think again, because they are popping up on pages faster than you can turn on the oven. I like to die-cut shrink film, rough it up with sandpaper, rubber stamp an image, and add detail with chalks and colored pencils. Once baked,

the film shrinks down to about one-eighth its original size and the color really intensifies, leaving you with a small, vividly detailed embellishment, customized for your layout.

For a completely overwhelming experience, visit a local bead store. The variety of beads will be staggering, but you are guaranteed to find just what you need to accessorize your layout. Even mass-consumer stores are starting to carry poetry beads and other 3-D embellishments. Who knows? You could be wandering the aisles looking for toilet paper and discover the perfect scrapbook treasure.

We bought Megan this Tinkerbell outfit for Halloween this year and now she wants to wear it all the time. We go every where with her in her costume. For Christmas my mom is going to buy her a snow white outfit to add to her wardrobe. She just loves to play dress up. I think we created a princess.

# Megan, our little princess

Beads add new dimension to a scrapbook page and are available in an endless assortment of colors and textures that makes it very easy to coordinate with any theme.

## MATERIALS

plain paper

patterned paper

thread

heart charm

beads

adhesive

foam adhesive

die-cutting
machine and dies

personal computer

1. Cut a 12" x 12" (30.5 cm x 30.5 cm) piece of patterned paper down to 8 ½" x 12" (21.6 cm x 30.5 cm). On the computer, create the journaling and run the trimmed paper through the printer. Attach the printed paper onto a solid colored 12" x 12" (30.5 cm x 30.5 cm) page leaving the solid color exposed along the right side.

2. Crop and mat photographs and arrange around the journaling. Print a title on the computer and attach it to the page.

3. Die-cut flowers out of two shades of pink paper. Cut away detail on the lighter pink flower and layer onto the darker pink flower. Place a small amount of strong adhesive tape in the center of each flower. Sprinkle beads over the tape and press with your finger to create the center of each flower.

4. Die-cut leaves out of green patterned paper.

5. Arrange the leaves and completed flowers along the left side of the page. Add foam adhesive to some of the flowers to create dimension.

6. Print a title on the computer on two lines. Separate the two lines, and apply a strip of strong adhesive to the top and bottom of the first title line. Add beads to the tape. Finish by stringing a gold heart charm and beads on thread that hang from the bottom of the second title line.

# Lowry Park Zoo

Glass beads add a certain sparkle and dimension to a page without much effort.

1. Dip a small paintbrush into glue and paint the glue into the biggest circles on the patterned paper.

2. Pour glass beads into the circles and swish them around, making sure all of the glue is covered. Use a craft knife to carefully edge around the circle, loosening all of the excess beads.

3. Gently shake off the excess glass beads onto a paper plate and pour them back into a bead container. Let the glue dry overnight to harden and give the circles a finished look that won't distract the eye from the beautiful paper.

4. Center a photograph on the top half of the paper between the circles and the edge.

5. Create the page title with stickers on vellum. Tear the vellum into squares and use a fine marker to edge around the letters so they stand out.

6. On the right page, punch out focal parts of some photos, glue them onto the page, and then cut out squares to frame them. Raise them with foam adhesive.

7. Double-mat the remaining photographs and place them on the page.

8. Print journaling onto vellum, and then cut to resemble the circles on the left page.

## MATERIALS

plain paper

patterned paper

card stock

vellum

letter stickers

glass beads

foam adhesive

glue

scissors

craft knife

journaling pen

fine marker

paintbrush

paper punch

personal computer

Westchase Elementary's first grade class went on a field trip to Lowry Park Zoo. Allie Banales and Sarah rode the merry-go-round (laughing the whole time), petted the stingrays in their pool (surprised at how soft and smooth they were), and were amazed at the size of some of the fish in the big tanks (bigger than our house)! They also loved watching the manatees with their sweet faces, but the best part was having lunch under the covered canopy.

# Ronald Letrick

Many patterned papers look just like fabric. A paper "ribbon" trimmed from a larger sheet appears dimensional but lays perfectly flat and partners well with fabric ribbon and word beads.

**MATERIALS**

plain paper

patterned paper

black ribbon, ³/₈"
(1 cm) wide

platinum ribbon,
⁷/₈" (2.2 cm) wide

platinum ribbon
corners

tag

word beads

adhesive

glue

scissors

1. Frame a square of striped paper (the one we show is 9 ³/₄" [24.8 cm] square) with four strips of ribbon and miter the corners. (The ribbon strips are created by trimming the edges from a coordinating patterned paper.)

2. Place the framed paper onto a larger sheet of coordinating patterned paper.

3. Mount the large photograph with photo corners to a mat that is slightly larger than the photograph. Mat a second time, leaving a larger border along the bottom of the photograph.

4. Mount the small photograph to a mat that is slightly larger than the photograph. Mat a second time, leaving a larger border along the bottom of the photograph.

5. Lace two beads with 9" (22.9 cm) and 6" (15.2 cm) pieces of black ribbon, tie a knot on the right side of the bead, trim the ends, and glue the threaded beads onto the mats.

6. Layer a solid colored journaling block onto coordinating patterned paper. Wrap the matted journaling block with ⁷/₈" (2.2 cm)-wide ribbon and the bead laced with black ribbon, knotted on both sides and trimmed. Mount onto a larger piece of solid paper and adhere to the page.

7. Hand-cut two flower clusters from patterned paper, adhere to the page, and place a small tag on top with the person's name.

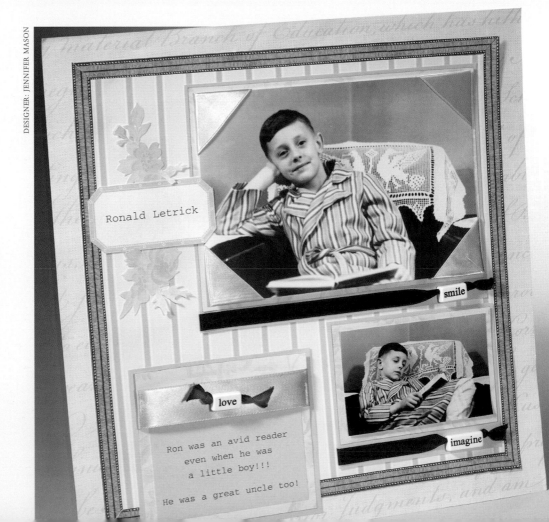

DESIGNER: JENNIFER MASON

DESIGNER: STEPHANIE BARNARD

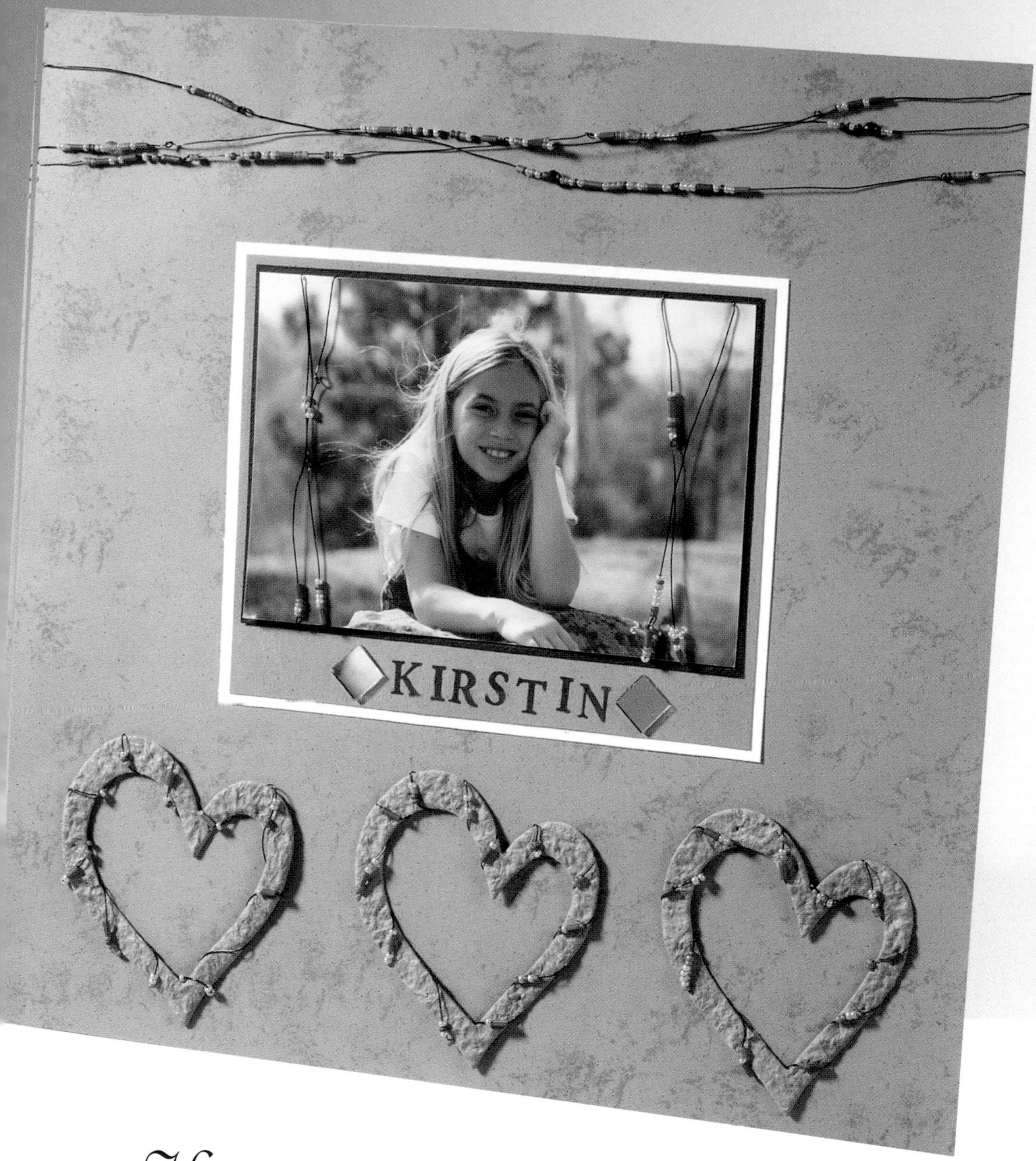

# *Kirstin*

Dimension and texture come together when wire and beads are added to handmade paper accents.

1. Add beads to wire, tying knots in various places, and wrap the beads around the photo.
2. Triple-mat the photo, leaving room in the second mat to add a stamped title.
3. Using glue dots, add mirrors next to the title.
4. Dip a sea sponge into a watermark ink pad and stamp onto the background card stock.
5. Adhere the photo to the layout.
6. Add beads to wire, tying knots in various places, and wrap around the background card stock.
7. Die-cut hearts out of handmade paper.
8. Wrap the hearts with the beaded wire and adhere to the layout.

## MATERIALS

**handmade paper**
**card stock**
**black 26-gauge wire**
**beads**
**mirrors**
**adhesive**
**glue dots**
**sea sponge**
**rubber stamps**
**ink pad, watermark**
**black ink**
**paper trimmer**
**die-cutting machine and heart dies**

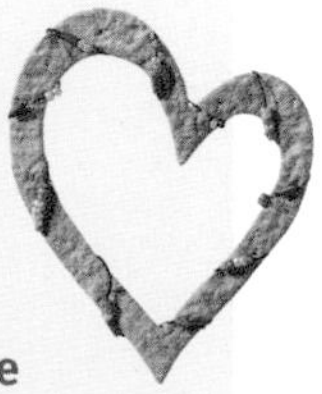

## MATERIALS

plain paper

iridescent-coated paper

card stock

ribbon

jewels

adhesive

glue dots

die-cutting machine and dies

# Our jewel

Jewels and ribbon add delight and charm to a layout. Complement a child's smile with jewel embellishments along with the actual ribbon worn in the photo.

1. Die-cut the title and adhere it to gold paper and iridescent-coated paper.
2. Add ribbon to the layout.
3. Mat the photographs with gold and purple iridescent-coated paper.
4. Add jewels to the ribbon and photo mat using glue dots.

# Simple sweet moments

Glass pebbles are a fun way to highlight little details
on a scrapbook page.

DESIGNER: CARA MARIANO

1. For the background, layer yellow paper on top of gold paper that has been cut slightly larger to create a border.

2. Die-cut the title out of red paper using the lollipop alphabet. Layer the letters onto orange paper and cut around them to create a small border. For variety, leave some letters on an orange rectangle instead of cutting around them.

3. Die-cut hearts out of a variety of colors. Layer the hearts onto a strip of red paper and position the paper at the bottom of the page, raising some with foam adhesive. Add highlights with a silver pen.

4. Crop and mat a photograph with red and orange paper.

5. Punch tiny hearts out of a variety of colors. Place a clear pebble over the hearts and position it on the page.

6. Journal around the pebbles to complete the page.

**MATERIALS**

plain paper

clear pebbles

foam adhesive

silver pen

paper punch

die-cutting
machine and dies

MATERIALS

**card stock**

**organza ribbon**

**wire**

**glitter**

**glue pen**

**scissors**

**die-cutting
machine and dies**

# Christmas card photo shoot

Add sparkle to any page by adding glitter to ribbon and wire.

1. Tear a strip from the top and bottom of the background card stock.

2. Place a piece of red organza ribbon in the space left by tearing out the strip and back it with white card stock.

3. Die-cut Christmas lights from red and black card stock. Trim the top from the red light and adhere it to the black light. Highlight the lights by using a glue pen to fill in the highlight area on the red bulb. Sprinkle red glitter on the glue and shake off the excess.

4. String the lights on wire and attach it to the top of the page.

5. Use a glue pen and glitter to highlight the mat for the focus photo.

DESIGNER: BECKY WHALEY-BUTLER

# Utah

Turquoise beads enhance the look of these southwestern photographs, but the mood is set with the watercolored background. Although the paper is flat, the watercolor layers create the feeling of dimensionality and set the tone for the entire layout.

1. Create the background page by layering watercolor washes. Start with a light color and add more paint as you layer to create dimension.

2. Paint 6" x 6" (15.2 cm x 15.2 cm) swatches of coordinating colors to use for die-cutting.

3. Die-cut three rectangle frames from black paper. Die-cut three zigzag frames out of the color coordinated watercolor swatches and position over the black frame.

4. Attach photos to the backs of the frames.

5. Die-cut two suns and embellish with watercolor circles. Place the suns on the page.

6. Title the page using die-cut letters.

7. Journal along the curves.

8. To finish, attach a string of turquoise stones with an aggressive adhesive.

## MATERIALS

plain paper

watercolor paper

turquoise stones

adhesive

watercolor paint

journaling pen

paintbrush

pre-cut die-cuts
or die-cutting
machine and dies

# You're never too old for Santa

Replicate the look of strings of Christmas lights with brightly colored beads that decorate a journaling card.

## MATERIALS

card stock

vellum

wire

beads

adhesive

foam adhesive

eyelets and eyelet setting tool

paper punch

personal computer

1. Use a paper punch to cut out three evenly spaced trees from the bottom of the layout, and place a coordinating color of card stock behind the trees.

2. Type the title on vellum. Create the title bar by cutting textured card stock and mounting it onto the background page.

3. Place the vellum title on the far right side of the title bar. On the left side, adhere one of the punched trees to the textured card stock with foam adhesive.

4. Mat the picture with a thin border and place on the same card stock used behind the trees, making sure to cover the width of the layout, but also leaving a small border on either side.

5. Type the journaling on vellum and attach the vellum to the card stock with eyelets.

6. String the beads on wire, alternating the main colors in the layout, and tuck the extra wire behind the layout through eyelets.

# Bubbles

The transparent quality of vellum and glass beads help to re-create the look of bubbles on a page. Attaching vellum to a less-than-perfect photograph with eyelets softens the image and takes focus off the photo underneath.

MATERIALS

card stock

vellum

mesh

watch crystal

stickers

adhesive

foam adhesive

chalk

eyelets and eyelet setting tool

lettering template

adhesive machine, such as a Xyron

1. Select the background paper. Select coordinating paper and trim approximately ½" (1.3 cm) all the way around.

2. Place a horizontal strip of mesh along the bottom quarter of the page. Embellish the mesh with stickers that relate to the photographs.

3. Cover one photograph with vellum and attach it to the photograph with eyelets at each corner.

4. Double-mat the other photograph and adhere both photographs to the page.

5. Mount the journaling block on top of the mesh, raising it with foam adhesive for added dimension.

6. Run vellum through an adhesive machine and cut title letters from it using a lettering template. Chalk letters lightly before adhering to the page. (Placing adhesive on the back of the vellum will cloud the transparent quality of the vellum, allowing greater visibility of the letters on the background page.)

7. Embellish the page with a few more stickers, overlapping the photographs for visual interest.

DESIGNER: KELLY JONES

**MATERIALS**

plain paper

card stock

journaling banners

photo corners

micro beads

embossing ink
and powders

water-based
lacquer

adhesive

scissors

white correction
pen

heat tool

stamping mat and
back-up paper

cleaning tray
and rag

rubber stamps

spray bottle and
water for clean up

# Beaded heart album page

Use special water-based lacquers to achieve a transparent raised coating that results in a truly three-dimensional finish.

1. Rubber stamp hearts and emboss on card stock using embossing ink and powder. Cut out the outlines, leaving small paper edges.

2. Apply a layer of water-based lacquer in one open area of the design at a time. Shake micro beads over the wet lacquer and shake the excess back into the jar. Allow to dry at least 30 minutes. Repeat with a second coat of beads.

3. Apply a smaller amount of water-based lacquer over part of the design for shading or accent, and apply a second color of micro beads. Allow to dry thoroughly.

4. Rubber stamp photo corners and banners, then emboss them using embossing ink and powder. Cut them out, leaving small paper edges.

5. Apply a contrasting color of 8 ½" x 11" (21.6 cm x 27.9 cm) paper to the left side of 12" x 12" (30.5 cm x 30.5 cm) background paper.

6. Apply photo corners to the smaller page, mat photos, arrange, and adhere into place.

7. Journal in banners with white correction pen, arrange the journaling around the photos, and adhere into place.

8. Arrange heart stickers along the right side, scatter around the photos, and adhere into place.

DESIGNER: DEE GRUENIG

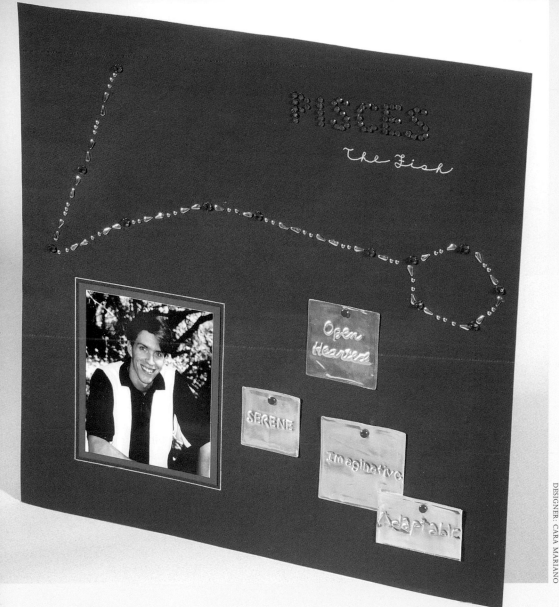

# Pisces

Iron-on rhinestones are an easy way to add color and glimmer to any scrapbook page. They iron onto paper just as easily as they do onto fabric or can be fastened with adhesive.

1. On 12" x 12" (30.5 cm x 30.5 cm) black paper, arrange the rhinestone alphabet letters at the top of the page and iron them onto the paper.

2. Underneath the title, arrange a design using metallic silver iron-on decorations. Once the design is what you want, iron it onto the paper.

3. Mat a photograph in red paper and attach it to the page. Draw a border around the photograph using a silver pen.

4. Die-cut squares out of silver decorative foil. On the computer, print on vellum paper the words that will go on the squares. The vellum will help in the placement and transfer of the words.

5. Place the foil on a soft surface, such as a mouse pad, and use a stylus tool over the vellum to transfer the letters onto the foil. Remember to transfer the words backwards so when the foil is turned over it will read the right way.

6. Attach the finished foil squares to the page using red brads.

## MATERIALS

plain paper

vellum

decorative foil

iron-on rhinestone alphabet

iron-on metallic silver decorations

brads

silver pen

stylus

die-cutting machine and dies

iron

personal computer

chapter three **Dimensional Pages** 271

# Best buds

Create a mini book for a special friend that is sure to become a keepsake. This mini book can have more or less pages, based on your preference, and can be altered to fit any occasion by changing the colors and embellishments. The checkered pattern of the book pages creates visual interest even before the pages have been decorated.

## MATERIALS

plain paper

textured paper

patterned paper

thread

alphabet beads

brads

clear page protector

adhesive

foam adhesive

adhesive machine, such as a Xyron

pre-cut die-cuts or die-cutting machine and dies

paper trimmer

personal binding system with discs

1. Select three sheets of four different colors of paper (for a total of twelve sheets) and arrange them in a repeating pattern for the inside pages.

2. Trim the first two colors (pink and green) to 8 ¼" x 3" (21 cm x 7.6 cm).

3. Trim the next two colors (yellow and blue) to 8 ¼" x 3 ¾" (21 cm x 9.5 cm).

4. Continue to trim the remaining colors in batches of two, each ¾" (1.9 cm) taller than the previous batch. The final pages will be 8 ¼" x 7" (21 cm x 17.8 cm).

5. Trim ¾" (1.9 cm) from the length of every other color beginning with the first sheet (pink). When all are trimmed, you will have created a wonderful checker-board pattern along the edge of the book. To vary the pattern, trim an additional ⅛" (3 mm) from the width of every other page beginning with the first page (pink).

6. Cut a front and back cover 8 ¼" x 7" (21 cm x 17.8 cm) from dusty pink paper or card stock. Mat a square of patterned paper and center it on the front cover. Attach a die-cut heart from textured paper and adhere it with foam adhesive to the matted square. String alphabet beads onto thread to create the title and attach to the cover with colored brads. (Adhesive can be used on the back side of the beads to make sure they stay in place.)

7. Trim a clear page protector 8 ¼" x 7" (21 cm x 17.8 cm) to fit over the front cover for protection.

8. Using the personal binding system with discs, punch holes in the left edge a few sheets at a time. The bottom of each sheet should always butt against the guide on the cutting tool. The clear page protector and front and back covers should also be punched.

9. Insert the discs into the punched holes.

10. Add photos, embellishments, and journaling to inside pages.

# Exotic Elements

## CREATING ACCENTS WITH FEATHERS, LEAVES, CLAY, RAFFIA, WOOD PAPER, AND TWIGS

Sometimes a gift from Mother Nature is just the thing to accent a layout. Pages that center on outdoor activities, such as a trip to the beach, a camping excursion, or a layout of your garden in full bloom, benefit nicely from the addition of natural elements. A seashell, feather, or a pressed flower can make a special memory even more vivid.

As funny as it sounds, you can actually purchase many natural elements, such as those listed above. Or, you can pick up a souvenir from the beach or the trail, clean it, and carefully add it to your layout. Shells can be glued directly to a page or tucked into a keepsake envelope. Other natural items, such as leather and cork, can be decorated, pierced, and cut to create decorative elements. Fragile dried or pressed flowers should be protected in an envelope or behind a page protector.

Clay is a fun material to work with and embellish. Polymer clay is available in many different colors, and you can

create your own by blending colors. After the clay is baked, it is neutralized and won't harm your pages. I like to create clay tags and use letter stamps to impress single words that complement my layouts. You can also make your own beads from polymer clay. (Don't forget to poke holes in the clay beads before you cook them if you plan to hang them.) Enjoy these layouts courtesy of Mother Nature.

DESIGNER: GRACE TAORMINA

## MATERIALS

card stock

raffia paper

dictionary page

photo corners

bronze wire

hemp twine

small envelope
and mailing tag
die cuts

cellophane window
mailing tag

wood beads

assorted
pressed leaves,
feathers, twigs,
and buttons

glue dots

rubber stamps

ink pads

scissors

colored pencils

grommet tools
and grommets

die-cutting
machine and dies

# Nature walk

Sometimes nature is the best source for embellishments. The title
bar on this page is suspended from a twig collected on a walk.

1. Stamp the title and cut it into a rectangular shape. Add two grommets to the top,
   then set aside.

2. Die-cut a small envelope and glue three flaps together to form an open envelope.

3. Stamp a title on the envelope, and then stamp a few coordinating images along-
   side the envelope title. Set aside.

4. Glue a dictionary page onto card stock and die-cut it into a tag. Glue a pressed
   leaf to the front of the die-cut tag. Loop hemp twine through the hole and add
   a couple of wood beads. Set aside.

5. Glue an additional pressed leaf on the inside of the cellophane window mailing
   tag. Loop natural hemp at the hole.

6. Mount a photo onto a piece of card stock. Trim around the photo to create a
   deckle-edged border.

7. Stamp a few coordinating images onto the scrapbook page, shading with colored
   pencils as desired.

8. Add two pairs of grommets to the right top of the page. Position the grommets to
   accommodate the width of a twig. Use bronze wire to secure the branch to the page.

9. Loop hemp twine through the rectangular title label and tie it onto the branch.

10. Glue the mounted photo to the page with photo corners.

11. Use glue dots to adhere additional embellishments, such as the pressed leaf
    in the cellophane window mailing tag, rust-colored raffia paper, buttons, and
    additional pressed leaves.

# Glenn and Cara

Explore the versatility and beauty of polymer clay with unique finishing, shaping, baking, and molding techniques.

1. Double-mat a photograph using colored corrugated paper and red handmade paper. Add decorative wire across the edges of the photograph and mats.

2. Place the finished picture on a black 12" x 12" (30.5 cm x 30.5 cm) background page.

3. Soften and roll out a piece of polymer clay and cut it into a square. Stamp names into the clay using alphabet stamps and punch a circle at the top so it can be hung. Stamp a heart into another piece of clay. Cut out the heart with a small circle cookie cutter or large pen cap. Repeat this three more times. Bake the square and circles according to polymer clay instructions.

4. After the clay is cool, arrange the circles with hearts onto small gold squares and attach to the background page.

5. Add four red eyelets underneath the photograph. Weave gold ribbon through the eyelets. Hang the finished clay square with the names from the ribbon and tie it in a bow.

6. Add a journaling square and gold circles around the page to create a finished look.

**MATERIALS**

plain paper

decorative handmade paper

corrugated paper

ribbon

decorative wire

polymer clay

foam adhesive

glue dots

alphabet stamps

rubber stamps

small circle cutter

eyelets and eyelet setting tool

paper punches

DESIGNER: CARA MARIANO

## MATERIALS

**plain paper**
**card stock**
**raffia**
**twine**
**adhesive**
**chalk**

# First signs of fall

Combine raffia, torn paper, and twine for a rustic effect reminiscent of a fall day.

1. Trim ½" (1.3 cm) on all four sides of background paper and mat onto contrasting card stock to create the frame.
2. Gather raffia to create a cornstalk effect and tie with twine.
3. Tear and chalk orange card stock to create the pumpkin.
4. Double-mat a photograph using two complementary colors of card stock.

first signs of fall

every year daddy excitedly decorates the front yard and stoop for fall. the day daddy puts up the cornstalks and positions the bail of hay is our family's first sign of fall.

Mckenna, OctobeR 2001

# It's a jungle out there

Give added emphasis to a journaling box by matting it on a stamped background that has been "stitched" with raffia.

1. Randomly stamp flowers onto card stock with watermark ink, emboss with clear embossing powder, and let cool. Repeat this process on another piece of card stock for individual flowers and the title piece to cut out later.

2. Stipple over the embossed papers with coordinating ink colors, and then buff with a paper towel to blend colors and take off excess ink.

3. Stamp the page title onto the extra piece of embossed paper, emboss with clear embossing powder, triple-mat, and adhere to the page. Place a translucent feather over the title.

4. Stamp the remaining title words, cut out, mat, and then mount to the background paper.

5. Cut out separate flowers, single-mat some and embellish some flower centers with raffia, raising some off the page with foam adhesive.

6. Cut a journaling block from coordinating card stock, stamp a border along the top edge with watermark ink, and emboss with clear embossing powder. Stitch raffia over part of the stamped border. Journal onto coordinating paper, trim, and mount to the journaling block.

7. Mat photos and adorn corners of two photos with raffia.

## MATERIALS

card stock

raffia

translucent feather

adhesive

foam adhesive

clear embossing powder

rubber stamps

ink pads, watermark

scissors

journaling pen

stipple brushes

paper towel

heat tool

# A place I love

Bring the feeling of the outdoors into your scrapbook with the addition of wood paper, which can give the illusion of dimension, especially when it is trimmed away and layered on a coordinating page.

1. Trim along the edge of the twig pattern with a craft knife. Place and adhere leaf paper with the twig overlapping the edge.

2. Double-mat the photo using contrasting card stock. Mount the matted photo to wood paper leaving an approximate 3" (7.6 cm) margin to the right.

3. Using glue dots on the back side, adhere wire across the face of the photo.

4. Mount buttons by using a hole punch and then threading wire and twisting over the top of the button. Place buttons in the top and bottom squares.

5. Record on the audio recording device a saying or nature sounds from a CD or other source.

6. Sponge colored ink onto the audio recording device. Decorate the button with wire coil and a button. Mount the coil and the button with a glue dot in the center of the audio recording device. Adhere the audio recording device to the page using glue dots.

7. Write the title heading along the left edge of the paper.

**MATERIALS**

twig paper

leaf paper

wood paper, such as Paperwood

card stock

brown craft wire

red buttons

audio recording device, such as the Memory Button

glue dots

craft knife

sponge

hole punch

# Love guest book

### MATERIALS

paper

vellum

gold foil

twig

elastic hair band

adhesive

removable white tape

brass stencil

hole punch

paper trimmer

adhesive machine, such as a Xyron

die-cutting machine and dies

personal computer

To emboss is to raise the design on the paper and is traditionally achieved with a brass stencil and stylus. Faux embossing involves cutting the design out of paper that matches the background and using adhesive to stick it on top. This guest book features circles and rectangles that have been adhered to the matching paper used for the cover, making it look embossed, but with a lot less time and effort than embossing the traditional way. The theme of the book can be altered by deleting the wedding information from the inside pages.

1. Cut the cover and inside pages to the desired size. The one pictured is 11" x 8 $\frac{1}{2}$" (27.9 cm x 21.6 cm). Judge the quantity of pages you will need by the amount of guests coming to the wedding. The front and back covers are lined with a slightly darker color to add interest and thickness. Punch two holes in the book. Base the distance between the holes on the length of the band that will be used for the binding.

2. Run paper through an adhesive machine to add an adhesive backing.

3. Create pairs of each rectangle by die-cutting or using the paper trimmer to cut strips that are $\frac{1}{4}$" x 1" (6 mm x 2.5 cm). Use die-cuts or craft punches to create pairs of circles in multiple sizes. Remove the backing from the top shape and stick to the matching circle or rectangle to double the thickness of each shape.

4. Use removable $\frac{3}{8}$" (1 cm)-wide white tape on the bottom and top of the front cover for a guide to position the rectangles to create stripes. Use loose rectangles of a different color as "placeholders" to accurately position each rectangle. (Placeholders are not fastened to the cover. They are only used as an aid to create stripes that are straight and evenly spaced.)

5. Randomly scatter the circles on the remainder of the cover.

6. Run a rectangle of gold foil an adhesive machine to add adhesive. Emboss the word "love" with a brass stencil. Multi-mat the embossed foil using varying shades of cream and tan.

7. For the inside pages, select a font and print the date, signature lines, and wedding couple's names on the computer.

8. The first sheet is a photograph of the wedding couple that has been photocopied on vellum.

9. Punch holes in the vellum and inside sheets that align with the cover holes.

10. Attach the matted embossed "love" to the cover. To complete the album, go to the hair accessory section of your local store and choose an elastic hair band in a coordinating color. Poke the elastic band through the top hole in the book. Insert a twig through the elastic band to hold the band in place. Stretch the band along the back cover and bring the other end of the band up through the remaining hole. Slide the other end of the twig through the elastic band and center the twig.

DESIGNER: SANDI GENOVESE

# templates

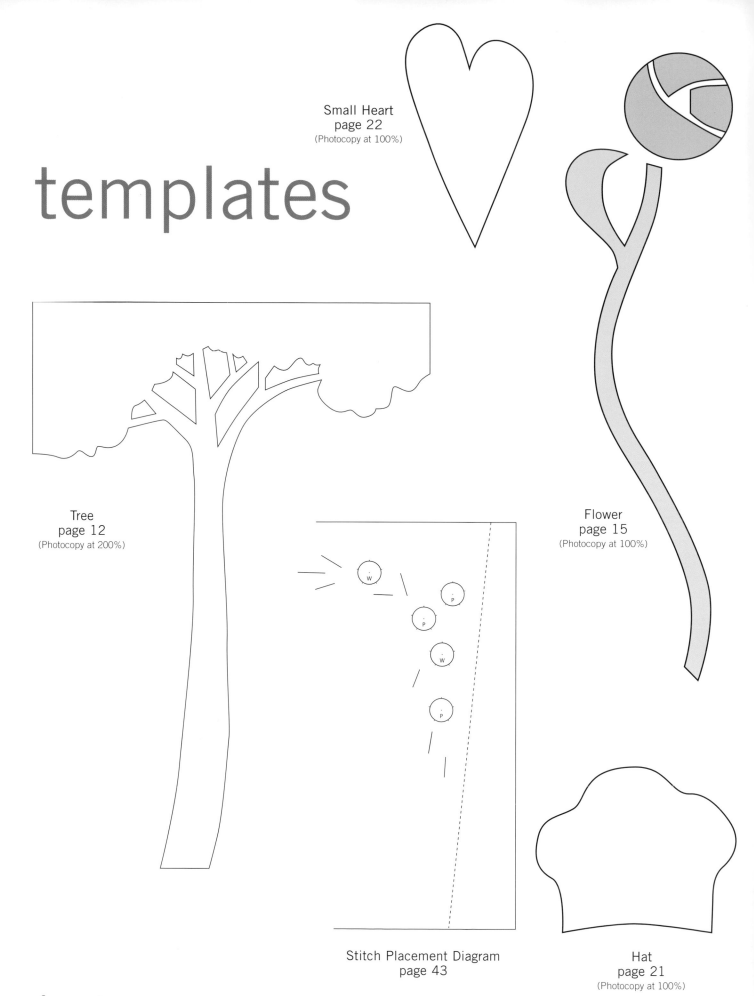

Small Heart
page 22
(Photocopy at 100%)

Tree
page 12
(Photocopy at 200%)

Flower
page 15
(Photocopy at 100%)

Stitch Placement Diagram
page 43

Hat
page 21
(Photocopy at 100%)

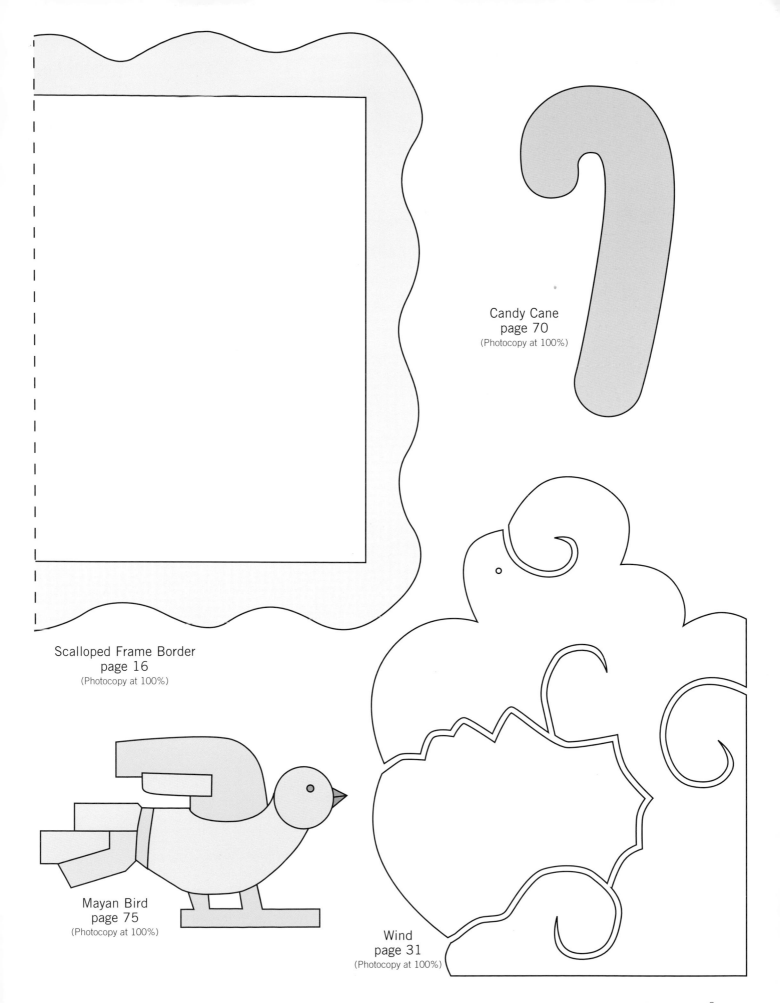

Candy Cane
page 70
(Photocopy at 100%)

Scalloped Frame Border
page 16
(Photocopy at 100%)

Mayan Bird
page 75
(Photocopy at 100%)

Wind
page 31
(Photocopy at 100%)

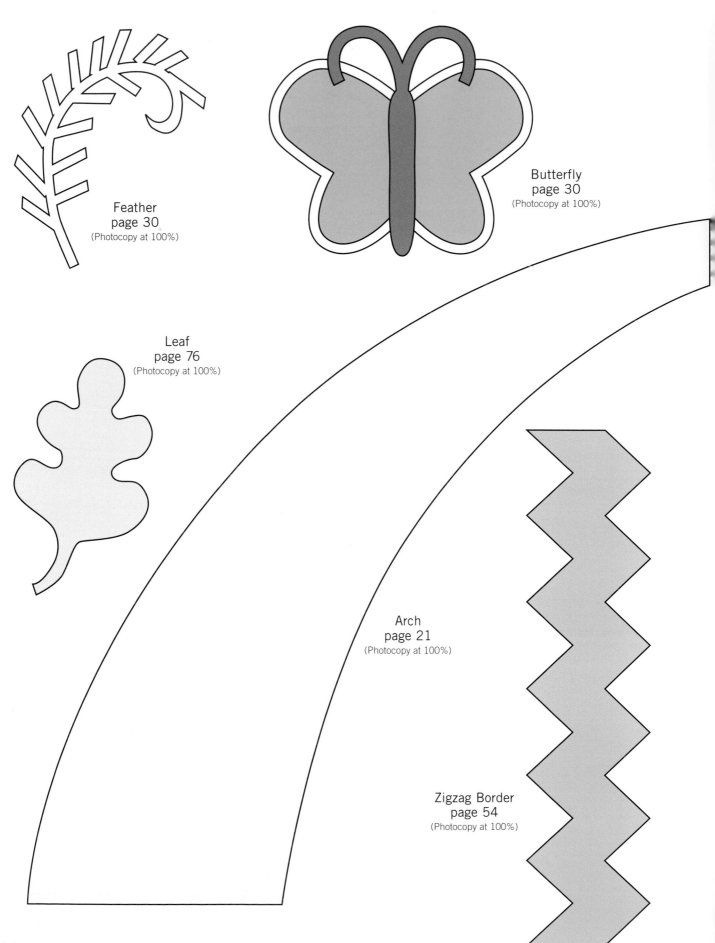

Feather
page 30
(Photocopy at 100%)

Butterfly
page 30
(Photocopy at 100%)

Leaf
page 76
(Photocopy at 100%)

Arch
page 21
(Photocopy at 100%)

Zigzag Border
page 54
(Photocopy at 100%)

Waves
page 97
(Photocopy at 200%)

Mask
page 30
(Photocopy at 200%)

Curvy Border
page 40
(Photocopy at 200%)

Large Heart
page 39
(Photocopy at 100%)

Spoon
page 21
(Photocopy at 100%)

Mayan Border
page 75
(Photocopy at 100%)

Flowers and Leaves
page 64
(Photocopy at 100%)

Palm Tree
page 49
(Photocopy at 100%)

Sun
page 48
(Photocopy at 100%)

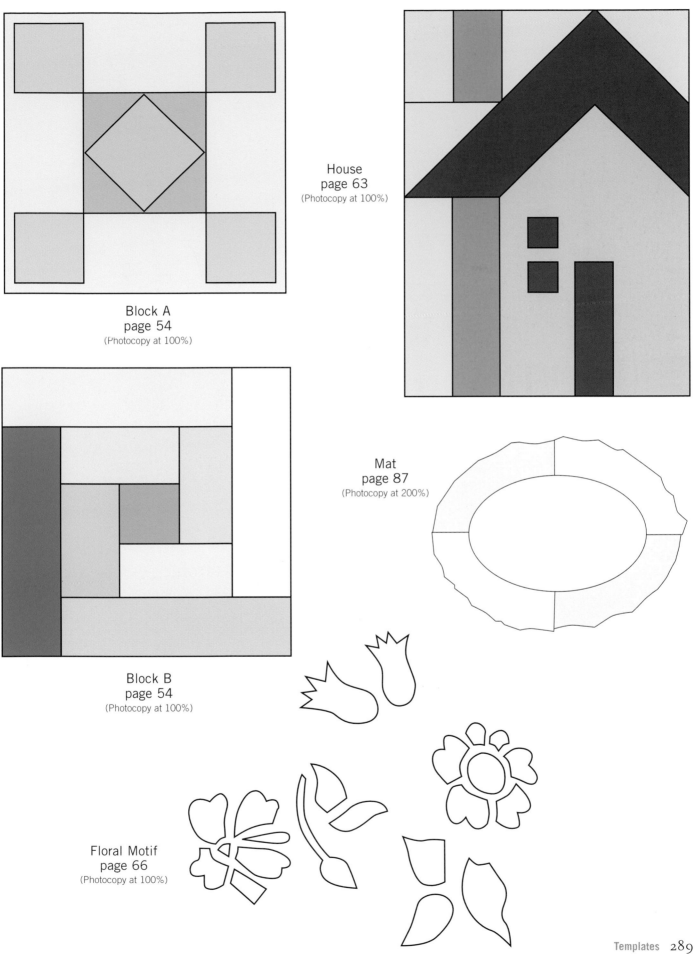

Block A
page 54
(Photocopy at 100%)

House
page 63
(Photocopy at 100%)

Mat
page 87
(Photocopy at 200%)

Block B
page 54
(Photocopy at 100%)

Floral Motif
page 66
(Photocopy at 100%)

Cake, Plate, and Candles
page 57
(Photocopy at 200%)

Christmas Tree
page 102
(Photocopy at 200%)

Moon and Star
page 55
(Photocopy at 200%)

Streamers
page 79
(Photocopy at 200%)

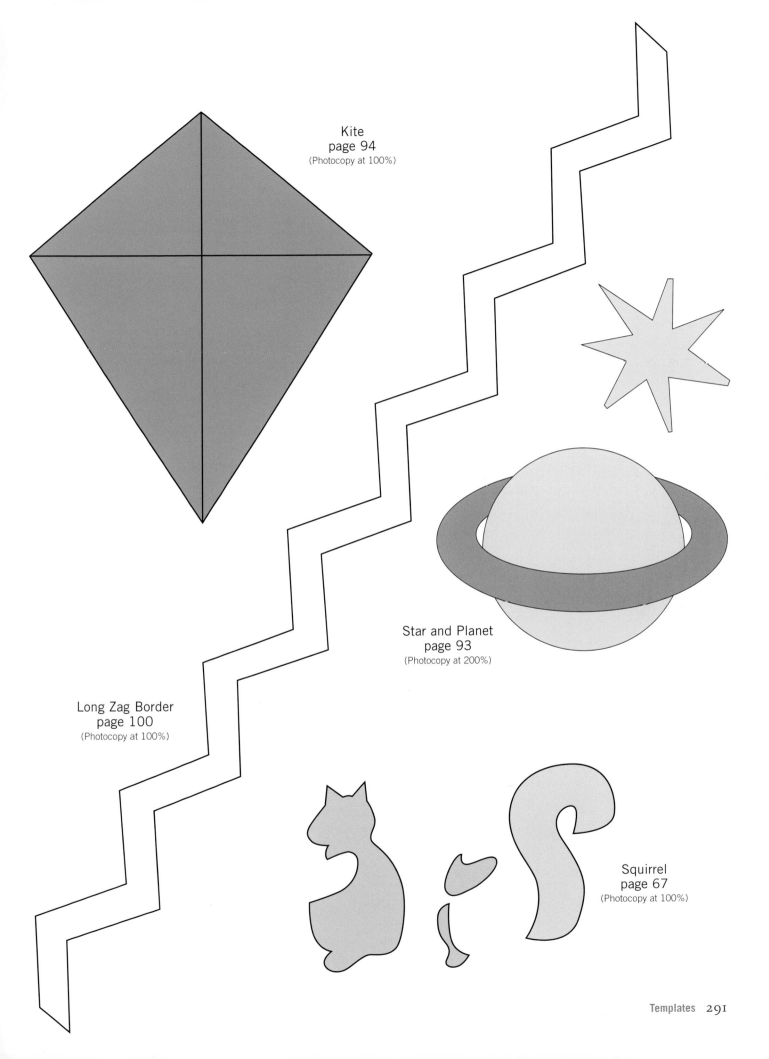

Kite
page 94
(Photocopy at 100%)

Star and Planet
page 93
(Photocopy at 200%)

Long Zag Border
page 100
(Photocopy at 100%)

Squirrel
page 67
(Photocopy at 100%)

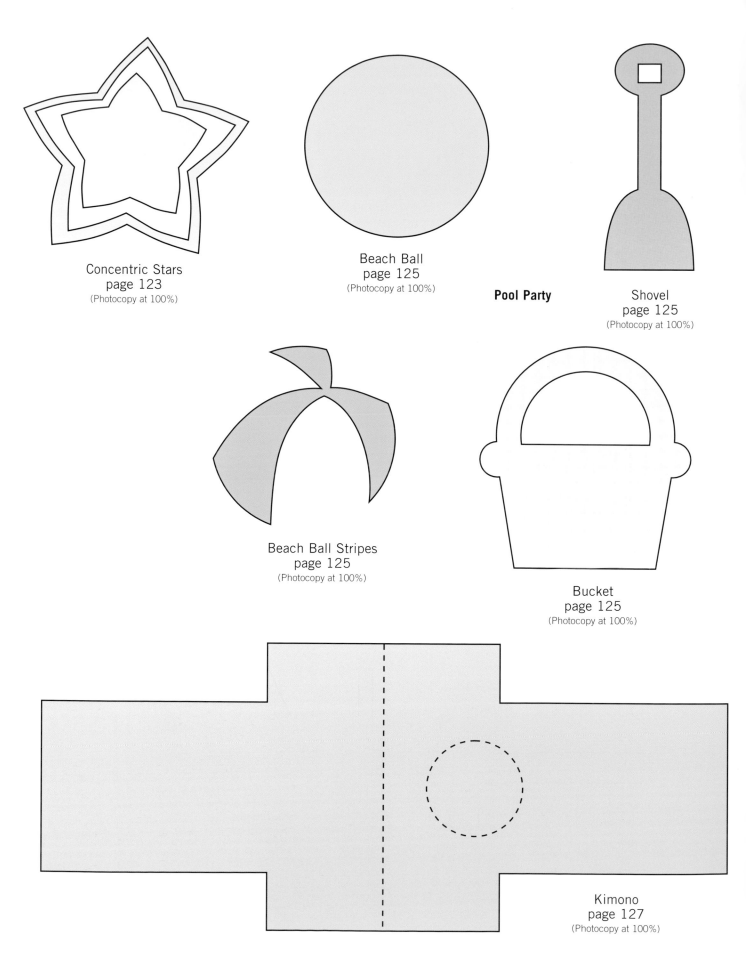

Concentric Stars
page 123
(Photocopy at 100%)

Beach Ball
page 125
(Photocopy at 100%)

**Pool Party**

Shovel
page 125
(Photocopy at 100%)

Beach Ball Stripes
page 125
(Photocopy at 100%)

Bucket
page 125
(Photocopy at 100%)

Kimono
page 127
(Photocopy at 100%)

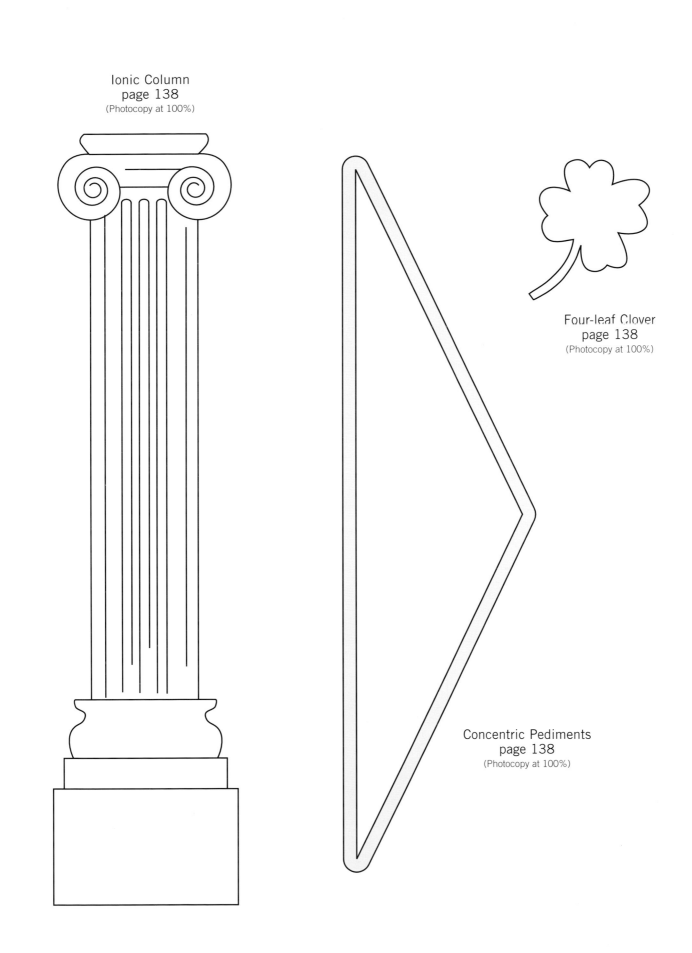

Ionic Column
page 138
(Photocopy at 100%)

Four-leaf Clover
page 138
(Photocopy at 100%)

Concentric Pediments
page 138
(Photocopy at 100%)

**Babies**

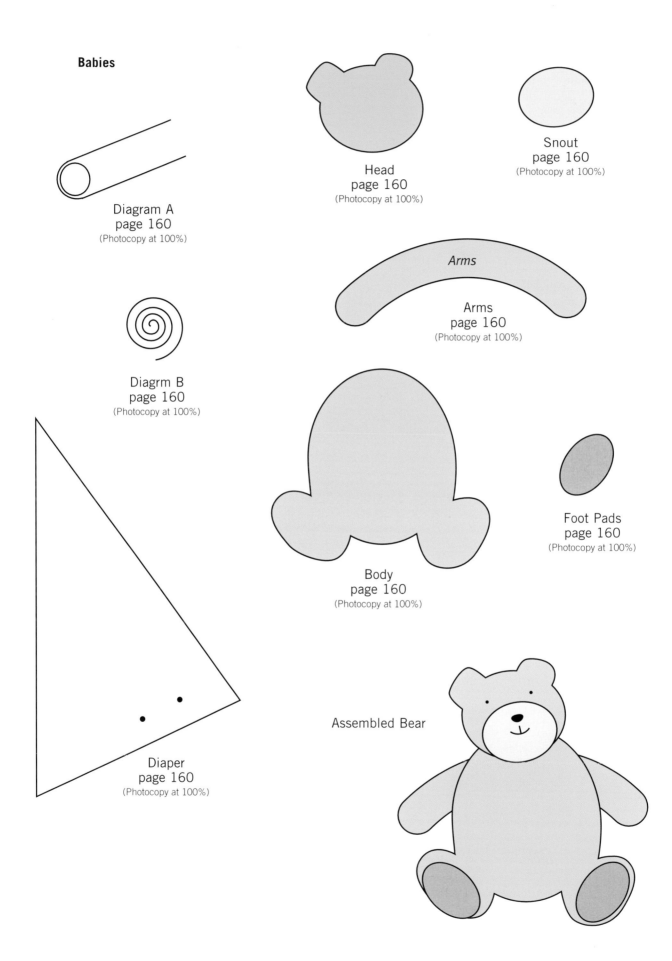

Diagram A
page 160
(Photocopy at 100%)

Head
page 160
(Photocopy at 100%)

Snout
page 160
(Photocopy at 100%)

*Arms*

Arms
page 160
(Photocopy at 100%)

Diagrm B
page 160
(Photocopy at 100%)

Foot Pads
page 160
(Photocopy at 100%)

Body
page 160
(Photocopy at 100%)

Diaper
page 160
(Photocopy at 100%)

Assembled Bear

**Having Fun**

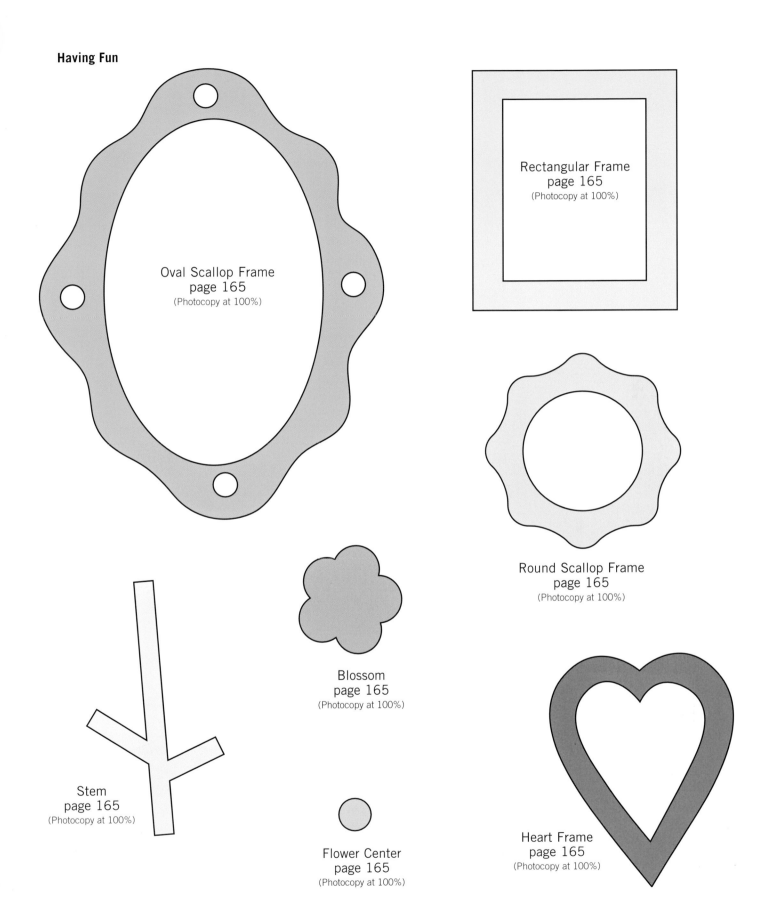

Oval Scallop Frame
page 165
(Photocopy at 100%)

Rectangular Frame
page 165
(Photocopy at 100%)

Round Scallop Frame
page 165
(Photocopy at 100%)

Blossom
page 165
(Photocopy at 100%)

Stem
page 165
(Photocopy at 100%)

Flower Center
page 165
(Photocopy at 100%)

Heart Frame
page 165
(Photocopy at 100%)

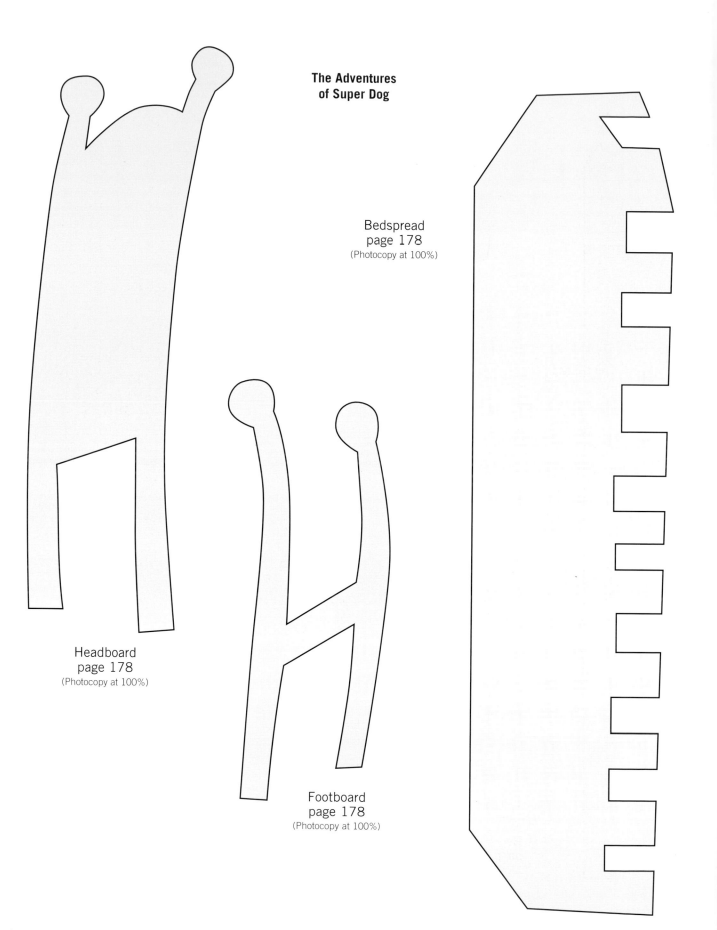

**The Adventures
of Super Dog**

Bedspread
page 178
(Photocopy at 100%)

Headboard
page 178
(Photocopy at 100%)

Footboard
page 178
(Photocopy at 100%)

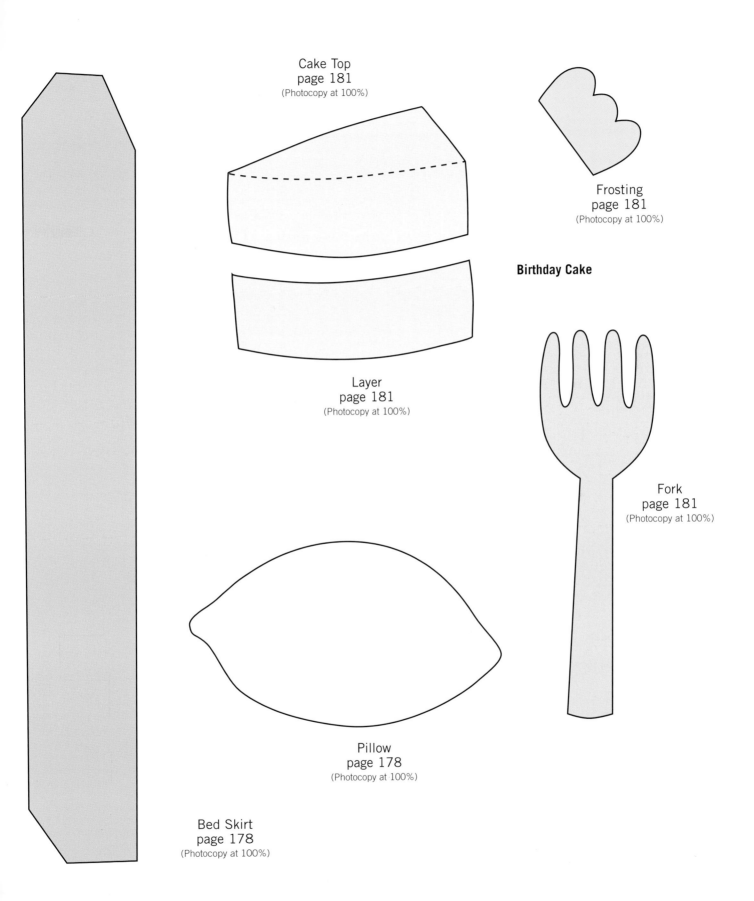

Cake Top
page 181
(Photocopy at 100%)

Frosting
page 181
(Photocopy at 100%)

**Birthday Cake**

Layer
page 181
(Photocopy at 100%)

Fork
page 181
(Photocopy at 100%)

Pillow
page 178
(Photocopy at 100%)

Bed Skirt
page 178
(Photocopy at 100%)

# Resources

**3M**
(888) 364-3577
www.mmm.com
*spray adhesive, laminating sheets*

**Anna Griffin, Inc.**
733 Lambert Drive
Atlanta, GA 30324 USA
(404) 817-8170
www.annagriffin.com
*paper, ribbon, vellum*

**Artistic Wire**
752 North Larch Avenue
Elmhurst, IL 60126 USA
(630) 530-7567
www.artisticwire.com
*wire*

**Aussie Scrapbook Suppliers**
www.scrapbooking.about.com
*supplies*

**Bazzill Basics**
451 East Juanita Avenue
Suite 10
Mesa, AZ 85204 USA
(480) 558-8557
www.bazzillbasics.com
*paper*

**Berwick Offray LLC**
www.berwickindustries.com
*ribbon*

**Canadian Scrapbook Stores**
www.welovescrapbooking.com/stores
*supplies*

**Canson**
21 Industrial Drive
South Hadley, MA 01075 USA
(413) 538-9250
www.canson-us.com
*paper*

**Clearsnap, Inc.**
www.clearsnap.com
*ink pads*

**Colorbok**
2716 Baker Road
Dexter, MI 48130 USA
(800) 366-4660
www.colorbok.com
*David Walker stickers*

**Craf-T Products**
www.craf-tproducts.com
*decorative chalk*

**Creating Keepsakes**
14901 South Heritage Crest
Bluffdale, UT 84065 USA
(801) 495-7230
www.creatingkeepsakes.com
*fonts*

**Creative Paperclay**
www.paperclay.com
*air-drying modeling clay*

**DMC**
www.dmc-usa.com
*pearl cotton*

**DMD Industries**
www.dmdind.com
*decorative paper*

**Daisy D's Paper**
www.daisydspaper.com
*paper*

**Darice**
www.darice.com
*tin snowflakes*

**Deluxe Cuts**
P.O. Box 8283
Mesa, AZ 85214 USA
(480) 497-9005
www.deluxecuts.com
*die-cut shapes*

**Design Originals**
2425 Cullen Street
Fort Worth, TX 76107 USA
(800) 877-7820
www.d-originals.com
*paper*

**Die Cuts With a View**
www.diecutswithaview.com
*faux metallic letters*

**DMC**
(888) 610-1250
www.dmc-usa.com
*embroidery floss*

**DMD Industries**
2300 South Old Missouri Road
Springdale, AR
72764 USA
(501) 750-8929
www.dmdind.com
*paper*

**Duncan Enterprises**
www.duncancrafts.com
*3-D paint*

**EK Success**
www.eksuccess.com
*pens and markers*

**Ellison Craft & Design and Ellison for Sizzix**
25862 Commercecentre Drive
Lake Forest, CA 92630-8804 USA
(800) 253-2238
www.ellison.com
*die-cutting equipment, die-cuts, wood paper, Rotatrim paper trimmer*

**Emagination Crafts, Inc.**
463 West Wrightwood Avenue
Elmhurst, IL 60126 USA
(630) 833-9521
www.emaginationcrafts.com
*paper punches*

**Fiskars**
7811 West Stewart Avenue
Warsaw, WI 54401 USA
(800) 950-0203
www.Fiskars.com
*paper crimpers, paper punches, paper trimmers, scissors*

**FoofaLa**
www.foofala.com
*hinges, decorative papers*

**Franca Xenia**
Bedfordview 2008
South Africa
+27 11 974 8464
www.paperworld.co.za
*supplies*

**Glitterex Corp.**
Cranford, NJ 07016 USA
(908) 272-9121
*glitter*

**Glue Dots International**
5575 South Westridge Drive
New Berlin, WI 53151 USA
www.gluedots.com
*adhesives*

**The Gold Leaf Company**
www.goldleafcompany.com
*composition gold leaf*

**Halcraft**
www.halcraft.com
*beads*

**Hallmark**
www.hallmark.com
*stickers*

**HERMA GmbH**
Ulmer Strasse 300
D-70327
Stuttgart, Germany
+49 (0) 711 7902 0
*supplies*

**Hero Arts**
www.heroarts.com
*rubber stamps*

**Hirschberg Schutz & Co.**
Union, New Jersey 07083 USA
(908) 810-1111
*decorative rhinestones*

**Hunt Corporation**
www.hunt-corp.com
*craft knives*

**International Scrapbook stores**
www.memorymakers.com/locator/store
*supplies*

**JewelCraft, LLC**
505 Winsor Drive
Secaucus, NJ 07094 USA
(856) 374-1234
www.jewelcraft.biz
*beads, wire*

**JHB International**
www.buttons.com
*buttons*

**Jolee's Boutique**
EK Success
P.O. Box 1141
Clifton, NJ
07014-1141 USA
www.eksuccess.com
*stickers*

**Kanban Card and Paper**
Unit 1, Jubilee Court
Bradford Yorkshire
BD18 IQF
United Kingdom
+44 1274 582 415
*supplies*

**Karen Foster Design**
P.O. Box 738
Farmington, UT 84025 USA
(801) 451-9779
www.karenfosterdesign.com
*paper*

**Magenta Style**
www.Magentarubberstamps.com
*scrapbooking paper*

**Magic Mesh**
www.magicmesh.com
*adhesive mesh*

**Magic Scraps**
1232 Exchange Drive
Richardson, TX 7508 USA
(972) 238-1838
www.magicscraps.com
*beads, buttons, seashells*

**Making Memories**
1168 West 500 North
Centerville, UT 84014 USA
(801) 294-0430
www.makingmemories.com
*plastic disks*

**Mary Engelbreit Studios**
6900 Delmar Boulevard
St. Louis, MO 63130 USA
(314) 726-5646
www.maryengelbreit.com
*stickers*

**Mary Uchida**
3535 Del Amo Boulevard
Torrance, CA 90503 USA
(800) 541-5877
www.uchida.com
*paper punches*

**Mead Corporation**
www.meadweb.com
*notebook*

**Me and My BIG Ideas**
30152 Esperanza Parkway
Rancho Santa Margarita,
CA 92688 USA
www.meandmybigideas.com
*stickers*

**Memory Lane**
www.memorylanepaper.com
*paper, eyelets*

**Memory Technology, Inc.**
32 East Red Pine Drive
Alpine, UT 84004 USA
(801) 756-6194
www.memorybutton.com
*memory buttons*

**Mrs. Grossman's Paper Company**
3810 Cypress Drive
Petaluma, CA 94954 USA
(800) 457-4570
www.mrsgrossmans.com
*stickers*

**Offray**
Berwick Offray LLC
9th and Bomboy Lane
Berwick, PA 18603 USA
(800) 327-0350
www.berwickindustries.com
*ribbon*

**Paper Adventures**
901 South 5th Street
Milwaukee, WI 53204 USA
(800) 727-0699
www.paperadventures.com
*paper, vellum*

**Paper Patch**
8325 South 4300 West
West Jordan, UT 84088 USA
(800) 397-2737
www.paperpatch.com
*paper*

**Pebbles Inc.**
www.pebblesinc.com
*paper*

**Personal Impressions**
Curzon Road
Sudbury Suffolk COIO 2XW
UK
+44 1787 375 241
www.richstamp.co.uk
*supplies*

**Pier 1 Imports**
www.pier1.com
*elephant paper clip*

**Plaid Enterprises**
P.O. Box 2835
Norcross, GA 30091 USA
(800) 842-4197
www.plaidonline.com
*acrylic paint, silk ribbon*

**Posh Impressions**
22600-A Lambert Street
Suite 706
Lake Forest, CA 92630 USA
(800) 421-7674
www.poshimpressions.com
*ink pads, rubber stamps*

**Provo Craft**
151 East 3450 North
Spanish Fork, UT 84660 USA
(800) 937-7686
www.provocraft.com
*bradlets, paper, stickers*

**PSX Designs**
360 Sutton Place
Santa Rosa, CA 95407 USA
(800) 782-6748
www.psxdesign.com
*ink pads, rubber stamps*

**QuicKutz**
1454 West Business Park Drive
Orem, UT 84058 USA
(888) 702-1146
www.quickutz.com
*die-cuts*

**Ranger Industries**
15 Park Road
Tinton Falls, NJ 07724 USA
(800) 244-2211
www.rangerink.com
*ink pads*

**Rebecca Sowers Fresh Cuts**
EK Success
P.O. Box 1141
Clifton, NJ 07014-1141 USA
www.eksuccess.com
*paper*

**Rhode Island Textile**
P.O. Box 999
Pawtucket, RI 02862-0999 USA
(800) 556-6488
www.ritextile.com
*hemp cord, twine*

**Rubber Stampede, Inc.**
2550 Pellissier Place
Whittier, CA 90601 USA
(800) 632-8386
ww.rubberstampede.com
*rubber stamps*

**Sakura of America**
30780 San Clemente Street
Hayward, CA 94544 USA
(510) 475-8880
www.gellyroll.com
*journaling pens*

**Sakura Japan**
1-6-20, Morinomiya Chuo
Chuo-ku
Osaka, 540, Japan
+81 (0) 6-6910-8824
www.craypas.com
*journaling pens*

**SEI**
1717 South 450 West
Logan, UT 84321 USA
(800) 333-3279
www.shopsei.com
*paper*

**Sanford Corporation**
www.sanfordcorp.com
*colored pencils*

**Stampendous**
www.stampendous.com
*embossing powder*

**Stamperia**
Box SRL
Via Orbassano 8
Vinovo Torino 10048
Italy
Phone: +39 011 9623833
www.stapmeria.com
*supplies*

**Stamper's Anonymous**
Williamsburg Square
25967 Detroit Road
Westlake, OH 44145 USA
(440) 250-9112
www.stampersanonymous.com
*ink pads, rubber stamps*

**Stampin' Up**
9350 South 150 East
Fifth Floor
Sandy, UT 84070 USA
(801) 601-5353
www.stampinup.com
*ink pads, rubber stamps*

**Sticker Studio**
www.stickerstudio.com
*stickers*

**Sticklers**
Scrapbook Times
1264 Tahoe Court
Orange Park, FL 32065 USA
(904) 276-7990
www.scrapbooktimes.com
*stickers*

**Strathmore Paper**
(800) 808-3763
www.strathmore.com
*paper*

**Therm O Web**
www.thermoweb.com
*double-sided adhesive*

**Two Peas in a Bucket, Inc.**
2222 Evergreen Road
Suite 6
Middleton, WI 53562 USA
(608) 827-0852
www.twopeasinabucket.com

**Versamark by Tsukineko**
Tsukineko, Inc.
17640 NE 65th Street
Redmond, WA 98052 USA
(800) 769-6633
www.tsukineko.com

*For orders outside North,
South, and Central America:*
Tsukineko Co., Ltd.
5-11-10 Arakawa,
Arakawa-Ku
Tokyo 116, Japan
+81 (03) 3891-4776
www.tsukineko.co.jp
*ink pads, rubber stamps*

**Westrim**
www.westrimcrafts.com
*wire*

**Xyron**
15820 North 84th Street
Scottsdale, AZ 85260 USA
(800) 793-3523
www.xyron.com
*adhesives*

# Contributors

**Stephanie Barnard**
Stephanie's Scraps
28461 El Peppino
Laguna Niguel, CA 92677 USA
(949) 831-2230
skbarn@juno.com

Stephanie Barnard is an accomplished author, designer, and teacher. She has written a book published by Design Originals, and has coauthored many other books. Her work appears in several top industry magazines.

**Jenna Beegle**
c/o Anna Griffin, Inc.
733 Lambert Drive
Atlanta, GA 30324 USA
(404) 817-8170
www.annagriffin.com

Jenna Beegle is a project designer for Anna Griffin, Inc., creating lovely things with beautiful papers. She teaches quilling, punch art, and heritage album–making at her local scrapbook store, and her work has been seen in *Memory Makers*, *Somerset Studio*, and several books.

**Kelly Carolla**
Mrs. Grossman's Paper Company
3810 Cypress Drive
Petaluma, CA 94954 USA
(800) 457-4570
www.mrsgrossmans.com

Kelly Carolla is a sticker artist at Mrs. Grossman's Paper Company, where she has worked since 2001. Kelly has a strong background in product development and

merchandising, in addition to extensive experience in crafts and stamping.

**Donna Downey**
Scrapbooks by Design
13646 Toka Court
Huntersville, NC 28078 USA
(704) 947-7598
www.scrapbooksbydesign.com

Donna Downey is a stay-at-home mom and runs a small scrapbooking-for-others company called Scrapbooks by Design to support her hobby.

**Shelli Gardner**
www.stampinup.com

Shelli Gardner is the CEO and cofounder for Stampin' Up!, one of the nation's leading manufacturers and distributors of decorative rubber stamps.

**Sandi Genovese**
c/o Ellison Craft & Design
25862 Commercentre Drive
Lake Forest, CA 92630-8804 USA
www.ellison.com
www.sizzix.com
(800) 253-2238

*See author's biography on page 304.*

**Michele Gerbrandt**
*Memory Makers* magazine
and books
12365 North Huron Street, #500
Denver, CO 80234 USA
(303) 452-1968

www.memorymakersmagazine.com
In 1995, Michele Gerbrandt recognized that the national scrapbooking community would benefit from an idea resource magazine—thus the first scrapbook magazine, *Memory Makers*, was born. Michele cohosts the *Scrapbook Memories* TV series for PBS and is a regular guest on HGTV's *The Carol Duvall Show* and DIY's *Scrapbooking*.

**Andrea Grossman**
Mrs. Grossman's Paper Company
3810 Cypress Drive
Petaluma, CA 94954 USA
www.mrsgrossmans.com
(800) 457-4570

Andrea Grossman is the founder of Mrs. Grossman's Paper Company, the oldest sticker company in the United States, where she serves as president and art director.

**Dee Gruenig**
Posh Impressions
22600-A Lambert Street
Suite 706
Lake Forest, CA 92630 USA
(949) 454-2609
www.poshimpressions.com

A longtime craft industry expert, author, teacher, and television guest, Dee has a Master's of Arts degree from Stanford University. She is the owner of Posh Impressions and the designer of Posh Impressions Rubber Stamps.

**Kelly Jones**
basj1995@yahoo.com

Kelly Jones calls herself a true scrapaholic. She has been published in *Ivy Cottage Creations*, *Creating Keepsakes*, and is a regular contributor in *Scrapbooks ETC.*

**Sherryl Kumli**
Mrs. Grossman's Paper Company
3810 Cypress Drive
Petaluma, CA 94954 USA
(800) 457-4570
www.mrsgrossmans.com

Sherryl Kumli is the coordinator of the sticker art department and assistant to Andrea Grossman at Mrs. Grossman's Paper Company, where she has worked since 1999.

**Julie Larsen**
Making Memories
P.O. Box 1188
1168 West 500 North
Centerville, UT 84014 USA
(801) 294-0430
www.makingmemories.com

Making Memories designers collaborated on these designs that incorporate the best of the company's popular Details collection. Making Memories, a 2001 Inc. 500 winner, is one of the nation's fastest-growing scrapbook and craft supply manufacturers.

**Cara Mariano**
c/o Ellison Craft & Design
25862 Commercentre Drive
Lake Forest, CA 92630-8804 USA
(800) 253-2238
www.ellison.com
www.sizzix.com

Cara is an accomplished designer at Ellison Craft & Design with a degree in photography from California State University,

Fullerton. Cara's designs have been featured in numerous Ellison and Sizzix ads and several popular magazines.

**Jenn Mason**
c/o Anna Griffin, Inc.
733 Lambert Drive
Atlanta, GA 30324 USA
(404) 817-8170
www.annagriffin.com

Jenn Mason, a project designer for Anna Griffin Inc., has a degree in graphic design, weaving, and textiles from the University of Michigan. Jenn has been teaching paper art classes for several years, both in her own studio and at local stamp and scrapbook stores. She is the author of *Pockets, Pullouts, and Hiding Places* (Quarry Books, 2005).

**Carol Rice**
Memory Technology, Inc.
32 East Red Pine Drive
Alpine, UT 84004 USA
(801) 756-6194
www.memorybutton.com

Carol Rice has been an innovator and award winner in the scrapbooking industry since 1991. She has had vast experience, first as an independent consultant and later as a co-owner of Memory Technology Inc.

**E. L. Smith**
c/o Ellison Craft & Design
25862 Commercentre Drive
Lake Forest, CA 92630-8804 USA
(800) 253-2238
www.ellison.com
www.sizzix.com

E. L. Smith is the art director for Ellison Craft & Design and the accomplished illustrator of Ellison's full-color project sheets. A graduate of Art Center School of Design in advertising, she is an avid watercolorist in her free time.

**Grace Taormina**
Rubber Stampede, Inc.
967-A Stanford Avenue
Oakland, CA 94608 USA
(800) 423-4135
www.rubberstampede.com

Grace Taormina is the design director at Rubber Stampede, Inc. She is the author of *The Complete Guide to Rubber Stamping* and *The Complete Guide to Decorative Stamping*.

**Barb Wendel**
Mrs. Grossman's Paper Company
3810 Cypress Drive
Petaluma, CA 94954 USA
(800) 457-4570
www.mrsgrossmans.com

Barb Wendel is a sticker artist at Mrs. Grossman's Paper Company, where she has worked since 1999.

**Becky Whaley-Butler**
Independent Designer
27741 Sinsonte
Mission Viejo, CA 92692 USA
(949) 457-8201

Becky Whaley-Butler is an avid scrapbooker who lives in Southern California. She worked in marketing for Ellison Craft & Design and her designs are currently featured on Sizzix.com.

# About the Authors

**TRICE BOERENS** has worked in the paper and craft industry for 23 years as a product designer, art director, and author. She has designed craft projects for kits and books, and has also designed consumer goods that include wall paper, linens, and jewelry. She is a graduate of Brigham Young University with a degree in Art Education and Graphic Design.

**SANDI GENOVESE** is a multitalented artist, author, and educator. She is the senior vice president and creative director of Ellison Craft & Design and hosts the daily television series *Scrapbooking* on the Do-It-Yourself (DIY) Network. She has written several books, including *Simply Sizzix*, *Creative Scrapbooking*, *Memories in Minutes*, *Creative Greeting Cards*, and *Sandi Genovese's Three-Dimensional Scrapbooks*, and is a frequent contributor to scrapbook magazines. Sandi is a regular guest on HGTV's *The Carol Duvall Show* and has demonstrated scrapbooking techniques on ABC's *Good Morning America*, *The View*, and other popular programs. She received *Creating Keepsakes* Magazine's 2001 Outstanding Achievement Award for her life-long contributions to scrapbooking and is a passionate ambassador for the craft.